The Folklore of the Freeway

The Folklore of the Freeway

Race and Revolt in the Modernist City

ERIC AVILA

A Quadrant Book

University of Minnesota Press
Minneapolis • London

QUADRANT

Quadrant, a joint initiative of the University of Minnesota Press and the Institute for Advanced Study at the University of Minnesota, provides support for interdisciplinary scholarship within a new, more collaborative model of research and publication.

http://quadrant.umn.edu

Sponsored by the Quadrant Design, Architecture, and Culture group (advisory board: John Archer, Ritu Bhatt, Marilyn DeLong, Katherine Solomonson) and by the College of Design at the University of Minnesota.

Quadrant is generously funded by the Andrew W. Mellon Foundation.

The University of Minnesota Press gratefully acknowledges financial assistance provided for the publication of this book from the César E. Chávez Department of Chicana/o Studies at the University of California, Los Angeles.

Portions of this book were originally published in "The Folklore of the Freeway: Space, Identity, and Culture in Postwar Los Angeles," *Aztlán: A Journal of Chicano Studies* 23, no. 1 (Spring 1998); copyright Regents of the University of California; published by the UCLA Chicano Studies Research Center Press; reprinted with permission; and in "East Side Stories: Freeways and Their Portraits in Chicano L.A.," *Landscape Journal* 26, no. 1 (2007): 83–97; copyright 2007 by the Board of Regents of the University of Wisconsin System; reprinted courtesy of the University of Wisconsin Press.

Published by the University of Minnesota Press
111 Third Avenue South, Suite 290
Minneapolis, MN 55401-2520
http://www.upress.umn.edu

Library of Congress Cataloging-in-Publication Data
Avila, Eric.
    The folklore of the freeway : race and revolt in the modernist city / Eric Avila.
    (A Quadrant book)
    Includes bibliographical references and index.
    ISBN 978-0-8166-8073-3 (pb)
    ISBN 978-0-8166-8072-6 (hc)
    1. Express highways—Social aspects—United States. 2. Urban planning—United States.
  I. Title.
    HE355.3.E94A95 2014
    303.48'320973—dc23
                                                                      2014001571

Printed in the United States of America on acid-free paper

The University of Minnesota is an equal-opportunity educator and employer.

20 19 18 17 16 15 14   10 9 8 7 6 5 4 3 2 1

To Ryan and Eric Avila

Contents

Preface   ix

Introduction: The Invisible Freeway Revolt   1

1. The Master's Plan
   The Rise and Fall of the Modernist City   17

2. "Nobody but a Bunch of Mothers"
   Fighting the Highwaymen during Feminism's Second Wave   53

3. Communities Lost and Found
   The Politics of Historical Memory   89

4. A Matter of Perspective
   The Racial Politics of Seeing the Freeway   119

5. Taking Back the Freeway
   Strategies of Adaptation and Improvisation   149

Conclusion: Identity Politics in Post-Interstate America   181

Acknowledgments   195

Notes   199

Index   223

Preface

The ideas that inform this book began as the flip side of an argument I made in a chapter of my first book, *Popular Culture in the Age of White Flight: Fear and Fantasy in Suburban Los Angeles*. In the first book I illustrated the way interstate highway construction in postwar Los Angeles supported a dominant civic culture organized around a new white suburban identity. That chapter explored the ways freeways sponsored racially exclusive patterns of suburban development and fueled a new paradigm of suburban development, better known as "chocolate cities and vanilla suburbs."

Whereas that chapter emphasized the freeway's compatibility with the emergence of "vanilla suburbs," this book delves into the cultural history of "chocolate cities" to explore alternative interpretations of the freeway and its place within the postwar urban landscape. *The Folklore of the Freeway* is a cultural history of interstate highway construction, a comparative urban history that explores the impact of freeway building on inner-city minority communities and the ways people in those communities expressed their experience of that process through cultural production. It is not a comprehensive history of interstate-highway construction, it does not delve into the intricacies of policy making, and it does not privilege the role of the state. By and large, that work has been done, and though it informs the following history of building interstates in cities, the chapters emphasize the contested meanings and conflicted experiences of that process.

The linking of "folklore" and "freeway" might raise theoretical qualms about this approach to the study of culture. My emphasis on the folklore of the freeway, on the cultural response to modernity and modernization, departs from an understanding of culture that pivots around the autonomous spark of human creativity and the singular genius of the studio artist. In the big historiographical picture, *The Folklore of the Freeway* situates itself within a more recent tradition of urbanist scholarship, largely Marxist in its orientation, trans-Atlantic, interdisciplinary, and eager to integrate culture into the study of political economy. The cultural portrait of capitalist urbanization, as it has evolved since the late nineteenth century, furthers my hunch that the idea of culture as epiphenomenal, as fluffy window dressing for the meaty drama of political economy, rests on an antiquated (read Eurocentric) notion of cultural hierarchy. In the rarified realm of museums and archives, culture might transcend mundane concerns, sequestered from the experience of daily life, but on the streets of the modern ghetto and barrio, culture provides one of the few avenues for empowerment and enrichment. Indeed, its creation is essential to the very identity of a community and its stubborn persistence against the daunting forces of erasure.

Though there are some necessary omissions from this comparative urban history, the cities that populate the following narrative harbor prominent examples of what I call the "folklore of the freeway," demonstrating a striking synthesis of structure and culture where the modernist city meets the postmodern city, where vigorous expressions of identity clash against the architecture of technocratic form and function. With apologies to my colleagues trained in the study of folklore, I use the term loosely, maybe licentiously, to suggest the ways ordinary people (at least those living near a freeway) express their understanding of a structure that casts its shadow over the experience of daily life.

This book is also a product of living in Los Angeles, the ultimate freeway metropolis. Few American cities rely on freeways to support a matrix of work, housing, and consumption that is both dense and decentralized. I spend a lot of time on freeways, and even as I suffer near-constant congestion ("rush hour" is obsolete in Los Angeles), I enjoy the privileges they still afford: convenient and autonomous access to the disparate points of public life in a vast metropolitan region teeming with the world's diversity. Yet such privilege is not accorded equally. As a burgeoning metro rail system takes shape, public transportation affords a modicum of the mobility that comes with automobile ownership. The city's bus system is one of the most extensive in the nation, like the electric trolley cars that once ran along city streets, but its riders have to organize unions to fight for basic service. Bicycle riding is also taking off: bike lanes have been widened and major boulevards are routinely closed for cyclists. It is back to the future in today's Los Angeles, where alternatives to the freeway metropolis are rapidly taking shape.

Los Angeles lays no particular claim to the folklore of the freeway, yet its uneasy mix of race, culture, and concrete generates a friction that finds expressive outlets in cities throughout the nation. In Los Angeles, as elsewhere, the freeway casts darker shadows over some communities than others, and to these shadows we turn our attention. Although the crusades of Jane Jacobs against modernist city planning in New York City are treated with skepticism in the pages that follow, I nonetheless share her appreciation for the experiences and perceptions of "very plain people, including the poor . . . the discriminated against . . . the uneducated . . . who tell with wisdom and eloquence about the things they know first hand from life." To that wisdom we now turn.

INTRODUCTION
The Invisible Freeway Revolt

In this age of divided government, we look to the 1950s as a golden age of bipartisan unity. President Barack Obama, a Democrat, often invokes the landmark passage of the 1956 Federal Aid Highway Act to remind the nation that Republicans and Democrats can unite under a shared sense of common purpose. Introduced by President Dwight Eisenhower, a Republican, the Federal Aid Highway Act, originally titled the National Interstate and Defense Highway Act, won unanimous support from Democrats and Republicans alike, uniting the two parties in a shared commitment to building a national highway infrastructure. This was big government at its biggest, the single largest federal expenditure in American history before the advent of the Great Society.

Yet although Congress unified around the construction of a national highway system, the American people did not. Contemporary nostalgia for bipartisan support around the Interstate Highway Act ignores the deep fissures that it inflicted on the American city after World War II: literally, by cleaving the urban built environment into isolated parcels of race and class, and figuratively, by sparking civic wars over the freeway's threat to specific neighborhoods and communities. This book explores the conflicted legacy of that megaproject: even as the interstate highway program unified a nation around a 42,800-mile highway network, it divided the American people, as it divided their cities, fueling new social tensions that flared during the tumultuous 1960s.

Talk of a "freeway revolt" permeates the annals of American urban history. During the late 1960s and early 1970s, a generation of scholars and journalists introduced this term to describe the groundswell of grassroots opposition to urban highway construction. Their account saluted the urban women and men who stood up to state bulldozers, forging new civic strategies to rally against the highway-building juggernaut and to defeat the powerful interests it represented. It recounted these episodic victories with flair and conviction, doused with righteous invocations of "power to the people." In the afterglow of the sixties, a narrative of the freeway revolt emerged: a grassroots uprising of civic-minded people, often neighbors, banding together to defeat the technocrats, the oil companies, the car manufacturers, and ultimately the state itself, saving the city from the onslaught of automobiles, expressways, gas stations, parking lots, and other civic detriments.[1] This story has entered the lore of the sixties, a mythic "shout in the street" that proclaimed the death of the modernist city and its master plans.[2]

By and large, however, the dominant narrative of the freeway revolt is a *racialized* story, describing the victories of white middle-class or affluent communities that mustered the resources and connections to force concessions from the state. If we look closely at *where* the freeway revolt found its greatest success—Cambridge, Massachusetts; Lower Manhattan; the French Quarter in New Orleans; Georgetown in Washington D.C.; Beverly Hills, California; Princeton, New Jersey; Fells Point in Baltimore—we discover what this movement was really about and whose interests it served. As bourgeois counterparts to the inner-city uprising, the disparate victories of the freeway revolt illustrate how racial and class privilege structure the metropolitan built environment, demonstrating the skewed geography of power in the postwar American city.

One of my colleagues once told me a joke: if future anthropologists want to find the remains of people of color in a postapocalypse America, they will simply have to find the ruins of the nearest freeway.[3] Yet such collegial jocularity contained a sobering reminder that the victories associated with the freeway revolt usually did not extend to urban communities of color, where highway construction often took a disastrous toll. To greater and lesser degrees, race—racial identity and racial ideology—shaped the geography of highway construction in urban America, fueling new patterns of racial inequality that exacerbated an unfolding "urban crisis" in postwar America. In many southern cities, local city planners took advantage of federal moneys to target black communities point-blank; in other parts of the nation, highway planners found the paths of least resistance, wiping out black commercial districts, Mexican barrios, and Chinatowns and desecrating land sacred to indigenous peoples. The bodies and spaces of people of color, historically coded as "blight" in planning discourse, provided an easy target for a federal highway program that usually coordinated its work with private redevelopment schemes and public policies like redlining, urban renewal, and slum clearance.

My colleague's joke also signaled a shared suspicion among city people of color that the interstate generation of freeway builders targeted their communities with malicious intent. This conviction persists in the barrios and ghettos of American cities. In a 1997 interview, for example, a former Overtown resident begged to understand why state officials routed Interstate 95 through the heart of Miami's historic black neighborhood: "Now all you white folk . . . you tell me the justification. . . . If that isn't racism you tell me what it is." In St. Paul, Minnesota, after Interstate 94 bisected the city's historic black neighborhood, a former resident explained his belief that the "white man's freeway" was built to "allow white people to get from downtown St. Paul to downtown Minneapolis five, ten minutes faster."[4] And as the following chapters illustrate, such racially inflected skepticism also finds recurring expression in the barrios of southwestern cities like East Los Angeles, where six major freeways ravaged the area during the 1960s, just as it transitioned into the nation's largest concentration of Mexican American poverty.

Beyond mainstream accounts of the freeway revolt and beyond conventional understandings of urban political struggle, city people of color have invented their own freeway revolt, waged through a wide variety of cultural practices rooted in diverse expressive traditions. The sum of this cultural work illuminates an entrenched conviction that highway construction during the postwar period constituted a calculated assault on urban communities of color. *The Folklore of the Freeway* homes in on that belief, its variants, and their expressions in the cacophony of American culture. It aims to listen to the voices and see the perspectives of people who experienced highway construction firsthand, whose communities were ripped up, gutted, ensnared, isolated, and altogether erased. The interpretative analysis considers a wide range of expressive cultural forms that address the place of freeways in the city and their consequences for everyday life. I describe this cultural work as the "folklore of the freeway," calling for an elastic definition of "folklore" that includes art, literature, poetry, music, dance, photography, murals, graffiti, theater, children's books, oral histories, autobiographies, sculpture, and film. Through such disparate modes of cultural expression, diverse city people convey their experiences and perceptions of a structure they know through an unwanted intimacy, forced by an interventionist state at the height of its power.

Hidden within this body of cultural work lies an *invisible* freeway revolt, invisible at least to scholars untrained or unwilling to engage with culture and its expressive forms. *The Folklore of the Freeway* delves into the symbolic realms of language and culture to broaden the scope of the freeway revolt, to contrast the organized, *visible* forms of protest against the freeway in the late sixties and early seventies with the disorganized, *invisible* expressions embedded in the contemporary cultural landscape of the American city. Here, I use the concept of *infrapolitics,* taken from the work of anthropologist James Scott and masterfully deployed by the historian Robin D. G. Kelley, to identify the hidden forms of resistance to the presence of the freeway in the city, beyond the visible end of the political spectrum. From graffiti on the freeway, to the satirical portrait of the freeway in inner-city words and images, this cultural work illustrates the infrapolitics of infrastructural development, underscoring the vital role of culture as a means of political expression among aggrieved communities of color and mobilizing awareness of environmental racism and its inimical consequences.[5]

In the context of urban history, infrastructure can make or break a community. In the United States, the historical development of urban infrastructure has both formed and followed the inscriptions of race, class, and gender on the urban landscape. Ample in more affluent communities, usually absent or minimal in historic concentrations of urban poverty, infrastructure does not serve its public equally. Some cities have a more equitable distribution of infrastructure than others, but many urban neighborhoods remain woefully underserved.[6] During the postwar period, the interstate highways sparked the development of new communities, new jobs, and new forms of commerce and enterprise, particularly for the great white suburban middle class of the postwar era. They did not (and do not) serve affluent communities very well because many in those communities successfully resisted local routing proposals, and they often decimated poor, working-class, and racialized neighborhoods, wholly vulnerable to the conclusions that highway planners derived from their meticulous data. These neighborhoods harbored the very conditions that infrastructure is designed to prevent—congestion, pollution, disease, crime—yet remained bereft of public investment. A better solution, in the logic of the time, was to simply eradicate these communities altogether through invasive public-works projects. Small wonder, then, that urban communities of color continue to express a pervasive belief that conquest and modernization are two sides of the same unlucky coin.

This book strives to listen to what inner-city people think about the freeways that fracture their communities and to open our senses to what is seen and heard in the shadows of the freeway, in the communities exempt from the dominant narrative of the freeway revolt. To some extent, *The Folklore of the Freeway* records long-standing grievances against the freeway and its presence in the inner city, but it moves beyond a simplistic narrative of victimization to explore a dynamic relationship between structure and culture, between the physical fact of the freeway and its refraction through the prisms of identity, language, and place. The surprising results of this investigation tell us not only what freeways do to inner-city people, but also what people do to inner-city freeways. Spatial justice remains elusive in the barrio and the ghetto, but there the freeway revolt continues.[7]

In thinking about the postwar era in general, and the 1960s in particular, the history of highway construction in urban America encapsulates a much broader sea change with lasting consequences for modern culture and society. Here is a *master* master plan, promulgated from the highest levels of a technocratic state at the height of its power, confronting forceful opposition in the cities, where a diverse citizenry rallied to protect its communities from evisceration. This struggle entailed winners and losers, but it also engendered new discourses of identity, community, and locality that challenged official rationales of progress, efficiency, and rational planning. The 1960s valorized these new modes of political expression, heralding a broader "cultural turn" that prioritized subjective feeling and experience over objective fact and data.

The shift from modernity to postmodernity has been theorized ad nauseam, but the materiality of that shift—its physical manifestations in the built environment—enables a more concrete comprehension of sweeping changes afoot. First on paper, then in practice, the modernist city emerged full-blown in the twentieth century from a set of structural interventions on the urban landscape. In the United States, modernist urban form debuted in a series of installations, erasing fragments of the city's past to produce a new infrastructure of concrete, steel, and glass. This included the construction of a national highway system designed to accommodate growing volumes of automobile traffic. The prioritization of vehicular traffic flow has been the very hallmark of modernist planning and design, from Paris and Los Angeles to Brasilia and Singapore, laying broad swaths of concrete above and below the city surface, segmenting urban space into discrete, isolated parts.[8]

The modernist city took shape through massive state intervention and centralized coordination, and it imposed a new set of values predicated upon progress, order, and efficiency. These values found powerful expression in their own mythology, designed in part to take the edge off the bulldozers and their brutal work. This myth, what anthropologist James Holston calls "the myth of the concrete," found powerful expression in postwar American culture, even in the technocratic discourse of highway policy, which invoked the sacred ideals of professional expertise and scientific objectivity. It turns out that these ideals were myths themselves, ruses for public policies tangled within local webs of material interest and mythic ideology. As a cultural history of American cities during the age of the interstate, this study describes some of that mythology, though it emphasizes the counterdiscourses to the myth of progress: the unexpected articulations of history, locality, and identity that surfaced in opposition to the highway-building program. These expressions of difference emerged from the gaps and contradictions pregnant within the modernist planning program, spawning new modes of urban experience and comprehension.[9]

Rooted primarily in historical analysis, *The Folklore of the Freeway* situates the urban history of interstate-highway construction within a broader set of social upheavals unleashed during the 1960s. The culmination of civil rights struggles and the eruption of racial violence in the cities, feminism's "second wave," environmentalism, the rise of multiculturalism and its embrace of epistemological diversity, the repudiation of a militarized state and its imperialist ambitions, a rejection of corporate consumerism, an insurgent appreciation of local history and its physical remnants, and, perhaps most of all, a deepening suspicion of progress and the science that bore this ideology: these profound changes redefined collective understandings of what constitutes knowledge, evidence, and politics and opened new avenues for comprehending human experience, perception, and agency. *The Folklore of the Freeway* follows the roads not taken in the literature, introducing alternative histories of highway construction and their diverse outlets for expression.[10]

This is a national story, albeit with some requisite omissions, comparing visible and invisible expressions of opposition to the interstate highway program. Although the narrative winds through the histories of Miami, St. Paul, El Paso, Boston, Seattle, Baltimore, New York, San Francisco, Oakland, and New Orleans, Los Angeles plays a lead role. Although a cultural history of urban highway construction needs scant explanation for a recurring focus on the freeway metropolis par excellence, Los Angeles models the very conditions that sustain a vibrant folklore of the freeway: its ubiquitous freeways and their marking of socioeconomic divisions, its history of civil rights struggle and racial unrest, and its diverse expressive cultures that deploy creativity and imagination in the absence of political and economic power. L.A.'s folklore of the freeway took shape under these conditions to mobilize opposition against highway construction and to generate awareness of its pernicious consequences. As these conditions remain broadly apparent in the cultural geography of the American city, and as more cities exhibit spatial and demographic trends pioneered in Los Angeles, they require new frameworks of study, new modes of analysis, and far more inclusive understandings of political struggle and agency.[11]

This is also a multiracial, multiethnic story, emphasizing race and racial conflict as primary categories of analysis. With explicit and implicit racial agendas, the planners and engineers who rammed freeways through cities

unwittingly provoked sharper articulations of racial difference and conflict. In some instances, their work hastened violent unrest in the ghettos
of American cities during the "long hot summers" of the mid-1960s. It coincided with the racialization of the inner city itself, in which poor people of
color, African Americans and Mexican Americans in particular, clustered
within the spaces abandoned by whites and white ethnics who fled for new
suburban frontiers. The centrifugal thrust of white affluence and enterprise
structured the concentration of racial poverty in precincts that gave birth to
the modern ghetto and barrio. Freeways helped seal the deal, erecting new
barriers that isolated and contained poor people of color. In this shifting geography of wealth and poverty, race displaced class as the discursive basis of
social conflict, dominating the national conversation. Urban highway construction played no small part in this process, ensuring an uncomfortable
and antagonistic relationship between freeways and city people of color.

The Folklore of the Freeway draws on the literature that has amassed
around the "postwar urban crisis," but it brings into the fold the voices of
racialized social groups who have been left out of that narrative. Like African
Americans, Mexican Americans also confronted the walls of racial bias built
into the restructuring of urban life after World War II. In the urban Southwest, highway construction led to severe consequences for the barrio, which
emerged alongside the formation of the modern ghetto.[12] This is, therefore, as
much a "brown–white" story as it is a "black–white" story, though the experiences of other racialized groups—Chinese Americans, Native Americans—
also populate the narrative, navigating through a folklore uttered mostly
in English, but with a few references in Spanish, Spanglish, Chinese, and
Hawaiian as well.

The Road from Paris to Honolulu

The Folklore of the Freeway delves into the dark side of modernization—
into the urban quarters of darker-skinned peoples to explore a more recent
chapter in the cultural response to modernity. An earlier chapter, which has
amassed its own library of scholarship, considers mid-nineteenth-century
France, where the modernist city was born by imperial fiat. Under the monar-

chy of Napoleon III, Baron Georges-Eugène Haussmann, prefect of the Seine, set out to retrofit the city of Paris with a new system of wide, uniform boulevards, fitted with rail lines, trees, and gas lamps. The new boulevards, touted as the summit of progress and modernity, were designed to accommodate the circulation of traffic, that creature of nineteenth-century urbanism that, like the crowd, threatened the order of city life and the maintenance of civil society itself. Haussmannization, with its own social, political, and military agendas, enforced a radical reorganization of urban space, exerting a new discipline over the flow of traffic and crowds.[13]

The monetary costs of Haussmannization paled in comparison to the social consequences. Tens of thousands of people were evicted from old buildings to make way for streets, bridges, quays, and buildings. The city's poor were banished to the periphery of the city, their homes replaced by government and commercial buildings or by new apartments beyond their means. The destruction of tens of thousands of old buildings, some of them notable monuments from the fifteenth to eighteenth centuries, compounded the toll that Haussmannization took. Haussmann himself invited accusations of vandalism by such writers as Louis Veuillot, Victor Hugo, Pierre des Essarts, and Paul Fournel. "Cruel demolisher," wrote Charles Valette in 1856, "what have you done with the past? I search in vain for Paris; I search for myself."[14] Still, despite its critics, Haussmannization created new opportunities for profit in Paris, prompting a boom in real estate speculation and commercial development, shifting vast sums of money into the hands of a rising bourgeoisie who claimed their stake in this new urban order.[15]

It is difficult to overstate the influence of Haussmann on a twentieth-century generation of American road builders who sought to reinvent their cities around the automobile. For Robert Moses, Haussmannization offered a useful lesson in hacking one's way through the built-up boroughs of New York City, and also in administering those bold interventions. In 1941, Moses wrote his own homage to Haussmann in the pages of *Architectural Forum*, expressing his admiration for Haussmann's vigorous approach to city planning.[16] Throughout his career, the New York power broker maintained an image of himself as the prefect of the Hudson, modeling his own designs for the Bronx's Grand Boulevard and Concourse after Haussmann's boulevards.

More than any single individual, Moses helped reconcile the mass proliferation of the automobile with the survival of the American city, especially
during the postwar period, when decentralizing policies threatened the economic stability and cultural relevance of traditional urban cores. Seeking the
carte blanche that Haussmann enjoyed in his rebuilding of Second Empire
Paris, Moses pursued an aggressive program of modernization that influenced an entire generation of American road builders in cities throughout
the nation. Ultimately however, toward the end of his career, as the freeway
revolt gathered steam, Moses discovered that Haussmannization did not
translate easily into the messy realities of American democracy.

Nonetheless, the structural transformation of Paris during the Second
Empire established a cultural framework for understanding the folklore of
the twentieth-century freeway. Haussmannization sparked an outpouring of
literary and visual expression that many scholars associate with the birth
of aesthetic modernism. Much of this work criticized the new urban order.
Émile Zola, for example, depicted the heavy toll that Haussmannization took
on the city's poor.[17] With agonizing detail, his novels described the ruthless patterns of displacement that enthroned a rising bourgeoisie. The poet
Charles Baudelaire took a more ironic stance toward these new social con-
frontations. Strolling the city's new boulevards, sometimes with a pet alliga-
tor on a leash, the flaneur translated his observations into verse that satirized
the pretense of the bourgeoisie and savaged the paradox of desperate poverty
in the heart of a newly gilded city.[18] The impressionists, on the other hand,
rendered a more ambivalent portrait of the new Paris. Standing with their
easels on Haussmann's boulevards, Claude Monet, Édouard Manet, Auguste
Renoir, Edgar Degas, and others depicted public scenes of pleasure and spectacle, fit for a city in the throes of gentrification. Yet their work also registered
the psychic toll of rapid modernization, inserting hints of alienation and exploitation into their image of the new Paris.[19]

Let this brief detour through Second Empire Paris remind us of a larger
historical effort to interpret structural forms of modernization through cultural expression, much broader in space and time than the purview of this
study permits. Cultural workers in the ghettos and barrios of the postwar
American city—muralists, poets, painters, musicians, choreographers, graf-

fiti writers, and photographers—inherit a *Western* tradition of interpreting modernization through creative expression, bringing their own experiences, memories, and judgments to bear on the vast and unwieldy canon of aesthetic modernism, which remains rooted in Eurocentric notions of cultural hierarchy. Like the Parisian working class during the Second Empire, city people of color in the age of the freeway bore the brunt of urban modernization programs. As with Haussmann's boulevards, the imposition of high-speed expressways on the precincts of the American city marked yet another expression of "capitalism in its essential form"—another instance of an interventionist state attempting to rationalize urban space and stimulate economic growth.[20] This work also favored the interests of an expanding middle class (who settled on the suburban fringe without having to sacrifice convenient and autonomous access to the city) while helping eradicate working-class slums and create new incentives for profit and gentrification.

But if we limit our reading of the folklore of the freeway to the language of class and class struggle, America's "race problem," to quote a homegrown discourse of race, remains stark in its absence. For one thing, the social conflicts engendered by urban highway construction were generally not articulated through the discourse of class. Through powerful union representatives, American workers expressed their undivided support for the interstate highway program and its promise of mass employment. On this issue, they stood on the side of their employers, rooting for more highways in more cities. Also, as a recent generation of urban historians has shown, highway construction conspired with other state-sanctioned programs—urban renewal, slum clearance, suburbanization, and public housing—to isolate urban communities of color, creating a "second ghetto" in the heart of American cities, and a "second barrio" in the urban Southwest.[21]

Such historical developments worked in tandem to enforce the racial re-segregation of urban America during the postwar period, even as the civil rights movement made greater strides toward racial equality. The spate of racial violence that erupted in American cities in the mid-1960s shocked white Americans who had insulated themselves within exclusive suburban enclaves, willfully ignorant of inner-city conditions of racial poverty. After riots in the Los Angeles neighborhood of Watts, 1965 became America's 1848, sparking more stringent demands for racial equality and drawing the world's attention to America's latest race problem. In the depths of inner-city despair, highway construction added insult to injury, fanning the flames of racial unrest. As one black former resident of the Rondo neighborhood of St. Paul said in 1964, just days after that city's worst racial conflict, "We've got cops busting down our doors and freeways destroying our neighborhoods. . . . Of course we're mad, what would you expect?"[22]

The following five thematic chapters ground the urban history of the freeway revolt and explore its diverse expressions in American culture since passage of the Interstate Highway Act in 1956. Chapter 1 provides a historical overview of highway construction in metropolitan areas and of its relationship to the broader transformation of the postwar American city. It begins with the experts and their mystique. The postwar generation of highway planners and engineers reached the peak of their profession during the 1950s, presenting themselves as the very personification of scientific expertise and empirical objectivity. Their technocratic reign ended in the following decade as freeway revolts erupted in cities across the nation, feeding on a deepening suspicion of state power and forcing substantial revisions of highway policy at both local and national levels. These scattered victories, however, only widened racial and class disparities in the city. Beyond the communities that successfully blocked specific highway projects, freeways hit hard, casting shadows over the experience of daily life and inspiring new expressions of political dissent, which are taken up by the following chapters.

Chapter 2 explores the history of the freeway revolt through the analytic lens of gender. In the aftermath of Betty Friedan's *The Feminine Mystique*, which no scholar has read as a feminist indictment of suburbanization, second-wave feminism forced a radical rethinking of social relations and of the spaces that enforced the maintenance of patriarchy. This chapter considers the indictment of the freeway as one of those spaces, analyzing cultural critiques of highway construction as a male pursuit. *The Feminine Mystique*, though often regarded as the opening salvo of second-wave feminism, also draws criticism from black and Chicana feminists as a narrow argument for equality for white middle-class women. This discrepancy is a central premise of this chapter, contrasting the experiences of white women who successfully organized their neighborhoods against highway construction—Jane Jacobs and her ilk—with those of Chicanas and other women of color who deployed creativity and talent in the absence of political and economic power to issue a sharp rebuke of highway construction as not only a racist but also a sexist enterprise.

Chapter 3 considers the aftermath of highway construction and local efforts to preserve the memory of communities lost under the freeway. Highway construction sparked a community's pride in its past, either as a political strategy against the invasion of bulldozers or as latter-day nostalgia for a bygone world. Race provides one means for comprehending this difference. During the age of the interstate, only those remnants of the urban landscape built by and for European Americans counted as historically significant. This Eurocentrism worked to the advantage of some neighborhoods, such as Soho in New York City and the French Quarter in New Orleans, whose defenders against federal bulldozers won a powerful weapon with passage of the National Historic Preservation Act in 1966. This act, however, did not save the black neighborhoods that won historical recognition long after they were destroyed. The chapter thus leaps to the 1980s, when African Americans in two cities, Miami and St. Paul, initiated concerted attempts to rebuild the cherished memories of communities lost to the freeway. Between these different stories with very different outcomes, this chapter illustrates the way freeways impaired not only a community's experience of space but also its sense of time.

Chapter 4 turns to the aesthetic dimensions of the freeway revolt in the history of American art since the age of the interstate. Related to the emergence of pop art, the noted portraits of freeways in painting and photography since the 1960s signaled an aesthetic engagement with new modes of urban experience that debuted in cities like Los Angeles, as well as a persistent disquiet with the ever-forward thrust of modernity, a favored theme in Western art since the Industrial Revolution. This work, however, pales in comparison to the Chicano portrait of the freeway in East Los Angeles, steeped in the riotous colors of a barrio aesthetic, which took shape as an integral part of the Chicano movement in the early 1970s. As East L.A. artists who made the barrio the subject of their work, David Botello, Carlos Almaraz, and Frank

Romero translated the immediacy of their experience with highway construction into colorful paintings that satirized, criticized, and aestheticized the structure of the freeway. Their *situated* perspective of the freeway in its barrio context contrasted sharply with the abstract imagery of white artists who emphasized the freeway's extraction from its physical and social environment. In exploring the image of the freeway in art and photography, this chapter illustrates the way the visual culture of the interstate era registered the racial conflicts engendered by metropolitan highway construction.

Chapter 5 retains some of its predecessor's focus on visual culture by exploring the problems and possibilities of living with freeways. The spaces under the freeway are familiar to city people of color, often associated with crime, vagrancy, drugs, prostitution, and other troubles that Marvin Gaye memorably described as the "Inner City Blues." Nonetheless, city people of color strive to reclaim this space through expressive cultural traditions, weaving it back into the fabric of their communities. The most spectacular example is San Diego's Chicano Park, where local artists and their supporters won the right to paint murals on the concrete piers that support the superstructure of a highway interchange. Chapter 5 surveys this and similar strategies of adaptation and improvisation, emphasizing the way urban communities of color take advantage of the freeway's proximity to assert their presence in the urban landscape.

The conclusion begins by exploring a recent twist in the folklore of the freeway. On the Hawaiian island of Oahu, the long-delayed construction of Interstate H-3 between Honolulu and Kaneohe Bay sparked an unexpected backlash among the descendants of indigenous Hawaiians, who rallied against the desecration of sacred ancestral lands. Invoking ancient superstitions and legends, the local cry of opposition against H-3 fueled a broader resurgence of Hawaiian folkloric traditions during the 1980s. After long and costly delays, the sixteen miles of H-3 ultimately opened in 1998, making it the most expensive road in American history. Its construction sparked defiant expressions of indigeneity and sponsored new levels of racial conflict on the Hawaiian Islands.

The fight against H-3, like the many cultural expressions and practices described in this book, signaled the unexpected consequences of building the modernist city. Even after the turmoil of world war, economic depression, and genocide and under the threat of nuclear annihilation, the executioners of the interstate highway program rested assured that their work made life better for all Americans, that it brought economic development, national security, and social progress—all powerful cultural ideals that found vibrant expression in the zeitgeist of 1950s America. They pushed history forward, claiming the mantle of national progress to build the largest public works project in human history.

Yet the sixties and seventies aroused deep skepticism toward these men and their achievement. Like policemen, soldiers, and other agents of state power, highway planners and engineers found themselves on trial for abusing public trust and colluding with powerful private interests. Neither guilty nor innocent, the technocrats who rammed freeways into American cities faced a changing public mood, largely unsympathetic to their expertise and authority. They saw their power capped by substantial reforms in federal highway policy, which mandated a new sensitivity to the contexts of nature, culture, and history. Today, contemporary ambivalence toward their work is once again altering the urban built environment in profound ways. Some cities are widening their freeways; others are tearing them down. Some cities have enacted costly new megaprojects to correct the mistakes of the interstate megaproject; Boston, for example, buried its elevated Central Artery to restore an organic urban whole.

So far, however, these remedies seem little more than aesthetic treatments that fail to address the broader inequities exacerbated by the aggressive push of urban highway construction after 1956.[23] This book explores these inequities and their expression in the cacophony of American culture. The folklore of the freeway entails its own freeway revolt, an unexpected consequence of the racial biases built into highway policy and practice during the interstate years. Obviously this was not the first, nor even the most egregious, instance of race bias in public policy, but unlike other institutionalized forms of racism, this example retains its stature in the physical landscape of the city, casting noxious shadows over poor, crowded neighborhoods that remain underemployed and underserved. This scenario resurfaces in the following pages, rendered through a set of words and images that assert the unique significance of diverse communities, histories, and identities and inspire new forms of community organization. They are the unexpected consequences of building the modernist city, whose creators planted the seeds of their own destruction.

The Master's Plan

The Rise and Fall of the Modernist City

The American city was in crisis after World War II. The suburbanization of business, retail, industry, and home ownership depleted the urban core of the riches it had hoarded over the past century or so. Against this backdrop, public officials at federal, state, and local levels, many reared within the managerial cultures of the Progressive Era and the New Deal, prescribed massive interventions to remedy what they diagnosed as an urban crisis. They confronted a conundrum of their own making. To counter the consequences of policies that promoted the decentralization of employment, consumption, and home ownership, they implemented bold measures to rescue the city from the threat of irrelevance.

History has made it clear that these efforts—urban renewal, public housing, slum clearance, and highway construction—produced their own urban crisis with lasting consequences; the effects persist today. Yet this approach to the American city was not conceived willy-nilly. Rather, it inherited a weighty tradition of thought and practice, from eighteenth-century Europe to twentieth-century America, fueled by the trans-Atlantic thrust of modernity and its twin engines, urbanization and industrialization. From Charles Fourier to Henri de Saint-Simon, Baron Haussmann to Otto Wagner, Ebenezer Howard to Daniel Burnham, Le Corbusier to Robert Moses, powerful new ideas emerged about the modern city and how to guard its successive explosions of wealth and population against the ever-present threat of total anarchy.

These ideas and the practices they inspired wrought the modernist city,

a European invention that marked a concerted effort to *design* a rational social order through the aggressive reorganization of urban space. It reflected
the state's effort to manage the crises induced by capitalist urbanization and
to advance society through enlightened architecture and planning. It enthroned the machine, not ambulatory human beings, as the arbiter of urban
spatial design, and it claimed the authority of reason and science, promising
to rescue humanity from its self-destructive attachments to history, community, and identity. A technical elite of men from Europe and America,
mandarins within the maturing disciplines of architecture, city planning,
civil engineering, and public administration, built this new civilization on
the rubble of the old, exporting bits and pieces of the modernist city to the
rest of world.[1]

The human circulation that streets provide has been an essential ingre-
dient of urban life since its earliest forms, but the nineteenth century introduced a new scale of movement in the city. Mechanized systems of mass
transportation demanded broader thoroughfares, introducing the boulevard
as a new urban realm. The mass adoption of the automobile in the twentieth century demanded more extreme solutions, like the Interstate Highway
Act of 1956, which implemented a national highway system both within and
between major metropolitan areas. City officials and their partners in the
private sector welcomed freeways to their cities, seeing them as job creators,
slum destroyers, and all-around growth generators. To that point, no city in
human history had been subject to such an audacious road-building scheme.
Its construction exacted the ruthless destruction of the urban fabric, uprooting hundreds of thousands, vastly enlarging the scale of metropolitan life,
and delivering new experiences of space and time.

To contextualize the following chapters' exploration of the folklore of
the freeway, this chapter lays out the momentous cultural shifts that ensued
during the age of the interstate, from the late 1950s to the early 1970s. This
epoch witnessed the rise and fall of the modernist city and the experts who
built it. It also introduced stringent new demands for social justice among
women, blacks, and other minority groups who shared a deep suspicion of
state power and its abuse by bureaucrats and technocrats. Many of these
groups defended the neighborhoods that grounded their identities against

the destructive work of highway construction. In this moment, the freeway revolt leveled a forceful challenge not just to planned segments of the interstate program, but also to the cultural ideals of progress that accompanied this monumental effort. Yet successful protests in some neighborhoods exacted a toll in others, especially those that lacked access to resources, connections, and the spotlight of media attention. In many American cities, a new highway infrastructure, built above or depressed below the surface of everyday life, presided over the birth of the modern ghetto and barrio. Just as old social divisions toppled under the force of civil rights struggle, the interstate highway program put new ones in place, recasting the age-old barriers of race and class into a stark new set of concrete lines.

Of Myth, Mystique, and Magic:
Building the Interstate Highway System

In hindsight, the interstate generation of highway engineers had easy justification for their work. "We were building freeways; we weren't saving the world." This is how one highway engineer, who wished to remain anonymous, described his thirty years of service to the California Division of Highways. Fair enough, but such modesty obscures the paradox of his profession's achievement. On the one hand, history could judge this work as right for its time. Under the Pax Americana that lasted for some twenty years after World War II, the national highway program greased the wheels of national prosperity. It brought jobs to millions of American workers, who built new roads and new communities. In turn, their work spawned new markets for jobs and consumers, unifying the nation around a national highway network built on a scale unprecedented in human history. This was a monumental and lasting achievement, ranking with the transcontinental railroad, the motion picture, the Panama Canal, the internal combustion engine, Hoover Dam, and Sputnik—game-changing feats that furthered modernity's imperative to annihilate space through time.[2]

On the other hand, this work brought massive destruction to the cities, laying waste to communities built across generations through the toil of migrants and immigrants. During the thrust of the interstate highway program, in the decade between 1956 and 1966, highway construction demolished some 37,000 urban housing units per year, displacing hundreds of thousands in cities across the nation. Other public and private redevelopment schemes compounded the havoc that highway construction had wrought on the American city, grinding distinctive neighborhoods and communities into dust, creating severe relocation problems in some neighborhoods, and leaving a legacy of environmental damage. Highway construction sapped cities of their human vitality, replacing bustling pedestrian life with dead and useless space. It depleted investment from mass transit programs and fueled the public's addiction to cars, oil, and gasoline. Yet as this and the following chapters consider, this program helped restructure the socioeconomic geography of the city by imposing new barriers along the lines of race, class, and gender.[3]

The California highway engineer was right: he and his cohort of state and federal engineers "weren't saving the world," but instead, they adopted a narrow outlook that precluded accountability for the consequences of their work. His reductive logic depended in part on the homogeneous ranks of his profession at midcentury. In most American cities, state highway engineers assumed responsibility for building the interstate highway system, with oversight from federal engineers in the Bureau of Public Roads (BPR). This professional group was made up almost exclusively of young to middle-aged white men, many from the rural Midwest, from middle- to lower-middle-class backgrounds. Many had served in one or both of the world wars, where they built bridges and roads for military operations. They did not enjoy the prestige of their colleagues working in Washington, D.C., or in private firms, and they made considerably less money. They worked in large organizations, often in teams, and were not encouraged to question their duties. They shunned publicity, avoided controversy, and had little tolerance for ambiguity. Their single mission was to build freeways to serve traffic; to let other considerations influence their work was anathema to their profession.[4]

Science provided a mantle of authority and the essential rationale. These men operated within a professional culture founded on the ideals of technical expertise and scientific objectivity. At the outset of the twentieth century, when automobiles were still playthings for the rich, roads were built haphazardly, through untested processes of trial and error. The Progressive Era, however, brought a new efficiency to road-building programs, led by a new set of technical experts who specialized in road construction and design. This culture of technical expertise took shape through the establishment in 1919 of the U.S. Bureau of Public Roads, which was a division first of the U.S. Department of Agriculture, then of the U.S. Department of Commerce, before its reincarnation as the Federal Highway Administration in 1966 (Figure 1.1).[5]

From the Progressive Era through the interstate era, the BPR was the sole arbiter of federal highway policy, largely through the leadership of Thomas H. MacDonald, who served as bureau chief between 1919 and 1953. From his post as a state highway engineer in Iowa, MacDonald took the helm of the BPR to forge a national highway policy that culminated with the National Interstate and Highway Defense Act in 1956, solidifying the authority of the engineer in the process. Eschewing the moral overtones of Progressive-Era reformers who invented modern public administration, MacDonald justified roadwork in strictly economic and technical terms, adopting the narrow view that "roads should be built by experts to serve cars."[6]

Under MacDonald's leadership, the BPR made highway construction and design a science, wrought from sophisticated research facilities that produced the hard data that shaped policy. Through its official journal, *Public Roads*, the bureau disseminated its research findings in a wide variety of areas, including research into the testing of building materials and soil composition, the visibility of highway signs, and the efficient utilization of mechanized construction equipment, as well as economic research on matters of fiscal policy and highway taxation. The Highway Research Board (HRB), established in 1919, became a clearinghouse for highway research, expanding its activities in subsequent decades through a Byzantine hierarchy of committees and subcommittees.[7]

Working with IBM in the 1930s, the BPR and the HRB developed methods for quantifying traffic flow, which provided an empirical basis for identifying principal traffic routes. The traffic survey captured the number of automobiles passing through a certain point within a given time frame. The points in the city with the most traffic indicated ideal vicinities for new

FRANK B. DURKEE   CHARLES H. PURCELL   GEORGE T. McCOY

CALIFORNIA HIGHWAY COMMISSION

HARRISON R. BAKER   HOMER P. BROWN   JAMES A. GUTHRIE

CHARLES T. LEIGH   F. WALTER SANDELIN   CHESTER H. WARLOW

FIGURE 1.1. The highwaymen: California Highway Commission, 1950. From *California Highways and Public Works* 29, nos. 9–10 (1950): 2.

highway construction. Also, origin–destination surveys located the areas that generated the most traffic, which supplied the data for desire-line maps, which charted the ideal routes of traffic in the city. These measurements became a professional jargon among highway planners and engineers, unintelligible to the lay public. The historian Bruce Seely argues that the algorithms and mathematical formulas that dictated the work of highway engineers generated a "scientific mystique" that insulated the profession from public accountability.[8]

Armed with hard data, state and federal highway engineers presented themselves as men of science, justified in their bold interventions into the urban fabric. Their authority rested not only on massive investment, empirical data, and centralized command but also on the heft of professional associations such as the American Association of State Highway Officials (AASHO), founded in 1914 to promote the legislation of a national, interurban highway system.[9] The AASHO's Standards Committee, chaired by MacDonald himself in the early 1920s and by senior BPR officials in subsequent decades, established a uniformity of measurements, materials, and procedures in standards for pavement, alignment and grading, intersections, grade separations, sight distances, signage, and passing zones. G. Donald Kennedy, AASHO president in the early 1940s, emphasized the centralized command of national highway policy and practice, noting that through AASHO's Standards Committee, MacDonald "determined geometric and structural design standards of the highway system in America, believe you me, and nobody else."[10]

Highway planners and engineers, though confident in their claims to rigor and objectivity, did not operate outside the play of political, economic, and cultural forces. They enjoyed the unanimous support of Congress, which passed the National Interstate and Highway Defense Act of 1956, the single largest federal investment in infrastructure in American history. This act increased federal excise taxes on gasoline, diesel fuel, motor vehicles, and tires; established the Highway Trust Fund to safeguard revenue exclusively for highway purposes; and made construction of the interstate system the centerpiece of the federal highway program. Consequently, federal highway spending more than quadrupled between 1955 and 1960, and the federal share of all capital spending on highway construction rose from 13 to 46 percent. The highway program became the single largest source of federal aid to the states by 1958, a distinction that lasted until the initiation of Great Society legislation in 1966. In urban areas, federal aid authorizations for interstate highway construction soared from $79 million to $1.125 billion between 1956 and 1960.[11] Such massive infusions of federal capital reflected a mandate for highway construction, elevating highway engineers to the peak of their profession.[12]

Highway engineers also drew support from a powerful cultural mythology that upheld their work as icons of progress and modernity. On the eve of the National Interstate Act, for example, Disneyland opened its Autopia Ride, one of the original thirteen attractions included in the park's opening in 1955. These were miniature gasoline-powered cars that ran along a one-mile-long multilane track, modeled after future freeway systems. This was in a theme park that strategically situated itself alongside the burgeoning route of Interstate 5, still making its way from San Diego to Los Angeles. The Autopia Ride centered automobiles and freeways within a utopian fantasy of the modernist city, which found mythic expression in the Tomorrowland section of the theme park (Plate 1).[13]

Autopia inherited the spectacular success of Norman Bel Geddes's Futurama exhibit, which debuted in 1939 at the New York World's Fair. As the BPR solidified its power during the 1930s, Futurama, a model of a city of one million people, enticed the public with previews of the expressway world: a moving panorama of experimental homes, industrial plants, dams, bridges, and office towers, linked by ribbons of high-speed highways. After waiting in a long queue to enter the exhibit building, visitors would sit in one of six hundred "moving sound chairs," gliding above a 36,000-square-foot model of the "city of tomorrow." "These are the express highways of 1960," a voice narrated over hidden loudspeakers. "Notice there are five different lanes, for various speeds, up to 100 miles an hour."[14]

Bel Geddes elaborated on this design in his 1940 book *Magic Motorways,* which offered "a dramatic and graphic solution" to the need for a national highway infrastructure. Somewhere between science fiction and rational planning, *Magic Motorways* outlined Bel Geddes's vision for a transcontinental highway system that would link major urban centers. In the tradition of modernist orthodoxy, Bel Geddes stressed the hierarchical separation of traffic channels through top-down renderings of urban freeways, enabling a God's-eye perspective of the city. This perspective, as chapter 4 argues, entailed its own rhetorical force that bolstered the case for an interstate highway system. By reducing the city's complexity to a Cartesian caricature of rectilinear lines, the God's-eye perspective, or what Jane Jacobs later criticized as "the Olympian view," made a visually compelling yet overly simplistic case for the modernist city.[15] Bel Geddes, a set designer by trade, packaged this perspective in treatises like *Magic Motorways* and in thrilling spectacles like Futurama. Even senior highway officials recognized the way the showman's "magic" mobilized national demand for a nationwide highway system. Frank T. Sheets, chief highway engineer of Illinois, recognized that "of every 100 people who are fed . . . into that awesome chamber of highway prophecy, 100 . . . exit with a very positive conviction that some heroic measures are needed, both in engineering, planning, and financing, if tomorrow's needs are to be met."[16]

That General Motors sponsored Futurama and Atlantic Richfield sponsored the Autopia Ride illustrates the corporate underpinnings of midcentury highway mythology. Highway planners and engineers worked closely with the executives of corporate America, who had organized themselves into a powerful highway lobby. The anchoring of corporations within the parameters of the central business district tied highway construction to the high stakes of downtown redevelopment, which ran especially high in an age of rapid decentralization. Highways opened new suburban markets, draining the cities of commuters and consumers. They could also channel people into the city, but only if it could retain its staple amenities: jobs, merchandise, arts, and entertainment. To maintain the centrality of cities in the changing economic and cultural geography of postwar America, leading executives waged a form of business activism that took shape through chambers of commerce, or through secretive committees of the rich and powerful: the New York Merchants' Association, the Penn Athletic Club in Philadelphia, the Greater Baltimore Committee, Greater Los Angeles Plans Incorporated (GLAPI), San Francisco's Committee of Eleven, Pittsburgh's Alleghany

Conference, the Greater Boston Chamber of Commerce, the Central Area Committee of New Orleans, Minneapolis's Downtown Council, the Cleveland Development Foundation, the Miami First Committee, and the Oakland Citizens' Committee for Urban Renewal (OCCUR). With close ties to city government, these elite coalitions pushed to build highways in the city. In the postwar logic of downtown redevelopment, freeways would not just ensure a steady influx of suburban workers and consumers; they would also help eradicate the blight that threatened downtown's imminent renaissance.[17]

Downtown elites were one constituent in a vast constellation of private interests that accrued around the construction of an interstate highway system. The automobile lobby, or "the Road Gang," included not only the usual suspects—automobile manufacturers and retailers, insurance companies, the producers of rubber, glass, and steel—but also oil companies, suburban retailers, housing developers, real estate associations, trucking companies, and powerful advocacy organizations like the Automotive Safety Foundation, the National Automobile Association, the American Association for Highway Improvement, the American Road Builders Association, and the Urban Land Institute. Yet the interstate program was not a conspiracy of the rich and powerful. It also enjoyed strong support from construction and trucking companies and from labor unions such as the Teamsters and the United Auto Workers, whose stake in building urban freeways contributed to an image of consensus around the interstate highway program. From elite downtown clubs to workingman's unions, the highway lobby put its trust in state and federal highway engineers as the agents of postwar redevelopment and modernization.[18]

Historical contingency added its own impetus to the national highway program. Although historians debate the martial impulse behind the 1956 Interstate Highway Act, the Cold War boosted rationales for the Federal Aid Highway Act. Its official name, the National Interstate and Highway Defense Act, resonated Cold War concerns about national defense. Two military men drafted the Highway Defense Act in its roughest form: Dwight Eisenhower, a former five-star general, and his ex-deputy Lucius Clay. During his travels in Germany, Eisenhower lauded the Autobahn as the "wisdom of broader ribbons across the land," and during his presidency he emphasized military concerns in his support for a national highway system. The onset of the Cold War heightened the need for contingency plans in the event of an air attack or land invasion of the cities. After World War II, decentralization was as much a military strategy as it was a social policy and an economic program, and the interstate highway emerged as a "top national economic and defense priority" and the vital lynchpin in the sprawling new military–industrial complex of the Cold War era.[19]

In this context, expressways assumed a bold new posture in the landscape of the postwar American city. Gone were the niceties of the urban parkway, heir to the garden city movement of the late nineteenth century and the descendant of garden suburbs, cemeteries, and parks. With carefully contrived landscaping, ornate bridges, sweeping vistas, and winding curves, the parkways of the 1920s and 1930s fostered a fleeting communion with nature in the rush of city life. By the postwar period, however, with the onslaught of mass suburbanization, the mandate for the expedient and efficient construction of a new traffic infrastructure precluded such frills, yielding a new austerity in freeway design. The Interstate Highway Act imposed a new set of federal design standards that prioritized maximum traffic flow, demanding wider freeways with more lanes, elaborate interchanges, and straighter lines that cut incisively into the urban fabric, unlike the earlier generation of state and municipal highways that snaked their way through the city's older neighborhoods. Typical of midcentury public architecture, the interstate generation of expressways demonstrated scant regard for spatial context. With broad swaths of raw concrete jutting above or sinking below the urban landscape, interstate highway architecture of the late 1950s matched the brutalism of public housing towers and urban renewal projects. Their imposing monumentality repudiated the pedestrian scale of the urban built environment, symbolizing the postwar stature of the engineer and his technical expertise.[20]

On the eve of the interstate era, the culture of highway planning and engineering was firmly rooted in the centralized authority of the BPR, which upheld a core conviction that empirical data was the key to building better highways for bigger volumes of traffic. Between the highway acts of 1944 and 1956, state and federal highway engineers reached the height of their power, becoming agents of infrastructural development, suburbanization, urban renewal, national security, and technological progress—technocratic elites whose "scientific mystique" won deference from congressmen, senators, and presidents. What began as a localized, fragmented, trial-and-error process had become by 1956 a project of national scope administrated by an elite corps of federal engineers who *disciplined* highway design and construction, applying science to new methods of research, organizing data, and establishing national standards through a far-reaching network of professional associations and trade publications.[21]

Highway engineers of the interstate era belonged to that body of experts who ruled American culture and society during the 1950s. Before the 1960s, Americans had put a great deal of faith in experts, who ended the Great Depression and brought the United States to an unrivaled position of global supremacy after World War II—why shouldn't they lead the way to a brave new world of jet travel, space exploration, multinational corporations, television, and nuclear power? Insulated within the mystique of science and the myths of popular culture, highway planners and engineers built a national highway system with the full confidence that their work was objective, impartial, and above the fray of social and political conflict. In hindsight, their expertise and their confidence—indeed, their very *objectivity*—were figments of their time. The mathematical formulas that dictated their work provided a ruse for the many political interests, public and private, that influenced the highway program, but in that moment, highway planners tore into the city fabric to implement a bold new geometry of superhighways. Science or no science, the job would get done. Never mind the social or environmental consequences, never mind the potential glut of automobiles or coordination with mass transit systems—the material goal was progress, at least until the 1960s, when that vague ideal died.

The Legend of Scrap Street

Napalm, the Bay of Pigs, the Watts riots, LSD, Las Vegas: in violent and ironic ways, these things induced a deep skepticism toward, or outright mockery of, the prospects of a utopian future, while *Silent Spring, One Flew over the*

Cuckoo's Nest, 2001: A Space Odyssey, and *The Structure of Scientific Revolutions* confirmed the basis of this doubt. The assassinations of John and Robert Kennedy and Martin Luther King Jr. and the murders of Malcolm X and Medgar Evers deepened a conviction that progress was dead. Everywhere, it seemed, the 1950s notion of a society advancing toward a more prosperous future died hard during the 1960s, leading to the 1970s, a decade of regret, doubt, and denial. The reigning ideals of progress could no longer justify their toll on humanity, at home or abroad.

In this cultural moment, the "highwaymen" lost their carte blanche to tear into the urban fabric.[22] The stirrings of what historians and journalists describe as the "freeway revolt" erupted in fits and starts during the 1950s and came to a head during the late 1960s and early 1970s, forcing a substantial revision of federal highway policy and administration. Despite its cachet, the term "revolt" is something of a misnomer, as it conjures an apocalyptic showdown that forced the state to its knees. That was not the case. In many cities—Boston, New York, Baltimore, New Orleans, Seattle, San Francisco, Los Angeles, San Diego—highway controversies were prolonged conflicts, escalating and de-escalating over long periods, often without clear resolution. Although these controversies yielded some modification of highway plans, freeways still punctured the urban core, linking downtown commuters to the spokes of a national highway network. The Highway Trust Fund, as well as the basic architecture of an interstate highway program, remained intact.[23]

Yet talk of a "freeway revolt" endures, not only for its market appeal but also for its heavy evocation of a particular moment in time. Its connotations of the grass roots—a "shout in the street"—suited popular idealizations of the 1960s as a decade of social unrest and challenges to authority.[24] Across the nation, citizens whose neighborhoods were threatened by the work of highway construction banded together, standing up to the bulldozers through an array of political strategies that drew public attention to the rampant destruction of urban neighborhoods. By forming neighborhood committees, leagues, and councils, by packing public hearings, by launching phone campaigns and petition drives, and by utilizing contacts in the media and city government, concerned citizens of disparate American cities made urban highway construction a public issue, drawing national attention to the wanton destruction of community resources and historic landmarks. Theirs was largely a struggle for self-preservation, but the urban groundswell of public opposition to the federal highway project echoed some of the broader issues that defined the political culture of the 1960s.[25]

First, citizen opposition to the highway program reflected growing concerns about the environment and its sustainability. San Francisco's version of the freeway revolt, for example, included a strong overlap with a burgeoning environmentalist movement. In 1969, the rerouting of the Junipero Serra Freeway, or Route 280, which engineers wanted to run along the shoreline of the Crystal Springs Reservoir, signaled a major victory for Bay Area environmentalists, who aimed to protect the city's water supply and recreational use of the coastline area. Antihighway activism also received a strong boost in 1970 with passage of the National Environmental Policy Act, the signature legislative victory of the environmental movement, which required environmental impact statements for all federally funded projects. Additionally, the Clean Air Act of 1970 and the Clean Water Act of 1972 bolstered the environmentalist case against freeways, sparking numerous local controversies over new highways and their threat to the quality of urban air and water.[26]

Not only did environmentalism influence opposition to urban highway construction, but so did a nascent historic preservation movement, which, as chapter 3 argues, shared much in common with the freeway revolt. The destruction of the cities' historic landmarks incensed many city residents, who shared a heightened consciousness of the historical value of the urban built environment. Opposition to highway construction in San Francisco and New York included a strong emphasis on the preservation of historic landmarks, but the preservationist impulse was strongest in New Orleans, where local residents mounted an impassioned defense of the Vieux Carré, or French Quarter. Though this area of New Orleans had deteriorated after a century of neglect, the proposed incursion of the Riverfront Expressway sparked a wave of sentiment and nostalgia. In New Orleans as elsewhere, passage of the National Historic Preservation Act in 1966 fueled local opposition to highway construction and other urban renewal programs that threatened the physical integrity of neighborhoods and landmarks that some constituencies recognized as historically significant.[27]

The 1960s also witnessed a revaluation of the neighborhood as the basis of civic life. After decades of master plans for regional development, the 1960s generation of urban Americans turned toward their neighborhoods as primary units of political mobilization. In the cities, identities were rooted as much in the physical space of the neighborhood as in shared cultural traditions and political values. Black nationalists pursued strategies of neighborhood empowerment in Harlem and West Oakland, hippies and the counterculture claimed the neighborhoods of Venice Beach and Haight-Ashbury, and gay and lesbian activists struggled to create safe spaces within the precincts of Greenwich Village, the Castro District, and West Hollywood. Jane Jacobs valorized these strategies in *The Death and Life of Great American Cities,* asserting the neighborhood as the most fundamental unit of civic life, while the children's television show *Sesame Street* established a multicultural pedagogy around the street and vibrant, diverse neighborhoods. The 1960s witnessed a grassroots push to reverse the sociological shift from gemeinschaft to gesellschaft, asserting these intimate spaces as the foundation of cultural and political life.[28]

A dawning sensitivity toward the natural environment, old buildings, narrow streets, and quirky neighborhoods thus inspired mounting opposition to urban highway construction, fueling impetus for a burgeoning freeway revolt. During the late 1950s, many communities were caught off guard, defenseless against the onslaught of highway-building bulldozers, but in the course of the following decade, outbursts of opposition in one city spurred protest in others. The freeway revolt became a national movement through the efforts of well-known critics and scholars who could put their opinions into national circulation. Wolf Von Eckardt of the *Washington Post,* Ada Louise Huxtable at the *New York Times,* Lewis Mumford, William Whyte, Herbert Gans, Jane Jacobs, Daniel Patrick Moynihan, Robert Caro—these authors showed little love for the suburbs. For the most part, New York was their home, and they brought their New York experiences and perspectives to bear on their critique of the federal highway program. Sharing their New York turf with the media, these writers helped *nationalize* the freeway revolt, fanning the flames of dissent in cities throughout the nation.[29]

Yet San Franciscans, not New Yorkers, fired the first shot. Even before the 1956 Interstate Highway Act, San Franciscans balked at the proposed construction of the Embarcadero Freeway, a double-decked highway that would span the city's eastern waterfront before veering west toward the Golden Gate Bridge (Figure 1.2). Their determined opposition to this one freeway spurred broader citywide protests against the official master plan for a highway grid that would have blanketed San Francisco's relatively small and densely developed terrain. Though this plan had the support of the mayor, the governor, and leading businessmen, a powerful coalition of neighborhood associations, environmental groups, and the *San Francisco Chronicle* succeeded in convincing San Francisco's Board of Supervisors to exercise its unique authority to veto the entire freeway system. Ultimately, San Francisco's master plan for interstate highways was whittled down to a single link connecting Highway 101 to the Oakland Bay Bridge and a truncated Embarcadero Freeway, which stood between the city and the western edge of the bay for thirty-three years before its demolition after a powerful earthquake in 1995.[30] This stunning defeat of the interstate coalition ultimately inspired the civil rights activist Harvey Milk to declare San Francisco "a city that breathes, one that is alive and where people are more important than highways."[31]

San Francisco's freeway revolt established a template by which white affluent communities successfully challenged downtown and suburban interests to stop the freeway. In 1959, for example, the California Division of Highways laid out its plans for the Beverly Hills Freeway, which was to run through the heart of one of California's wealthiest communities. In the early 1960s, the Beverly Hills City Council hired four separate engineering consulting firms to reexamine the state's recommendation for a Beverly Hills freeway. Not surprisingly, their reports drew conclusions very different from those of the Division of Highways, emphasizing the unique and special character of Beverly Hills and disputing the need for a freeway. Facing such well-informed opposition, the state ultimately scrapped its plans for the Beverly Hills Freeway, clearing a path for what local citizens touted as the triumph of "community values."[32]

Similarly, I-95, the great Atlantic Coast Highway that was supposed to link Florida to Maine, loops to a dead end on its way from Philadelphia to

FIGURE 1.2. New ramps to Washington and Clay Streets from Embarcadero Free-way, San Francisco, August 15, 1965. From Charles W. Cushman Collection, Indiana University Archives, P14845.

New York. Federal plans for I-95 charted a straight line across central New Jersey, through the heart of Princeton, and into upper Manhattan via the George Washington Bridge, but in the 1970s, the residents of the New Jersey townships of Hopewell, Princeton, and Montgomery filed a lawsuit against the federal government to stop I-95, insisting that it would destroy the rural character of their communities. After much legal wrangling, the New Jersey Department of Transportation pulled its support for the missing link of I-95 in 1980, prompting federal cancellation of the project in 1982. This "victory for the people" left a yawning gap in I-95 and perennial congestion on the quaint roads of central New Jersey.[33]

In other cities, however, opposition to highway construction drew in broader segments of the population. Boston's version of the freeway revolt, for example, pitted the Massachusetts Highway Authority and Boston's downtown establishment against Irish and Italian Catholic charity organizations, the Chinese Merchant's Association, women's clubs and leagues, and low-income advocacy groups. When controversy ensued in Cambridge over the proposed construction of the Inner Belt, umbrella organizations like the United Effort to Save Our Cities and the Greater Boston Committee on the Transportation Crisis (GBC) formed to block not just the Inner Belt but the entire Boston Master Highway Plan. The support of black Boston was key in this strategy because Massachusetts highway engineers planned to erect a massive highway interchange in the heart of Roxbury, Boston's black neighborhood. Kill the interchange, kill the master plan: such was the logic behind the GBC's solicitation of Roxbury's Black United Front (BUF), an umbrella organization of some forty community groups.[34]

With the BUF on board, Boston's freeway-fighting coalition impressed one *Boston Globe* reporter as a "Great American Melting Pot," but for black Boston, fighting freeways did not top the list of community priorities, even as Boston's Department of Public Works was claiming rights of way in the South End and in Roxbury by the mid-1950s. Rather, from the perspective of the BUF, including its leader, Chuck Turner, a dashiki-garbed professor from Northeastern University whose beat-up Saab sported a poster of Malcolm X, joining the GBC signaled an opportunity to press for issues more vital to black Boston: jobs, housing, tenants' rights, schools, police relations, urban renewal, and welfare reform. Yet even this grand coalition could not surmount Boston's age-old racial tensions. Representatives from Boston's white working-class neighborhoods resented the participation of "outside agitators" in the city's freeway-fighting coalition, and Irish Americans from Charlestown quit the GBC altogether, drawing charges of racism from Turner and other black participants in the coalition.[35]

Yet despite these frictions, the coalition strategy seemed to work, sort of. In 1970, Governor Francis Sargent (Figure 1.3), who, as Boston's commissioner of public works, had once advocated for building the Inner Belt, finally called a moratorium on all further highway construction in the Boston area, killing plans for the Inner Belt, the Southwest Expressway, and the Route 2 extension. Boston's fight against the freeway seems truer to the spirit of "community values" than the well-heeled rebellions of Princeton and Beverly Hills,

FIGURE 1.3. Governor Francis W. Sargent speaks to Inner Belt protestors on the steps of the Massachusetts State House, Boston, 1969.

but privilege and prestige played no small part in this story as well. It did not hurt the GBC's cause that the proposed route of the Inner Belt would impinge on the precincts of Harvard and the Massachusetts Institute of Technology (MIT), two of the nation's most prestigious universities. Some saw nothing less than the fate of humanity at stake in the freeway's threat to these bastions of privilege and power. One MIT spokesman claimed that "the continuation of Western civilization itself might well depend on not interfering with any of these MIT facilities."[36]

In 1967, from his office in between Harvard and MIT, the assiduous mayor of Cambridge, Daniel Haynes, shrewdly enlisted the heavyweights of these powerhouse institutions, establishing the Mayor's Committee on the Inner Belt, which included John Kenneth Galbraith of Harvard's economics department; Kevin Lynch, professor of city planning at MIT; Daniel Patrick Moynihan of Harvard and MIT's Joint Center for Urban Studies; the noted urbanist Lewis Mumford; and Talcott Parsons, president of the American Academy of Arts and Sciences. These men brought to the people's fight against the Inner Belt not only their professional heft but also their technical proficiency, which at least matched, even surpassed the expertise of Boston's highway engineers and planners. The report drafted by the Mayor's Committee charged error and bias in the conclusions of the Department of Public Works, deflating the scientific mystique that empowered Boston's technocrats. According to some scholars of Boston's freeway revolt, this marked the first time that "highway planners confronted not just the affected households with their predictable concerns . . . but also a group of peers who could mount a challenge in professional terms."[37]

Yet the prestige of Harvard and MIT, as well as the prejudice of Boston's white working class, seem conspicuously absent from local interpretations of Boston's freeway revolt. Today, on the rear exterior wall of what is now a Trader Joe's in Cambridgeport, just off Memorial Drive, one finds the fading image of *Beat the Belt,* a mural painted by Cambridge artist Bernard LaCasse in 1980. This is Cambridge's *Guernica,* a portrait of a community under siege. On one side, a massive bulldozer is painted in a bureaucratic shade of grey, labeled "Federal Inner Belt I-95." The white man driving the bulldozer faces a band of diverse community members, whose defiant postures loom larger than the bulldozer itself. White and black, young and old, men and women—Cambridge's diverse citizenry raises fists and brooms against the bulldozer. The artist's use of color and scale underscore a narrative that has become local legend: the cancellation of the Inner Belt was a multiracial victory of working people who organized against daunting odds to hand Boston's technocrats a stinging defeat (Figure 1.4).[38]

Similar interpretations came from other communities organizing against freeways. In Greenwich Village, where community members pooled their talent and their connections to organize against Robert Moses's plan for the Lower Manhattan Expressway (LOMEX), local playwrights took their community's case to the stage. Robert Nichols, cofounder of the Judson Poets Theater and lead architect for the 1969 redesign of Washington Square Park, wrote *The Expressway,* a play that parodied the local fight against LOMEX. The play is about the plight of Scrap Street, a "distinguished ethnic commu-

FIGURE 1.4. *Beat the Belt,* by Bernard LaCasse, Cambridge, Massachusetts, 1980.
   Courtesy of the Cambridge Arts Council.

nity" in the city of Metropole. Facing the looming threat of a proposed expressway, the citizens of Scrap Street concoct the Scrap Street Defense Plan,
plotting to assassinate the mayor and other prominent supporters of the
highway, including auto executives and union chiefs. They turn to two experts in civil resistance, an African and an African American. "Zip-Bakongo,
Premier of the East African Republic of Senegal," explains to the people of
Scrap Street how he united small villages in the fight against colonial rule.
"Remember," he tells the people of Scrap Street, "you are their blacks. You
can only free yourselves in this way." After that, "Joe Hill" comes to speak.
A Freedom Rider from Alabama and a charter member of the Congress of
Racial Equality, he gives the gory details of his fight for integration in the
South and enjoins his audience to go "face to face with the real agents. Not a
system, but a real person. You can't get a system to listen to you, but you can
get a person to listen." In the final scene, the people of Scrap Street come up
with a plan: as the mayor's motorcade comes to dedicate the new expressway, the citizens of Scrap Street throw themselves onto the roadway, and
they all die. The motorcade moves on, ignoring the carnage in the street.[39]

For all its West Village quirks, *The Expressway* sheds light on the white-ness of the freeway revolt. The play pokes fun at the pomp of city officials, the bigotry of union leaders, and the media hype that surrounds the open-ing of new expressways, but it also reveals the desperation of local citizens who turn to two black "missionaries" who bring *soul* to an otherwise soul-less struggle. This is a familiar relationship between blacks and whites in American cultural history: whites finding in blacks, or other people of color for that matter, a surrogate for authentic experience or a channel for emo-tive release. Or maybe the play just reflects the fashion of the time: a claim to political legitimacy in a dawning age of multiculturalism and rainbow diversity. With its downtown brand of dark humor, *The Expressway* presents Scrap Street as a parable for understanding the symbolic role of black people in a white community's fight against the freeway.

This vexing dynamic also had real-world parallels in the freeway revolt of Baltimore, a city notorious for its bitter history of racial segregation and conflict. There, public outcry over highway construction sparked fleeting il-lusions of black–white harmony. In August 1969, a diverse crowd of working-class and middle-class blacks and whites packed public hearings in Baltimore over the proposed construction of the East–West Expressway. One witness described the freeway controversy as "the greatest boon to race relations in years," and another angry woman told highway officials, "You did one good thing. You brought black and white together and this is a beautiful thing."[40]

Yet this instance of interracial unity in Baltimore was the exception, not the rule. It must have been amazing to see black and white citizens unite in opposition to the freeway, especially after the explosion of racial unrest in April 1968, which claimed six lives and left much of black Baltimore in ruins. In the racially polarized climate that ensued after the riots, the Re-location Action Movement (RAM) and the Movement against Destruction (MAD) brought blacks and whites together, creating a united front against highway construction. But this display of interracial solidarity came too late for black Baltimore, whose neighborhoods had withered under slum-clearance programs and plans for highway construction, on the books since the 1930s. Proposals for the East–West Expressway, for example, damaged black neighborhoods by inducing disinvestment and abandonment. Suddenly RAM and MAD come along in 1969, hailed as marvels of interracial solidarity, fighting to stop an expressway from eradicating the tattered remnants of black neighborhoods well in decline. At best, these freeway-fighting coalitions turned a blind eye to the long-standing isolation and deterioration of black Baltimore; at worst, they strove to defend a spatial status quo sanctioned by formal and informal patterns of racial segregation.[41]

The Paths of Least Resistance

Viewed in the broader context of the American city and its postwar transformation, the freeway revolt, as we know it, did not address, let alone alleviate, the increasingly separate and unequal geography of race in postwar America. The age of the interstate encompassed a mounting crisis in the cities, a crisis of race and poverty, and while white, affluent communities tapped into local political networks to fight the freeway and its place in the city, urban black and brown Americans found themselves trapped within the parameters of a new highway infrastructure. As the modern ghetto and barrio took shape, freeways added insult to injury, ravaging neighborhoods that were already bearing the brunt of disinvestment, deindustrialization, and decline.[42]

Highway planners, like others charged with the responsibilities of planning and managing cities, targeted not people of color but the spaces in which they lived. As far back as the 1930s, federal blueprints for urban expressways presumed a racial hierarchy of spaces, following precedent established by the Home Owners' Loan Corporation (HOLC) and the U.S. Federal Housing Administration (FHA). In 1939, for example, Thomas MacDonald issued *Toll Roads and Free Roads,* a master's master plan, the first comprehensive study ever made of the national highway system. This report synthesized the data amassed by the traffic surveys conducted by state highway departments, outlining the construction of a 26,700-mile freeway system that was to connect major urban centers.[43] The report emphasized the need for a Robert Moses–style intervention, asserting, "Only a major operation will suffice—nothing less than the creation of a depressed or elevated artery that will convey the massed movement pressing into, and through, the heart of the city." The authors of *Toll Roads and Free Roads* took a *noir* outlook on the American city, advocating urban expressways as a means of erasing "the mean clutter of narrow streets" and the "decaying slum areas" that "embarrass the movement of twentieth century traffic." Whether or not these "indeterminate areas" supported stable, cohesive communities did not concern BPR engineers; what mattered was the potential of building a cost-effective link between the urban core and the "fast growing outlying suburban areas."[44]

Another BPR report of 1944, *Interregional Highways,* retained the urban focus of *Toll Roads and Free Roads* but drafted more specific details about routing procedure. This report, issued by a presidential committee chaired by Thomas MacDonald, advocated a muscular federal role in routing freeways through cities. It outlined a master plan for 39,000 miles of interregional highways, some 5,000 miles built in cities of 5,000 or more. It also prescribed another 5,000 miles for the construction of undetermined circumferential and distributing routes, so that urban miles now made up one-quarter of the total.[45] In a section titled "The Principles of Route Selection in Cities," the report recommended that new urban freeways "should penetrate within close proximity to the central business area," but it did not specify whether these new routes should pass through or by the central business district, leaving this decision to state and municipal authorities. Though it elided the exact details of routing procedure, *Interregional Highways* nonetheless identified a few ideal locations for new expressways, such as parks and other tracts of public land, as well as the banks of rivers and streams that led to the urban core, which exhibited a "very low order of development—neighborhoods of cheap, run-down houses and shacks, abject poverty, squalor, and filth."[46]

As the doctrines of the highway planning profession at midcentury, neither *Toll Roads and Free Roads* nor *Interregional Highways* explicitly noted the racial character of certain urban neighborhoods, but there was no need. These reports inherited the racialized discourse of mid-twentieth-century planning, which recognized the city's mix of race, ethnicity, and poverty as "blight." By the late 1930s, federal agencies like the Home Owners' Loan Corporation and the Federal Housing Administration had codified the racial composition of an urban neighborhood as the primary criterion for identifying blight in the city. The HOLC considered many aspects of a neighborhood in addition to its racial profile, including the condition of its housing stock and its proximity to industry. Yet of the nine evaluative categories listed on the HOLC appraisal form, or the "city survey file," the social composition of the neighborhood, or its "inhabitants," ranked first. Within that category, the first subcategory, before "ethnic and nationality groups," "laborers," or even "foreign born," was the percentage of "Negros." Blacks, in other words, were singled out as the most conspicuous symptom of urban blight.[47]

The last entry on the city survey file was simply a blank space, room for the appraiser to write his impression of a particular neighborhood. In redlined areas—that is, areas accorded a D grade and assigned the color red on HOLC maps—the term "blight" was ubiquitous, as in "This area is thoroughly blighted and is thereby accorded a low D grade." This specific quotation is taken from the HOLC file on Boyle Heights in Los Angeles. The HOLC savaged East Los Angeles. Not only was it declared "hopelessly heterogenous," but it was said to be "literally honeycombed with diverse and subversive elements." In other redlined areas of Los Angeles, HOLC appraisers made explicit connections between blight and highway construction. For the community of Lincoln Heights, for example, with a Negro population estimated at 5 percent and a mix of "Armenian, Japanese, and Mexican workers," the HOLC appraiser noted that the area "seems ideal for the placement of a new highway project."[48]

There is no smoking gun that directly links the work of the HOLC and FHA with that of the BPR, but race shaped the federal response toward the American city in a variety of ways.[49] Thomas MacDonald recognized the potential to coordinate urban highway construction with urban renewal and slum-clearance programs, planning urban expressways not only to facilitate traffic flow between city and suburb but also to eliminate the "blighted areas contiguous to the very heart of the city." This two-birds-with-one-stone strategy had powerful support from private agencies like the Urban Land Institute, a national association of downtown developers and real estate agents, and the Automotive Safety Foundation, a key player in the automobile lobby. Public entities like the Highway Research Board also endorsed this view, promoting highway construction as the salvation of the inner city, a tool for eradicating blight and arresting the development of slums.[50]

Such talk of expressways, slums, and blight among the city's most powerful public and private interests did not bode well for urban communities of color, which slipped further into decline during the age of the interstate. The blighted areas targeted for demolition by expressway plans and urban renewal programs were often the outcome of discriminatory housing policy and practice. World War II sparked demands for new housing among white and nonwhite newcomers to the city, but African Americans faced a dearth of options. Although the exigencies of wartime production engendered severe housing shortages for everyone, most new housing built after the war was made off-limits to African Americans through both formal and informal measures. The HOLC and FHA discouraged investment within the boundaries of redlined areas and colluded with the discriminatory practices of mortgage lenders, real estate agents, business owners, and white home owners to arrest black mobility and to fortify a new set of racial, spatial, and economic barriers.

This backdrop is crucial to understanding the role of highway construction in the racial crisis of the American city. Across the nation, state highway departments, with the blessing of federal authorities, gutted cohesive black neighborhoods. In Detroit, where highway planners were careful to minimize disruption of middle-class neighborhoods, highway projects like the Oakland–Hastings (later Chrysler) Freeway, the John C. Lodge Freeway, and the Edsel Ford Freeway tore into middle-class and working-class black neighborhoods, destroying the most prominent churches and businesses anchoring black Detroit. As in Baltimore, these highway projects created a no-man's-land *before* their construction by inducing abandonment and decline. Displaced residents, deprived of housing assistance, faced higher rents charged by predatory landlords who had little incentive to maintain their properties. A staunch advocate of inner-city highway construction, Detroit's mayor Albert Cobo, reckoned such hardship as "the price of progress."[51]

Interstate highway construction enforced a similarly bleak transformation of West Oakland's black community. Even before passage of the Interstate Highway Act, West Oakland had fallen into a pattern of decline as redlining and suburbanization depleted the resources that sustained an African American neighborhood of port and rail-yard workers through the 1930s and 1940s. The community's bay-front location and its proximity to the port of Oakland made the area an ideal site for the convergence of three massive highway projects during the mid-1950s, destroying the cultural and commercial heart of black Oakland. This work left West Oakland in tatters: what had been a centrally located, stable working-class community had become by the late 1950s a disaggregate collection of vacant lots and dilapidated housing. Both East Bay suburban communities and downtown Oakland benefited from this new highway scheme, but the residents of West Oakland found themselves trapped in what had become a ghetto. Later, the addition of a Bay Area Rapid Transit (BART) line further severed West Oakland's connection to the rest of the city, destroying the last remnants of what had been a cohesive community of middle- and working-class families (Figure 1.5).[52]

Interstate highway construction had especially vicious consequences for black neighborhoods in the urban South, largely because local highway officials, like other public servants, also served as agents of white supremacy. In his dual capacities as Alabama's state highway director and leader of the White Citizen's Council, for example, Samuel Engelhardt led the local fight against school desegregation while he planned the routing of Interstate 85 through Montgomery's black neighborhood. After vocal community protest, Engelhardt took advice from federal highway officials and did nothing, so as to "let the dust settle" before he sicced federal bulldozers on a defenseless black neighborhood.[53] In Nashville, Tennessee, blacks fought unsuccessfully against the routing of Interstate 40, which veered from its straight-line path across the city to bisect their neighborhood. In many of these cities, blacks had limited means of voicing their opposition. Cities like Birmingham, for example, excluded African Americans from public hearings before highway officials, maintaining a strict policy of Jim Crow. In these cities, as in Columbia and Kansas City, Missouri; Charlotte, North Carolina; Atlanta; and New Orleans, federally funded highways were instruments of white supremacy, wiping out black neighborhoods with clear but tacit intent.[54]

Despite the claims of some big-city mayors, such destruction was not an unfortunate consequence of progress. Rather, it was the product of individual decisions made within institutional frameworks, pushed by powerful private interests tied to downtown redevelopment. Highway builders and

FIGURE 1.5. The I-580/I-980 interchange under construction in West Oakland, California. From Department of Public Works, *Annual Report, 1968–1969* (State of California, 1969), 73.

FIGURE 1.6. The construction of I-94 in the Rondo neighborhood, St. Paul, Minnesota, circa 1962. Courtesy of the Minnesota Historical Society.

the city officials who approved their work had options. In the late 1940s, for example, St. Paul's planning department considered two proposals for routing an east–west highway to link the central districts of Minneapolis and St. Paul. The central route ran directly along an east–west line between the two cities, which would wipe out the Rondo neighborhood, one of the few urban black neighborhoods of the upper Midwest. The northern route, however, ran northwest from St. Paul to Minneapolis, following a rail line that skirted industrial areas. Although some highway officials pressed for the northern route to preserve both white *and* black neighborhoods, Minnesota's State Highway Department adopted the central route, against both internal dissent and the vociferous protest of Rondo's community leaders (Figure 1.6).[55]

A similar debate occurred in Miami. Since the late nineteenth century, the neighborhood of Overtown sheltered its black population, a diverse mix of African Americans and Afro-Caribbeans, who created a thriving neighborhood that by midcentury had developed a bustling interracial nightlife. By 1950, on the eve of the interstate era, some 45,000 African Americans had settled in Overtown, forging a cohesive community of working-class and middle-class African Americans, anchored by schools, homes, churches, businesses, and community-service organizations. The coming of Interstate 95 in the early 1960s, however, destroyed this community, displacing some 30,000 residents, most of whom relocated to Miami's "second ghetto," in such outlying areas as Brownsville, Opa-Locka, and Liberty City. By 1975, Overtown's population had dwindled to fewer than 10,000 and had become a deracinated landscape of vacant lots and abandoned buildings in the shadow of a massive freeway interchange.[56]

Yet Overtown could have been spared. In 1955, the Miami Planning and Zoning Board, emphasizing neighborhood preservation, presented a plan that would have left this legendary neighborhood intact. The economic logic of preserving a neighborhood that supported a thriving nightlife scene around big-name acts seems obvious today, but the Miami First Committee, a coalition of downtown businessmen, realtors, and politicians, threw its weight behind an alternative expressway plan that slashed directly through the commercial heart of Overtown. Ultimately, the Florida State Road Department adopted this plan, eviscerating what was once a hot spot on the map of African American culture.[57]

Through both malicious intent and benign neglect, interstate highways tore into the heart of African American neighborhoods in cities across the nation, reflecting a broadly shared recognition that black bodies and black spaces had no place in a racialized civic realm. For urban communities of color, the coming of the freeway posed a dilemma in political strategy. Local residents could organize in opposition, as they did in cities from Nashville to Los Angeles.[58] In many black communities, African Americans relied on local institutions to organize neighborhood councils and steering committees. Churches usually played a central role in such efforts, as both meeting places for the community and as cherished landmarks in danger of destruction. Business leaders often took leading roles in voicing opposition to high-way construction, and civil rights organizations like the National Association for the Advancement of Colored People (NAACP), the Urban League, and the Congress of Racial Equality (CORE) also played supporting roles, especially as the civil rights movement gathered steam. Yet these efforts remain outside the narrative scope of the freeway revolt largely because they won few victories, leaving black neighborhoods vulnerable to the worst consequences of the interstate highway program.

African Americans, like other Americans, were not unified in their opposition to highway construction. Black community leaders in Miami, for example, were divided over proposals for highway construction. The editors of Miami's black newspaper, the *Miami Times,* editorialized in support of the city's expressway plan in 1957 and again three years later, voicing its approval for a local expressway bond issue, emphasizing the theme of progress: "We cannot afford to take a backwards step." Similarly, the Greater Miami Urban League issued its approval of the expressway plan that would ravage Overtown, though it qualified such support by noting pressing concerns about housing and relocation issues.[59]

Lacking the community resources that enabled some black communities to protest highway construction (even if unsuccessfully), Mexican Americans and Mexican immigrants had even less means by which to defend their neighborhoods. The experience of Graciela Valenzuela and her family underscores this predicament. Initially settling in Boyle Heights after immigrating from Mexico in the early 1960s, Graciela and her husband Abel received a letter from the California Division of Highways, stating that work was beginning in the area and that their home, where they were raising three children, lay in the proposed path of a planned freeway. The letter specified procedures for relocation, outlined state assistance, and served three month's notice. Moving farther east, to Whittier, another community of East Los Angeles, the family found a larger home, removed from the chaos unleashed on Boyle Heights. Years later, however, they discovered that their first home, where their first child had been born, remained intact; the freeway that was to come crashing through had been rerouted. They had moved for nothing.

Graciela and her husband Abel were immigrants from Mexico who were working long hours, earning two incomes, and raising three children who spoke Spanish at home and learned English in school. They did not protest their official instructions. They did not organize petition drives or disrupt public hearings or write letters to the editor or chain themselves to bull-dozers. They played by the rules as specified by the Division of Highways (and as translated by their children), accepting modest compensation and moving when told to move. They remained in East Los Angeles, unfamiliar and unwelcome in other parts of the city.[60] Their story helps explain the absence of visible freeway revolt among city people of color. For many Mexican Americans in particular, language was an obvious barrier, as were the daily demands of work and settlement. For their part, the Valenzuelas, newcomers to the United States, were eager to play by the rules: to speak English, encourage their children to succeed in school, obey the law, and avoid its discipline; if that meant having to relocate for the work of highway construction, such was the price of success in the United States.[61]

Defiant or compliant, urban communities of color stood on the losing end of the fight against the freeway. Just as interstate highways hit their communities, urban Americans of color faced bigger fights: for jobs, housing, health care, education, and protection from the law, especially law enforcement. The interstate era only added insult to injury. Deindustrialization, disinvestment, white flight—all consequences of urban restructuring after World War II—gutted urban communities of color and racialized a new geography of wealth and poverty in postwar America. This is not to wax nostalgic for black urban life before the interstate era, but under stricter regimes of segregation, paradoxically, American cities nurtured bustling minority communities, anchors of communal support and economic opportunity. In the absence of other options, these communities provided gateways to the middle class—the very model of social cohesion and economic vitality that Jacobs extolled in *The Death and Life of Great American Cities*. The destruction of these communities during the 1950s and 1960s, through urban renewal and highway construction, halted this development, precipitating the long hot summers of racial violence.

Of course, black and brown communities were not the only neighbor-hoods eviscerated by highway construction. In the gut-wrenching "One Mile" chapter of *The Power Broker,* Robert Caro recounts the story of Robert Moses hacking his way through stable neighborhoods of the South Bronx, displacing tens of thousands of working-class and middle-class Jewish, Italian, German, Polish, and Irish Americans. East Los Angeles had its version of this story, as did many other urban enclaves of Old World ethnicity. Across the nation, highway construction leveled Jewish neighborhoods, Little Italys, Germantowns, Poletowns, and Irish neighborhoods, some of which were later repackaged as touristic touchstones for younger generations of white ethnic Americans seeking fleeting connections to their urban immigrant past.[62]

White ethnic Americans felt the brutal push of urban renewal and highway construction, but unlike people of color, they could join the exodus to the suburbs. Indeed, the construction of interstate highways facilitated that dispersal. Italian Americans who lived in the Temescal neighborhood of West Oakland, for example, tell heartbreaking stories of the freeway's destruction of an Italian American community. Yet few remained within the precincts of the old neighborhood; many relocated east of the Oakland Hills, to the newer suburban communities of Orinda, Moraga, Walnut Creek, and Lafayette.[63] Postwar housing developers, such as William Levitt on the East Coast or Joseph Eichler and Fritz Burns on the West Coast, welcomed the descendants of Italians, Jews, and Irish immigrants into their new suburban melting pots. In some instances, as in Lakewood, California, Jewish developers built communities open to new patterns of religious diversity, mixing Jews, Protestants, and Catholics. Undergirded by the policies of the HOLC and the FHA, these private developments expanded the boundaries of white racial identity during the postwar era, but their success depended on their proximity to the streams of commerce and consumption that flowed along a new interstate highway system.[64]

The interstate era encompassed a remarkable revision of white identity, or what historian Nell Irvin Painter describes as the "third enlargement" of American whiteness. White Americans of the 1960s could embrace either their whiteness or their ethnic roots, depending on where they lived. Whereas the suburbs nurtured the melting-pot ideology of whiteness, by the early 1970s the cities harbored a new public language of ethnicity and heritage. Black nationalism and multiculturalism inspired this language, as the American descendants of European immigrants quit the melting pot and embraced their ethnic heritage as a badge of pride, not shame. As Matthew Frye Jacobson argues, this new articulation of white ethnicity did not disrupt but, rather, bolstered white privilege, giving short shrift to the history of slavery and conquest and instead celebrating a myth of "Ellis Island whiteness." As the chapters of this book illustrate, highway construction played a paradoxical role in the postwar revision of white identity. On the one hand, it sponsored the creation of new suburban melting pots, which consigned ethnic expression to the private sphere. But on the other hand, the urban politics of fighting freeways sparked impassioned exhortations of white ethnic identity and heritage, particularly in older neighborhoods built by earlier generations of European immigrants. White flight had already sapped the vitality of these neighborhoods, but their casings could accommodate a repackaged nostalgia for a distant immigrant past, suited for tourists and preservationists in the new service-oriented economy of American cities during the 1970s and 1980s.[65]

The Snake in the City

The highways that stand in today's cities are not innocent spaces. Despite the objective posturing of highway planners and engineers, despite the reams of published data that justified their conclusions, and despite the heft of a profession replete with its own schools, trade journals, and associations, the freeway in the city ultimately followed the spatial coordinates of power, money, and ideology. More than a dedicated channel for efficient traffic flow, the urban freeway boosted the stakes of downtown redevelopment, serving as powerful agents of slum clearance and in many instances, of "Negro removal." It dealt its destruction unevenly, dictated by the prejudice, expediency, and resources of the time.

The freeway revolt halted the momentum of the highway juggernaut, reducing the ambition and scope of this monumental endeavor. Like the Summer of Love or the Age of Aquarius, this grassroots movement has earned its place in the folklore of the 1960s. A scrappy phalanx of neighbors, shopkeepers, community activists, parishioners, and parents, bound by the ties of shared history and neighborhood proximity, huddled behind homemade signs and banners to stop the onslaught of highway-building bulldozers, unraveling the master plans of technocrats and bureaucrats. Their victories, won through sheer determination and shrewd political tactics, have entered the canon of postwar urban history. From a broader perspective, the freeway revolt dealt a lasting blow to the modernist city project, with its ambition to rationalize urban space around the automobile and to sort out the complex functions and processes of urban life. Freeways, like the stark housing and office towers that sprouted on the urban scene during the 1960s, were the concrete expression of modernist ideals, but their imposition from the top down sparked a backlash from the bottom up—a grassroots defense of tradition and community and their localized context of streets and neighborhoods. This was the postmodern moment, the death knell of master plans and its metanarrative of progress.

But the freeway revolt, as we know it, does not fit easily into stereotypes of the 1960s as an epoch of progressive social change. How to reconcile this white neighborhood uprising with the simultaneous crisis of race and poverty in the inner city remains a historiographic riddle, for fighting freeways did not entail a concomitant struggle against the entrenchment of urban racial poverty, it did not challenge the new patterns of racial segregation enacted by highway construction, and it did nothing to secure a more equal footing for African Americans and other peoples of color in the political geography of the city. In some cities, whites were willing to forge alliances with blacks in their fight against the freeway, but only when it served the interests of their particular communities, which took shape within historic frameworks of racial segregation. If anything, the freeway revolt, as it played out in Baltimore, San Francisco, New York, New Orleans, and elsewhere, enforced the aggressive push of gentrification, further whitening the precincts of the urban core for tourist consumption and luxury lifestyles. In this context, the freeway revolt rallied its participants, wittingly or unwittingly, in defense of the spaces wrought by racial and class privilege. The paths that urban freeways took in the course of their construction followed not the dictates of empirical science but, rather, the subjective axes of racial and class power; but the path that freeways *did not* take followed those coordinates as well. That is why there is no Beverly Hills Freeway.

Noting the disparate outcomes of black versus white resistance to highway construction in Baltimore, one black activist aptly described the politics of fighting freeways: "The snake, if not racist, certainly seems to know that white is more threatening to it than black."[66] This insight provides a starting point for my investigation of alternative histories of urban highway construction. In contrast to the dominant narrative of the freeway revolt, city people of color have a different story to tell and a different way of telling it. By and large, that story is not one of triumph; rather, it is one of reckoning—of coming to terms with the freeway and its monolithic presence in the landscape of daily life. It is a story of remembrance, and of some nostalgia for the "good old days," before the onslaught of bulldozers and the rush of commuting traffic. It is an ironic story, rendered through wit, sarcasm, satire, and other imaginative forms of cultural appropriation. And though it is usually a story of utter destruction, it is not one of defeat, for the very act of telling this story through traditional and inventive cultural forms signals the continuing struggle against the freeway and its towering presence in the racialized quarters of American cities.

Like a prism refracting a beam of light, the city dispersed the freeway into various strands of meaning and significance. Chapter 2 takes up the interpretive strand of gender, which emerged through feminism's "second wave" of the 1960s and 1970s. Although women took separate roads to feminism, urban women of diverse classes, races, and ethnicities earned a prominent, though largely unrecognized, place in the history of the freeway revolt, through polemics, politics, and poetry. Some changed the course of freeways, thus changing the course of urban history; others changed public consciousness, leveling a gendered critique of the freeway and its benefit to what we used to call "mankind."

2 "Nobody but a Bunch of Mothers"

Fighting the Highwaymen during Feminism's Second Wave

She towers over the city below, clutching a car in her hand. Her miniskirt and bikini top reveal long sturdy legs and heaving breasts. Traffic has come to a halt as people flee their cars in terror. The police cannot stop the destructive march of this buxom giant, who visits her feminine wrath on the city. It's the Fifty-Foot Woman, and the freeway between her legs is about to topple (Figure 2.1).

A 1958 B movie, *The Attack of the 50-Foot Woman* tells the story of an abused woman who grows to giant size through an alien encounter and gets even with her philandering husband. The movie belongs to a category of 1950s science fiction films that made the city its mise-en-scène. The urban science fiction film rendered a spectacular portrait of urban destruction, deploying innovative visual effects to dramatize the fall of civilization. And by 1958, at the very moment of their debut on the urban scene, freeways fit squarely within the iconography of the urban science fiction film, a concrete symbol of progress in its latest incarnation. And though it was built to last, this freeway met a quick demise at the hands of an angry woman.[1]

The image suggests an undercurrent of anxiety about women and their threat to the man-made icons of progress, at least in the galaxy of 1950s American popular culture. Yet, as with the many social fantasies and anxieties encoded within movies, TV programs, and radio hits, this image struck a chord of authenticity in the political culture of the 1960s. With the onset of the freeway revolt, diverse women in cities throughout the nation expressed their ambition to pulverize freeways and the plans for their construction.

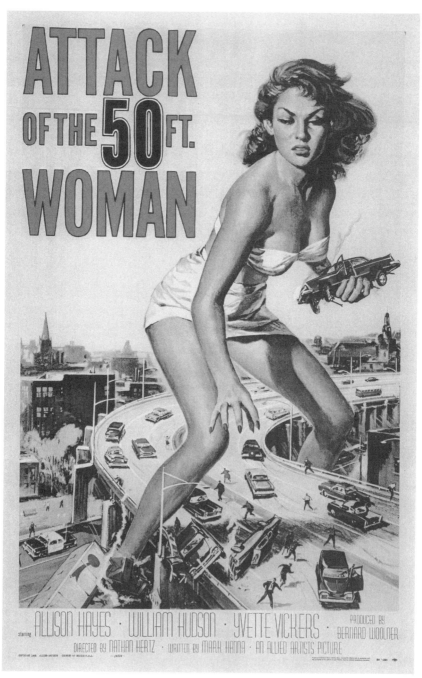

FIGURE 2.1. *Attack of the 50-ft. Woman,* promotional poster, 1958.

They took leading roles in organizing opposition to urban highway construction and asserted a gendered critique of that work through creative forms of cultural expression. Their disparate efforts illuminate a gendered discrepancy between the cadre of male planners and engineers who built freeways, the "fraternity" that Jane Jacobs chided in *Death and Life,* and the women who challenged their efforts in order to defend the spaces of family, neighborhood, and community. Though men and women of diverse neighborhoods united in opposition to highway construction, there are gendered expressions of this conflict that resonated throughout the political culture of the 1960s. Amid the surge of feminism's so-called second wave, women stepped outside the boxes of 1950s stereotypes to openly question the premises of urban highway construction, casting doubt on the benefit of freeways to "mankind"—a popular term in the civic discourse of postwar America.[2]

The dominant narrative of the freeway revolt slights the intellectual and organizational leadership of white women, but it altogether ignores the voices of women of color, who mustered their own version of the freeway revolt through creative forms of cultural expression, even after freeways had decimated their communities. This chapter is thus a tale of two struggles: of white metropolitan women—mothers, homeowners, and shrewd organizers—who assumed leading roles in their communities' fight against highway construction, and of working-class women of color, who summoned artistic talent and creative imagination to assert an indictment of highway construction as both a sexist and a racist enterprise. Their divergent experiences with highway construction illustrate racial and class disparities in the fight against the freeway, but the combined force of their efforts sheds light on the gendered dimensions of the freeway revolt and its diverse expressions in American culture.

Freeways and the Suburban Mystique

In Alison Lurie's 1965 novel, *The Nowhere City,* Paul Cattleman, recently graduated from Harvard with a history PhD, and his wife, Katherine, leave the cozy comforts of Cambridge so he can work as company historian for the Nutting Research and Development Corporation, an electronics firm located in West Los Angeles. The newlywed couple rent a stucco bungalow in Mar

Vista, a tract-housing community built for aircraft workers during the late 1940s. As Paul begins to discover the pleasures of Los Angeles, which include a furtive dalliance with a beatnik waitress in Venice Beach, Katherine frets at home, bedridden from allergies in Southern California's arid climate, clueless about her husband's affair. She hates Los Angeles, clinging to East Coast stereotypes of the city as artificial and crass. Of particular distress to Katherine is the imminent arrival of Interstate 405, which by the mid-1960s was gouging its way north, to the San Fernando Valley, and south, through the housing tracts of aircraft and aerospace workers.[3]

The coming of the freeway induces an obsessive paranoia in Katherine, who counts the growing number of vacancies on her street. Each abandoned home leaves her even more uneasy and with greater regret for accompanying her husband to Southern California. Lurie's portrait of marital dysfunction implicates the freeway, which undermines the stability of domestic life. The freeway threatens to demolish the couple's new home, and it provides an easy conduit for her husband's infidelity, as he speeds across the city's new freeways in a Corvette Stingray to pursue an extramarital affair. For this inconsolable wife, life in Los Angeles is not the suburban utopia pictured in advertisements and TV shows; it is a lonesome trap verging on destruction.

Katherine's predicament in *The Nowhere City* is more than the product of one writer's vivid imagination. This portrait of a woman's confinement resonated throughout feminism's "second wave," which surfaced during the 1960s, largely among college-educated white women who reinvigorated a feminist tradition that had begun in England and America in the late nineteenth century.[4] This renewed push for gender equality escalated during the tide of affluence that pulsed outward from cities toward a thriving suburban fringe. The democratization of suburban home ownership, and all the mobility that that entailed, exacted a price from a new generation of white suburban women who asked, Is this all?, wondering if they had sold their soul, or at least their dignity, confidence, and agency, in order to live the suburban dream. This was how Betty Friedan posed the question in her 1960 best seller, *The Feminine Mystique*, which some view as the opening salvo of second-wave feminism. Here Friedan targets the suburban home, calling it a "trap," as well as "the ugly and endless sprawls which are becoming a national problem." This new spatial arrangement, Friedan argued, forced a generation of white suburban housewives into a stultifying regime of isolation and immobility.[5]

A few perceptive scholars have corroborated this argument, arguing that during the postwar period, the very organization of suburban space enforced traditional notions of gender hierarchy. Although these scholars emphasize the biases built into the mass-produced, suburban tract home, highway construction played its part as well. By opening up new territory for suburban development, and by separating the private world of home from the public realm of work on an unprecedented scale, postwar highway construction created new spaces for the reinstatement of sexual divisions of labor. The 1950s witnessed its own "cult of domesticity," a postwar rehash of the nineteenth-century bourgeois ideology that consigned women to the private sphere of home and family and expected men to fulfill their responsibilities in the public realm of the city. This ideology came back to trouble a new generation of suburban women, coercing them into the domestic spaces created by a national flurry of housing and highway construction.[6]

Women and the Freeway Revolt

Yet the resonant portrait of the alienated suburban housewife also included a degree of myth and stereotype. In spite of the "feminine mystique," women actually stood on the front lines of political activism in postwar America, across the spectrum of identity and ideology and across metropolitan space, in both inner city and suburb. As Michelle Nickerson and a more recent generation of historians have shown, the mid-twentieth century introduced a new politics of motherhood, a gendered political formation in which women publicly invoked their maternal responsibilities as a basis of political activism. Unlike the Progressive-Era generation of middle-class women reformers, these "housewife activists" were not uniformly middle class, nor were they primarily concerned with uplifting or reforming the lot of the less fortunate. Rather, they situated themselves as mothers and housewives within their own communities, organizing to defend their boundaries from the perceived threat of an outsider attack. By the 1930s, a new political woman emerged "who worked to keep her family and neighborhood intact—to maintain as much normalcy and security as possible."[7]

Women stood on the front lines of various social movements throughout the postwar period, from anticommunism to antiwar. On the left, women challenged the structures of patriarchy and their constraint of feminine mobility and opportunity. But on the right, women emphasized their duties as mothers and housewives to protect their communities from perceived external threats, whether from Washington, D.C., Moscow, Wall Street, or the inner city. Washington bureaucrats were a favorite target among this generation of conservative women; they spoke out against the perceived excesses of the federal government, a reaction against the New Deal order and its immediate effects. These "mothers of conservatism" organized themselves through a shared sense of maternal responsibility, voicing a collective suspicion of federal bureaucracy and its reach into the realms of everyday life, especially in those areas, such as education and housing, that had an impact on the domestic sphere of family and home.[8]

Like the landmark 1954 case *Brown v. Board of Education* the Federal Aid Highway Act of 1956 provoked women to organize themselves, often as mothers and housewives, against federal incursions into the domestic sphere. Without taking sides on the left or right, white metropolitan women, from well-heeled and working-class communities alike, in both city and suburb, entered the fray of local politics to defend their neighborhoods against the ravaging effects of highway construction. Unlike many of the mothers of conservatism, these freeway-fighting women struggled to defend the physical, not the racial, integrity of their neighborhoods. Yet like their conservative counterparts on the front lines of neighborhood activism, they had a deep mistrust of federal bureaucracy during the 1950s and 1960s, while also defying popular stereotypes of June Cleaver housewives who avoided political confrontation. Through both class privilege and ethnic identity, these outspoken white women brought the politics of neighborhood and motherhood to bear on the public transcript of the freeway revolt.

Postwar New York provides an illustrative example. With varying degrees of success, white women, as housewives, mothers, and stalwart activists, organized themselves and their communities against the work of

Robert Moses. Robert Caro, for example, wrote about the "housewives of East Tremont" in the famous "One Mile" chapter of *The Power Broker*. On April 23, 1953, some three hundred housewives from the Bronx neighborhood of East Tremont, mostly from working-class Jewish immigrant households, chartered several buses to travel to City Hall to pack a Board of Estimate hearing that had initiated condemnation proceedings for their neighborhood. The housewives brought with them homemade signs that called Moses's Cross Bronx Expressway "Heartbreak Highway" and included a map of an alternate route drafted by the Bronx engineering society that would have spared the homes of East Tremont. Despite their concerted push into the male lair of municipal power, however, the housewives of East Tremont ultimately lost to Moses and his ironclad determination to push the expressway through their neighborhood.[9]

In the gentrifying neighborhoods of Lower Manhattan, however, mothers and housewives scored more decisive victories in the fight against the freeway. It was in these precincts that Jane Jacobs built her reputation as a streetwise activist, taking on the city's most powerful figures and, through her polemic writings, provoking a paradigm shift in the culture of city planning. A mother and housewife who forsook the suburban dream for city living, Jacobs summoned her experiences as a mother of three, as well as her extensive connections in media and government, to wage a civic war against highway officials in New York City to preserve the social and cultural life of Lower Manhattan. Though she rejected political labels, her stalwart activism against urban renewal and highway construction and her collaboration with other indignant Greenwich Village mothers exemplified the politics of motherhood that surfaced in postwar America.

Jacobs and other Greenwich Village mothers, for example, fought to save Washington Square Park from automobile traffic in the 1950s. Moses wanted to widen and extend Fifth Avenue southward along a depressed route through the park, linking growing volumes of traffic that coursed between Midtown Manhattan and downtown. The urbanist Lewis Mumford attacked this plan, calling it an act of "civic vandalism" that would "cut the square into two unrelated halves . . . endanger[ing] pedestrians and children and reduc[ing] a precious recreation space."[10] Through their mutual involvement in the Parent–Teachers' Association (PTA) of Public School (PS) 41, Jacobs, along with two other Greenwich Village mothers, Shirley Hayes and Edith Lyons, established the Joint Emergency Committee to Close Washington Square to All but Emergency Traffic. This small but determined group of women won an early victory in 1952, persuading the city's Board of Estimate to put a temporary halt on plans for the expressway, prompting the *New York Times* to report, "New Traffic Plan/Project That Would Put New Roads in Washington Sq. Park Upset by Women."[11]

Jacobs credited Hayes with being the driving force behind the committee. An aspiring actress and the wife of an advertising executive who gave up her career to raise four children and, later in her life, a charter member of the National Organization of Women (NOW), Hayes collected 16,000 signatures against official plans for a Washington Square expressway, as well as the endorsements of politicians, newspapers, twelve parent–teacher associations, and the Lions Club. She took an extreme position, pushing for an outright ban on traffic from Washington Square. She even garnered the support of Eleanor Roosevelt, a one-time resident of the square. One local observer recalled that Hayes "and the mothers kept insisting and wouldn't give up."[12]

In many ways, this was a mothers' struggle. The PTA of PS 41, one of the oldest schools in the New York City Department of Education, played an essential role, providing an institutional forum for local mothers to develop strategies to preserve the square for their families. Jacobs later spelled out this concern in *The Death and Life of Great American Cities* by recounting the battle of Washington Square as a local effort to improve "certain city uses, such as children's play, strolling, and horsing around, at the expense of vehicular traffic."[13] Children played a prominent, if symbolic, role in the battle of Washington Square, making posters and attending rallies with their parents. Hayes marshaled her sons to stand by her side in defending the square, and toward the culmination of the controversy, Jacobs enlisted her three-year-old daughter, Mary, to hold one end of a ceremonial ribbon that signaled community ownership of the square. Not unlike the way in which white antihighway activists in Cambridge, Massachusetts, enlisted immigrant and African American families to represent their interests in the

FIGURE 2.2. Mothers and children protest plans for the Lower Manhattan Expressway, New York City, 1962. Allyn Baum/The New York Times/Redux.

struggle against the Inner Belt highway, the mothers of Greenwich Village put their children's face on the fight to save Washington Square (Figure 2.2).[14]

Ultimately, this strategy worked. The city's Board of Estimate finally killed the proposal for the Washington Square expressway in 1959, handing Greenwich Village mothers a stunning defeat of Robert Moses at the height of his power. Not only was it a victory for Jacobs and her allies, but it also sparked national demands for citizen participation in the highway-planning process. As Robert Fishman notes, Hayes's Joint Emergency Committee became "the mother of all citizen activist groups," and its tactics—collecting signatures, rallying local officials, writing editorials, and packing public hearings—inspired nationwide strategies to defeat state plans for highway construction. With college degrees, home equity, dual incomes, inherited wealth, flexible hours, and contacts in media and government, the mothers of Greenwich Village staged a form of political theater, asserting the rights of pedestrians over automobiles in a gentrifying neighborhood.[15] Their efforts also reflected a larger flurry of organizational activism among middle-class women across the political spectrum during the 1950s, women whose sense of civic engagement spurred a new zeal for canvassing, speaking, writing, establishing committees, and other local forms of organizational activism.[16]

The Greenwich Village mothers also took advantage of their connections to local news outlets like the *Village Voice,* the first-of-its-kind alternative newspaper that reported on community issues. Throughout the controversy, the *Voice* diligently covered the efforts of the PTA mothers, stressing the roles of Jacobs, Lyons, Hayes, and their allies in the confrontation. The paper's editor in chief, Dan Wolf, tirelessly editorialized in support of the Greenwich Village mothers, and the columns of Mary Perot Nichols (then wife of Robert Nichols) kept a sympathetic focus on the struggles against highway construction and urban renewal in New York and other cities throughout the nation. Nichols, a close associate of the PTA mothers at PS 41 and a founding member of the Greenwich Village Planning Committee, used her columns in the *Voice* to lambast the city's efforts to introduce more car traffic into Lower Manhattan. In the following decade, Nichols continued this journalistic form of activism by writing extensively against the proposed incursion of the Lower Manhattan Expressway and by vigilantly reporting other antihighway battles in cities like New Orleans and San Francisco.[17]

The stakes were high in Greenwich Village, especially as the pace of gentrification picked up in the neighborhood during the 1950s and 1960s. In her classic 1961 polemic *The Death and Life of American Cities,* Jacobs cast Greenwich Village as a community under siege. The neighborhood was under siege, but not just from vilified public officials like Robert Moses. It was also convulsed by gentrification, seeing its celebrated mix of artists, intellectuals, and bohemians displaced by an invasion of developers, architects, ad men, and interior designers. An apartment boom stoked speculation about the "rebirth [of] a neighborhood that may become one of the most fashionable in Manhattan." *Partisan Review* editor William Barnett wrote about the upswing in Greenwich Village's real estate market in his *New York Times* article "Bohemia Gone Bourgeois." The neighborhood's quirky streets still provided respite from Manhattan's tedious grid, and Washington Square

Park retained some of its scruff, but Greenwich Village was no longer "the new American capital of Bohemia"—a title that went to the East Village in 1964.[18] The changing socioeconomic profile of the West Village sharpened a local sense of insiders versus outsiders and cultivated a certain pride, maybe a bit xenophobic, in neighborhood distinction. When Moses targeted the area around Washington Square for a slum-clearance program in 1951, the indignant editors of *Interiors* published a retort loaded with a sense of Waspish entitlement:

> Whatever it lacks in streamlined convenience, this picturesque section has one thing to distinguish it from the six other slums with which it was grouped for demolition purposes: it is a *community,* with a strong group sense which is quite unrelated to literary clichés about the village Bohemia overrun with Mimis and Rudolfos. It is a neighborhood settled by a homogenous, self-supporting and self-sufficient group, bound by its own culture and traditions.[19]

This was the Greenwich Village that Jane Jacobs touted as the exemplar of "good city form" in *Death and Life.* Like women on the rightward end of the political spectrum, Jacobs attacked the state from a position of racial and class privilege, emphasizing its infringement on neighborhood autonomy. She brought her maternal concerns to bear on this perspective, reiterating the details of a mother's life in New York City—taking kids to school, gossiping with neighbors, running household errands, and scheduling PTA meetings, music lessons, and chorus recitals. Her real emphasis, however, was on the spaces that enclose these routines, stressing the importance of streets, sidewalks, and stoops to the chores of parenting. In Jacobs's New York, these spaces sustained the familial relationships that had been consigned to the private sphere by Victorian Americans of the nineteenth century. Like many urban women, however, Jacobs rejected these partitions as impractical and irrelevant, staking the right of mothers and children to the public spaces of the city.

Jacobs situates her critique within a broader attack on the gendered inequities built into the modernist city, emphasizing the discrepancy between the environments planned and designed by men and the needs of women who live in these environments. She attacked the "paternalistic, if not authoritarian" prescriptions of Ebenezer Howard and Le Corbusier, the founding fathers of twentieth-century planning orthodoxy. In her blunt assertion that "most city architectural designers and planners are men," Jacobs criticized the planning "fraternity," not only for its destruction of cities but also for its construction of suburbs. Like Friedan and Lurie, Jacobs repudiated the suburban isolation of women that second-wave feminists deplored. She argued that suburbs let men off the hook, leaving the chores of "normal, daytime life," to "impossibly vacuous housewives."[20] Throughout the chapters of *Death and Life,* Jacobs pauses to attack the interstate highway program and its impact on city life, but she singles out the consequences for women. She argues that urban highway construction both destroyed the spaces vital to the welfare of families and children and sponsored the growth of suburbs that confined women to a life of household drudgery.

Death and Life also provoked gendered expressions of conflict around the ideals of city planning regnant at midcentury. Its arguments upset some of the male experts, who compromised their posture of technocratic or journalistic objectivity by resorting to chauvinism and condescension. During a public hearing on the Washington Square controversy, for example, Moses bellowed, "There is nobody against this—nobody, nobody, nobody but a bunch of mothers!" Moses's rebuke of mothers matched the sexist rants of Jacobs's one-time ally, the urbanist Lewis Mumford. Bitter, perhaps, over her sour review of his recent book *The Culture of the Cities,* Mumford, in turn, savaged *Death and Life* in the *New Yorker.* His review essay, "Mother Jacobs's Home Remedies," ridiculed the book as "schoolgirl howlers," admonishing a woman for insinuating her way into the male preserve of city planning and politics. *Death and Life* provoked other public outbursts of male chauvinism. Similarly, in 1962, *Scientific American* dismissed the book as the screed of an "angry young woman," and Edward Chase, writing for *Architectural Forum,* ridiculed Jacobs as a "militant dame." Branded a naive schoolgirl, a cantankerous old maid, or a caustic feminist by her staunchest male critics, Jane Jacobs aroused sexist caricatures of outspoken and politically savvy women within the male-dominated culture of midcentury planning.[21]

Jacobs might have expected this kind of animosity, given the way she singled out the sex of her target in *Death and Life*: "the men with great visible egos" who thought it was "radical and exciting" to build broad swaths of highway above, below and on the surface of the urban fabric.[22] These men clung to the "outmoded fantasies" of Le Corbusier or Norman Bel Geddes, whose "dream cities" of the 1920s and 1930s had little relevance to the contemporary needs of diverse city dwellers in the 1960s. Jacobs insisted that these fantasies belonged to "the generation of New York's Robert Moses," a generation whose time had passed. To underscore the deluded state of midcentury planning, Jacobs even rendered a subtle portrait of Moses in drag, a man who "cling[s] to old intellectual excitements, just as some belles, when they are old ladies, still cling to the fashions and coiffures of their exciting youth."[23]

The final act of Jane Jacobs, before her move to Canada in 1968, was her leadership in the local fight against LOMEX, the southernmost leg of a tripartite system of expressways that would have cut across the island of Manhattan. LOMEX was slated to follow the path of Broome Street, linking the Holland Tunnel in the west with the Williamsburg and Manhattan Bridges in the east, slicing through Greenwich Village, Soho, Little Italy, Chinatown, and the Lower East Side.[24] A national celebrity after the publication of *Death and Life,* Jacobs took the helm of a coalition of small business owners, neighbors, attorneys, journalists, artists, and other concerned citizens determined to defeat Moses and LOMEX. The details of this battle, which stretched across three mayoral administrations during the greater part of the 1960s, are well known, but Jacobs emerged as the unlikely symbol of a powerful grassroots movement. Crediting the efforts of women like Shirley Hayes, Jacobs organized the Joint Committee to Stop the Lower Manhattan Expressway and staged other forms of political theater that won admiration and notoriety. She wore gas masks to Board of Estimate meetings; she interrupted planning officials in public hearings; and she destroyed a stenographic machine that recorded the minutes of a State Department of Transportation hearing in 1965. This last stunt prompted Jacobs's arrest for attempting to incite a riot, but criminal charges were dropped after Jacobs agreed to pay a fine for disorderly conduct.[25] Finally, after years of waffling on the issue, Mayor John Lindsay withdrew the proposal for LOMEX in his reelection campaign of 1969, conceding that pushing for expressways in Manhattan was "as close to political poison as a candidate could get" (Figure 2.3).[26]

FIGURE 2.3. Kill the Xpressway Now! Jane Jacobs (*center*), 1962. Fred W. McDarrah/
Premium Archive/Getty Images.

So maybe, at least in the mind of Moses and his "fraternity" of midcentury planners, Jane Jacobs was the fifty-foot woman, laying waste to the
best-laid plans of New York's planning establishment. Her polemics inspired
new approaches to urban planning and design, but they also overlapped with
contemporary forms of public activism among conservative women, who
shared her suspicion of state power and maternal commitment to defending
their neighborhoods against federal overreach. Jacobs looks even more like a
mother of conservatism if one considers *Death and Life* as a defense of racial

and class privilege. She railed against the interventions of government and its audacious figureheads but said nothing about the radical forces of capitalism that ravaged her neighborhood, pushing out factories, affordable housing, and struggling artists while enforcing broader disparities of race, wealth, and poverty. Her color-blind polemic altogether ignored these patterns of rising inequality, even as they made a starker imprint on the landscape of the postwar American city. Such ignorance of structural inequality might make Jacobs a mother of neoconservatism, as opposed to outright conservatism, but assigning pithy labels distracts from her forceful presence in urban public life during the postwar period and her unique power to shape the discourse of the freeway revolt.

Other metropolitan mothers took up Jacobs's struggle, even in suburban settings. In the affluent Seattle suburb of Bellevue, for example, Nancy Rising emerged from the ranks of her local PTA in 1963 to organize against the proposed incursion of Interstate 605, which the Washington Highway Department planned to serve the suburban growth areas of Redmond, Kirkland, Bellevue, and Renton. As president of her local PTA, Rising led a local effort to block a proposed zoning change in her community, which taught her the skills needed to fight policy changes that affected her neighborhood: how to develop strategies, how to do technical research, and how to challenge public officials. Rising applied these skills to a bigger fight against I-605, the so-called East Side Freeway, which, on the fast track to completion, threatened to displace Rising's "beautiful, secluded Bellevue home" and her children's school. She organized the East Side League, which represented some twenty-three community-based organizations. Although Rising was the logical leader for the league, she ceded that post to a young political novice, Jerry Kuenhoel, thinking that suburban men would resent a woman in charge. Still, Rising remained the force behind the league, using local school offices to mimeograph fliers, pamphlets, petition forms, and form letters. As in New York City, this was another mothers' fight against the interstate, and the *Seattle Times* reported, "Mothers and children combed the Bellevue and Lake Hills area with leaflets and petitions."[27]

Having learned how to fight civic battles, Rising handled public relations for the campaign against the East Side Freeway, working with contacts in media and government. After a packed public hearing in December 1968, with over a thousand in attendance, the East Side Freeway simply died a slow death. State and city officials issued no further public statements on the proposed highway, and in 1969 the Highway Omnibus Bill, which included funds for the East Side Freeway, appeared before the state legislature.[28] State senator Marvin Durkan, a close associate of Rising and an outspoken advocate for mass transit, introduced an amendment to delete this inclusion, and the bill passed with this amended deletion. The East Side Freeway simply died in its tracks. Though the East Side League stopped holding meetings, Rising went on to win a seat on the Bellevue City Council in late 1969.

Other suburban women ventured into the inner city to fight freeways. Baltimore's freeway revolt, for example, gathered steam after Lucretia Fisher fell in love with the dilapidated charm of the city's historic waterfront. Described by the *Baltimore Sun* as "a matron from suburban Ruxton," Fisher discovered the Fells Point neighborhood one evening in 1965 after a concert at the Peabody Institute. The area's redbrick buildings and cobblestone streets, built during the Revolutionary period, struck Fisher as having the potential to become "another Georgetown, only better."[29] The neighborhood had fallen into disrepair, however, thanks in part to plans for the East–West Expressway, an Inner Harbor crossing that, like San Francisco's Embarcadero Freeway, threatened to sever the city from its historic waterfront. Fisher, known affectionately as "Lu" among friends, arranged tours of the neighborhood for her affluent suburban friends, and they began buying up properties in the area to renovate for a rapidly expanding market of young urban professionals. Their slumming produced results, giving rise to such effective grassroots organizations as the Expressway Committee, the Fells Point Improvement Association, and the Society for the Preservation of Federal Hill, Montgomery Street, and Fells Point. Fisher also enlisted the support of her contacts in local government, including City Councilman Thomas Ward and local developer James Rouse, later known for the festival marketplace that many cities, including Baltimore, adopted as a strategy of urban redevelopment in the 1970s and 1980s.[30]

Although the incursion of suburban money drew some suspicion among the white working-class residents who remained in the neighborhood, Fells

Point became Fisher's turf, especially after she opened a popular museum devoted to local history in one of the many buildings that she purchased. She garnered the active support of the Daughters of the American Revolution and the Maryland State Society Daughters of the American Colonists, who helped Fisher in sponsoring local events like the Fells Point Fun Festival in 1967, which attracted thousands of people and became an annual rallying point for local opposition to the Baltimore highway system. After extensive wrangling at the local, state, and federal levels and after other grassroots organizations representing Baltimore's diverse communities joined the fight against the freeway, Fisher's tireless and costly efforts paid off: in 1972, attorneys for the Society for the Preservation of Federal Hill, Montgomery Street, and Fells Point won a court injunction against the East–West Expressway, which ultimately never got off the drawing boards.[31]

Another woman who played a leading role in Baltimore's freeway revolt was Barbara Mikulski, as of this writing in her fourth term as U.S. senator from Maryland. Like Rising, Mikulski began in her career in public service by fighting freeways, not as an urban mother or a suburban matron but simply as a tough community organizer from a working-class neighborhood. Yet in the spirit of the time, she asserted her opposition to Baltimore's highway program through a sharpened sense of white ethnic pride. Representing the white working-class communities of Canton, Highlandtown, and Fells Point, Mikulski assumed leadership within the Southeast Baltimore Community Organization, a nearly all-white coalition of some ninety neighborhood organizations and groups united to oppose urban expressway construction.[32] Assuming leadership in an organization that later played a central role in fighting efforts to desegregate Baltimore's schools, Mikulski spoke on behalf of the white working-class ethnic neighborhoods of Baltimore. She rejected contemporary visions of integration, adopting a "community first" approach that favored coalitions among communities shaped by long-standing patterns of racial segregation. This strategy enabled Mikulski to speak out on behalf of white ethnic rights. For example, at a public hearing in Baltimore's Highlandtown neighborhood, originally a German settlement on the outskirts of Baltimore proper, Mikulski spoke as a "young Polish American," likening the threat of highway construction to the loss of the American Dream:

My great grandparents [and] grandparents . . . came to this country looking for an American Dream. The dream was that through hard work and honesty they could own a home that no King, Kaiser or Czar could take from them on some whim. Now, in 1971, the dream has turned into a nightmare. The State Roads Commission and City Hall are taking from us the very homes we have struggled for all of our lives.[33]

Mikulski went on, saying, "The only people served by this expressway are people living in the county and they aren't paying for it. We ethnic Americans (the ones who didn't move to the suburbs) are paying for it with our homes, our neighborhoods, and our taxes."[34]

By this time, Mikulski, the great-granddaughter of Polish immigrants, was already speaking out on behalf of white ethnic America. Writing an op-ed piece in the *New York Times* in September 1970, Mikulski issued a stinging rebuke to "phony white liberals, pseudo black militants and patronizing bureaucrats," asking, "Who Speaks for Ethnic Americans?" "The Ethnic American is forgotten and forlorn," she wrote, on behalf of "40 million working class Americans who live primarily in 58 major industrial cities like Baltimore and Chicago." These were the people whose roots "are in Central and Southern Europe," who "have been in this country for one, two or three generations," and "who have made maximum contribution to the USA, yet received minimal recognition." She emphasized the historic discrimination faced by white ethnic Americans, recounting the restrictions placed on immigration from southern and eastern Europe during the 1920s and the derogatory labels invented for Americans of Italian, Polish, and German descent. The one place where the ethnic American "felt the mastery of his own fate," however, "was his own neighborhood": the "urban villages," places "where people knew each other"—places that sustained "warmth, charm, and zesty communal spirit."[35]

"But here we are in the 1970s," Mikulski continued, and "the ethnic American is losing ground economically. He can't even buy a home in his own neighborhood because FHA loans are restricted to new suburban housing." The Little Italys and Polish Hills of urban America faced the threat of extinction, and ethnic Americans, at least those who resisted the impulse to move to the suburbs, found that "the only things being planned for [their] neighborhood[s] are housing projects, expressways and fertilizer factories."[36]

Mikulski thus articulated her opposition to highway construction in Baltimore through a certain politics of identity, though not the politics of motherhood or class privilege. As Matthew Frye Jacobson reminds us, the early 1970s brought a white ethnic revival in the United States, inspired in no small part by the perceived success of racialized social movements during the 1950s and 1960s. Ethnic awareness, rooted in the diverse neighborhoods of American cities, engendered a "whole new syntax of nationality and belonging," but it upheld existing patterns of racial inequality. It strove mainly to relocate the center of a normative whiteness from "Plymouth Rock whiteness" to "Ellis Island whiteness." The very threat of highway construction to the physical enclaves of Ellis Island whiteness—Boston's North End, New York's Lower East Side, San Francisco's Little Italy, and Southeast Baltimore— helped galvanize public articulations of white ethnic solidarity. The future senator thus helped solidify her political reputation by appropriating the discourse of the civil rights movement to defend Baltimore's enclaves of white ethnicity against the onslaught of interstate highways.[37]

The politics of fighting freeways were long, drawn-out affairs, with incremental victories and daunting setbacks. The battles took shape at all levels of government and implicated diverse social actors, across the divides of race, class, and gender. Yet in cities throughout the nation, a visible pattern emerged in which women, from both posh suburbs and gritty urban quarters, manned the front lines of the *visible* freeway revolt, mobilizing organized expressions of political protest to resist federal plans for highway construction. By defending neighborhoods steeped in class privilege or Old World ethnicity against federal intervention, these women stood outside the leftward shift of American politics during the 1960s. Not only did they corroborate a conservative mistrust of federal government, but they also defended historic patterns of racial segregation and mimicked the discourse of civil rights in the interests of white communities. Their organizing skills also foreshadowed the late-twentieth-century politics of NIMBYism, especially for some suburban women, like Rising, who defended her backyard against invasive state policies.

It is tempting to group some of these women within the growing ranks of white conservative women who helped tip the balance of late-twentieth-century American politics toward the right, but assigning labels obscures the gendered contours of the freeway revolt. Besides, not all white women who fought freeways did so on behalf of their own communities. In Miami, Elizabeth Virrick stands out as an exception to this pattern, a "one woman crusade" against the destruction of Miami's black community by expressway construction. Virrick crossed racial lines in her campaign for open-housing laws in Florida, drawing interracial support. A resident of Miami since the 1920s, Virrick organized the Coconut Grove Citizens Committee for Slum Clearance in 1948 to improve black housing in Miami's Coconut Grove section. When Interstate 95 threatened Miami's historic black neighborhood, Virrick emerged as a sole crusader for housing and relocation assistance. She challenged elected officials, badgered staffers in city and county agencies, and cultivated local press. She also reached out to housing reformers in other cities, corresponding with federal housing officials and writing articles on housing inequality in her monthly publication, the *Ink Newsletter*. Denouncing Miami's proposed expressways as "great Frankenstein monsters," Virrick demonstrated how white women could look beyond their whiteness to insert a racial critique into the discourse of the freeway revolt.[38]

From New York to Miami to Seattle, white women of the interstate era defied stereotypes of the isolated suburban housewife by fighting freeways, yet they also shared a growing mistrust of the federal government and its interventions. Although their politics defied ideological labels, their stories nonetheless inflected the folklore of the freeway. Movies like *The Attack of the Fifty Foot Woman* underscored women's threat to man-made infrastructure, but other realms of postwar American popular culture dramatized the unique power of women to protect their homes and communities from destruction. In 1961, the same year that Random House published *Death and Life*, a rival company, Simon and Schuster, issued *Make Way for the Highway*, another of its Little Golden Books (a series of small, affordable children's books that began in 1942). The book tells the story of a "little old woman" who faces down highway-building bulldozers. "I'm sorry ma'am, but we have to take this house down," the workers tell the woman. "No you don't," she replies. "The new highway goes right through here," the men insist. "No it doesn't," she says. When the Big Boss is summoned to resolve the dispute, he calls on the Bigger Boss to investigate. Before this supervisor arrives, the workers surreptitiously reroute the freeway on behalf of the old lady's wishes, leaving her home intact.[39]

Like many children's stores, *Make Way for the Highway* offers a simplified parable for grown-up complexities. In 1961 many men and women faced the dilemma of highway construction, evicted from their homes to make way for the many freeways built under the National Interstate and Defense Highway Act. This story resonated within the flurry of highway construction that ensued during the late 1950s and early 1960s. It dramatized the destruction of homes and nature. It described the many machines used to build highways. It emphasized the layers of bureaucracy: from the construction crews to the "big bosses" to the "bigger bosses." And it lionized the ordinary women who brought bulldozers to a halt by insisting on their right to protect their property.

From stories about giant women to little old ladies, American popular culture was shifting its focus to women on the front lines of the freeway revolt. Jane Jacobs, Shirley Hayes, Nancy Rising, Lucretia Fisher, Barbara Mikulski, and Elizabeth Virrick inspired much of this discourse, their victories packaged by a national culture industry into films and books for mass consumption. In other neighborhoods, however, women of color inserted their own voices into the discourse of the freeway revolt. Lacking access to the resources, opportunities, and connections that empowered women in whiter or wealthier communities to successfully challenge the interstate program, women of color drew on cultural traditions, artistic talent, and historical experience to render their own freeway revolt, asserting a deeper indictment of the freeway as an instrument of racial, class, and gendered oppression.

Feminism under the Freeway

From the Barrio Historico of Tucson, Arizona, for example, the Chicana poet Patricia Preciado Martin wrote "The Journey" in 1988 to preserve her memories of her elderly aunt and the strolls they used to take through the streets of the barrio. The poem takes the reader through the sentimental details of that journey: coming to the convalescent home to meet her aunt, holding her arm as they walk slowly past the old house where her aunt was born, basking in the fresh air of a spring day. Martin remembers the sensory pleasures: the smell of fresh flowers, the sight of the "gleaming white towers" of St. Augustine's Cathedral, the sound of pigeons fluttering overhead, the warmth and brightness of the sun, and the cool breeze off the Santa Cruz River, when it used to have water.

In the mid-1950s, however, Arizona highway officials, following the procedures outlined in the BPR report *Interregional Highways*, ran Interstate 10 between the western edge of Barrio Viejo and the eastern bank of the Santa Cruz River. Martin pauses in "The Journey" to criticize this work:

> The freeway had cut the river from the people.
> The freeway blocks the sunshine.
> The drone of traffic buzzes like a giant sleeping bee.
> A new music in the barrio.[40]

A similar critique finds expression in the poetry of the Chicana feminist Lorna Dee Cervantes, who grew up on the outskirts of San Jose in the Mexican American barrio of Sal Si Puedes. In partnership with the BPR, San Jose transportation authorities added Highway 280 to the Interstate Highway System in 1955, linking San Francisco and San Jose. In the late 1960s, construction of the San Jose portion of I-280 cut through the heart of Sal Si Puedes with little community opposition. This community of migrant farmworkers resided in a neighborhood that had been redlined in the early 1940s. Property values in the area were low, making it vulnerable to the placement of infrastructural projects like federal highways. The neighborhood was also racially segregated, separated from San Jose's white neighborhoods by a railroad line that ran north to San Francisco.[41]

This was the world of Lorna Dee Cervantes, the daughter of itinerant Mexican farmworkers, who remembers the coming of the freeway and its division of her neighborhood. She inscribed that memory into a 1977 poem, "Beneath the Shadow of the Freeway," which has earned lasting recognition within Chicana/o literary culture. It is a nostalgic remembrance of a lost community, but it is also a sharply gendered critique of highways and highway builders. Like Martin, Cervantes emphasizes the relationships among women in the family. She remembers her "woman family"—her mother and grandmother—and the fleeting men who came and went. Wayward men contrast with these women, and the sanctuary of her grandmother's home, "the house she built with her own hands," is a central image of the poem. More striking, however, is the contrast between the home and the freeway, "the blind worm wrapping up the valley from Los Altos to Sal Si Puedes." The freeway fills Cervantes with dread: "Every day at dusk as grandma watered geraniums, the shadow of the freeway lengthened." The "cocky disheveled carpentry" of her grandmother's home contrasts sharply with the perfect symmetry of the man-made freeway. The freeway, the poet suggests, was built by men, men infatuated with movement, mobility, and, most of all (from the perspective of a fatherless child), escape. Two central oppositions thus gird "Beneath the Shadow of the Freeway": men's movement versus women's anchoring, and the freeway's movement versus the stability of a grandmother's home. Wrapped in such contradictions, the narrator concludes, "in time, I plant geraniums, I tie my hair in braids, and trust only what I have built with my own hands."[42]

In 1981, Cervantes published "Freeway 280," a poem about the freeway's erasure of the barrio and the stubborn survival of its cultural traditions. The first stanza of the poem reminisces on the world destroyed by the freeway:

> Las casitas [The little houses] near the gray cannery,
> nestled amidst wild abrazos [hugs] of climbing roses
> and man-high red geraniums are gone now.
> the freeway conceals it all beneath a raised scar.

Yet "under the fake windsounds of the open lanes," she discovers thriving traces of that world:

> in the abandoned lots below, new grasses sprout,
> wild mustard remembers, old gardens
> come back stronger than they were,
> trees have been left standing in their yards.

> Albaricoqueros [apricot trees], cerezos [cherry trees], nogales [walnut trees] . . .
> Viejitas [old women] come here with paper bags to gather greens.
> Espinaca [spinach], verdolagas [purslane], yerbabuena . . .

Cervantes describes the staples in Mexican American food culture, mostly ignoring the structure of the freeway, except for its destruction of the community that cultivated the land. Cervantes herself had left this community, following the wry imperative built into the very name of her neighborhood. In Spanish, *sal si puedes* means "leave if you can." As the nickname for many Mexican American communities in the urban Southwest, Sal Si Puedes signals a homegrown injunction to leave the barrio, to go out and up toward new possibilities and opportunities. For immigrant groups in U.S. history, this has been the dream of the second or third generation: to move into the mainstream or into new realms of personal and professional satisfaction, untethered from ethnic and family ties. Cervantes herself admits to having taken this path to pursue her love of learning and letters, but ultimately she comes back: back to the site of the old barrio, now buried under a freeway, where old women return to reap the harvest they were forced to leave behind:

> Once, I wanted out, wanted the rigid lanes
> to take me to a place without sun,
> without the smell of tomatoes burning
> on swing shift in the greasy summer air.
>
> Maybe it's here
> en los campos extraños de esta ciudad [in the strange fields of this city]
> where I'll find it, that part of me
> mown under
> like a corpse
> or a loose seed.[43]

Cervantes offers her poems like the *cerezos, verdolagas,* and *nogales* that grow in the "strange fields" beneath the freeway. California's highway builders destroyed the barrio community that cradled Cervantes's youth, but her poetry illustrates how its "seeds" continue to bear fruit, sowing new perceptions about the particular forms of spatial injustice that afflicted Mexican

American communities during the age of the interstate. Like the new grasses that sprout in the abandoned lots beneath the freeway, the author prepares herself to come "back stronger," ready to embrace her culture and community after its evisceration. "Freeway 280" and "Beneath the Shadow of the Freeway" are the seedlings of this culture, reasserting Chicana cultural traditions in the aftermath of destruction.

This theme of cultural regeneration under the freeway is discussed further in chapter 5, but its gendered dimension bears consideration here. Women bring life, even to the deadening spaces created by men. This message finds more poignant expression in the work of the Chicana muralist Judith Baca, who knows the desolate spaces of urban infrastructure well. Baca spent much of her youth in Pacoima, a satellite barrio of Los Angeles on the northeastern fringe of the San Fernando Valley, bisected by three major freeways.

Baca also lived close to the Pacoima Wash, a concrete flood-control channel and a tributary of the Tujunga Wash, a larger channel that courses through the San Fernando Valley, where she created the *Great Wall of Los Angeles* in the 1970s, the work that solidified her international reputation as a muralist. The *Great Wall*, a half-mile-long mural painted on the concrete retaining wall, is really a historical timeline—a linear sequence of vignettes of the history of Los Angeles and California, emphasizing the perspectives of marginal social groups. Toward the end of the mural, in the section titled "Division of the Barrios and Chavez Ravine," Baca portrays a Chicano family torn apart, father and son on one side, mother, daughter, and another son on the other. A serpentine freeway writhes between and around these figures, and its supporting columns crash into the homes of the barrio below. This portrait of a Chicano family ravaged by infrastructure resonates with the history of many Mexican American families in the Los Angeles area during the 1950s and 1960s, as it reflects Baca's own experiences growing up in the San Fernando Valley (Figure 2.4).[44]

Baca had another opportunity to insert her point of view into the city's built environment when she accepted an invitation from the city of Los Angeles to paint a mural on the retaining wall of its central freeway artery. In 1983, in preparation for the 1984 Summer Olympic Games, the Municipal Arts Council commissioned Baca to take over a stretch of the 110 freeway to

DIVISION OF THE BARRIOS & CHAVEZ RAVINE

FIGURE 2.4. Judith F. Baca, "Division of the Barrios and Chavez Ravine," detail from 1950s section of *The Great Wall of Los Angeles*, 1976–83. Located in the Tujunga Wash flood-control channel in the San Fernando Valley. Acrylic on cast concrete, 13 × 2,400 feet. Photograph courtesy of SPARC, www.sparcinla.org.

paint *Hitting the Wall: Women in the Marathon* (1984), a visual tribute to the first women allowed to compete in an Olympic marathon.[45] The painting appeared on the surface wall of the Third Street underpass of Interstate 110, the central corridor of the sprawling L.A. freeway system. Construction of this freeway, which borders the western edge of the city's downtown core, began in the late 1950s in conjunction with urban renewal and slum clearance programs. Its placement in the downtown core presented the California Division of Highways with the unique challenge of having to integrate the freeway into the grid of surface streets. Their approach entailed a sequence of raised overpasses that cross the freeway at Ninth, Sixth, Fourth, and Third Streets, enabling drivers to glide seamlessly between the freeway and the streets of downtown. When the freeway was completed in 1971, the *Los Angeles Times* heralded the 110 corridor as "Downtown's New Main Street."[46]

Yet this example of freeway architecture rarely draws admiration today. Not only is it one of the most congested roadway segments in the nation, but it also incites recent charges of class warfare among activists and urban critics. The construction of the 110 corridor destroyed the last remnants of Bunker Hill, a pocket of working-class racial and ethnic diversity that HOLC officials targeted in 1939 as a "slum area in need of rehabilitation."[47] Obliterating its dilapidated Victorian buildings, the new freeway debuted in conjunction with a new corporate citadel built in the early 1960s; the centerpiece of the new development was the monumental Music Center, a pavilion of glass and concrete that was Los Angeles's answer to New York's Lincoln Center, and the Water and Power Building, a translucent building of thin concrete planes interspersed with rectangular walls of glass. As a new generation of elites staked their claim over this brave new world, the 110 freeway *spatially* fortified class privilege against the threatened incursions of workers, immigrants, and the homeless. In a city wracked by violent episodes of social unrest in 1965 and again in 1992, what had been a feat of engineering had become a concrete symbol of exclusion in an environment given over to corporate and commercial interests.[48]

Yet *Hitting the Wall* illuminates another dimension of L.A.'s class struggle: the struggle of community activists and artists to humanize the inhuman environment of "Fortress L.A."[49] With the assistance of a municipal arts program that worked with at-risk youth, Baca painted the image of a female athlete in the throes of victory: a marathon runner breaks the tape of the finish line, lunging toward the viewer; her arms are stretched out in triumph as sunlight floods the background scenery. Baca's treatment of the freeway's surface wall enhances the visual impact of the mural. From both sides of the mural, the viewer sees not the smooth concrete surface of modern freeway architecture but rather what appears to be crudely shaped stone blocks, forming a wall that conjures Mesoamerican architecture. As the runner crosses the finish line, she breaks through the wall, which crumbles into rubble at the foot of the mural (Figure 2.5).

Using paint, skill, and imagination to transform a modern freeway into an ancient wall gives force to the idea of feminine strength. This, to put it crudely, is the main message of the mural. But there is a subtler comment

FIGURE 2.5. Judith F. Baca, *Hitting the Wall: Women in the Marathon*, 1984. Acrylic on cast concrete, 20 × 100 feet. Fourth Street off-ramp, Harbor Freeway (I-110), Los Angeles. Sponsored by the Olympic Organizing Committee for the 1984 Olympics. Photograph courtesy of SPARC, www.sparcinla.org.

on the structure and meaning of the freeway itself. We wonder if this 1950s feat of architecture and engineering can withstand the forceful arrival of women on equal footing with men. To bolster this point, Baca also painted a pylon across the roadway from the mural with an image of massive stone-carved blocks, suggesting the collapse of the entire overpass. Thus, although the mural celebrates the victory of women, it disputes the sturdiness of the freeway. Instead, the artist renders the freeway, as other feminist critics have done through art, literature, and poetry, as the precarious product of a man-made society on the verge of collapse. Given the gendered meanings assigned to the automobile, the gendered division between urban and suburban space, and the heroic myth of modernity as a masculine enterprise, it is possible to see how Baca strives to *feminize* the freeway: to make it speak to the particular experiences of women and to subdue its rigid geometry to an alternative social vision that enables women to compete and to win within the contested terrain of city life.

Baca and Cervantes express a uniquely *Chicana* relationship to the freeway, a relationship structured not by choice but by design. Master plans for interstate highway construction in the urban Southwest targeted their neighborhoods, forcing an intimate knowledge of public infrastructure that indelibly marks experience and memory and their expression through cultural forms. In a similar vein, Helena Maria Viramontes, a Chicana writer of fiction and poetry, remembers growing up in the East Los Angeles community of City Terrace, which had been torn up in the late 1960s for construction of the interchange between Interstate 710 and State Route 60. Viramontes retains in her mind's eye the sight of fallen trees with their roots exposed and remembers stories of people finding human bones unearthed from cemeteries maimed by highway construction crews. If you came across the "bones of the forgotten," she remembers being told, "you were supposed to throw them back into the earth."[50]

Viramontes wondered what happened to the people dislocated by highway construction: what were their stories, what mark did they leave on the landscape, and what is left of those markings after the advent of the freeway? Such questions inspire much of her fictional writing, especially her 2007 novel *Their Dogs Came with Them,* a semiautobiographical story about East Los Angeles in the age of the freeway. Like Martin and Cervantes, Viramontes subordinates the stories of men to the stories of women in the novel, weaving the interrelated experiences of four teenage Chicanas trapped within a community under siege by bulldozers and police helicopters. She asserts gendered conflict as a basic premise, writing of the daily struggles of women against the financial, sexual, or punitive instincts of male authority. Fathers are absent from the narrative, as are uncles, brothers, and grandfathers. There is a priest, but he is cast as an irrelevant symbol of a bygone past. This is a Chicana story—a working-class and a uniquely racialized story, but primarily a story of young women caught between the immigrant past of previous generations and their L.A. future. *Their Dogs Came with Them* explores the tensions between tradition and modernity, a common theme in much of

Chicana/o art and literature, but by focusing on the singular perspectives and experiences of young Chicanas, it breaks with patriarchal conventions that emphasize male perspective and power.[51]

This is also a story about freeways and what they do to people and their environment, or to put it simply, about the conquest of East Los Angeles by public infrastructure. The novel begins with an epigraph from Miguel León-Portilla's *Broken Spears,* an Aztec account of the Spanish conquest of Mexico written in 1962:

> They came in battle array, as conquerors, and the dust rose in whirlwinds on the roads. Their spears glinted in the sun, and their pennons fluttered like bats. They made a loud clamor as they marched, for the coats of mail and their weapons clashed and rattled. Some of them were dressed in glistening iron from head to foot; they terrified everyone who saw them.
>
> Their dogs came with them, running ahead of the column. They raised their muzzles high; they lifted their muzzles to the wind. They raced on before with saliva dripping from their jaws.[52]

Conjuring the arrival of the Spanish war machine in the Aztec capital of Tenochtitlán, Viramontes employs conquest as a metaphor to convey the predicament of East Los Angeles in the age of the freeway. She laces her narrative with vivid descriptions of the East L.A. landscape, emphasizing the assault on East Los Angeles by the California Division of Highways and its pack of bulldozers hungry for homes, schools, and churches. Barely into the first few pages of the book, we learn about "the earthmovers, Grandmother Zumaya had called them; the bulldozers had started from very far away and slowly arrived on First Street, their muzzles like sharpened metal teeth making way for the freeway."[53] Bulldozers accompany the swarm of helicopters with bright spotlights that descend on East Los Angeles at night, allegedly on the hunt for rabid dogs. The "ghettobirds," inner-city sarcasm for helicopters, belong to the Quarantine Authority, which controls access to those streets and blocks that lie outside the path of interstate highways.

Viramontes gives the gory details of an unwanted intimacy between freeways and living, breathing human bodies: "The pulverizing dust of heaved up earth and cement" invading pores, nostrils, lungs, ears, and eyes; the din of rushing cars and jackhammers; the clashing and rattling of bulldozers and excavators; the floodlights that turn night into day; the musk of dredged earth; trenches gouged between neighbors; the haze of exhaust and dust; the sight of electrical wires dangling from broken cement and of severed tree roots jutting from mud walls—Viramontes renders a sense of the freeway's total assault on human sensation and perception, inducing impressions of East Los Angeles as "another planet, a crater of another world mixed into [the] real world all at the same time." Freeways also stifle pedestrian life, discouraging the presence of what Jacobs recognized as "eyes on the street" that monitor and regulate public behavior. When a young Chicana is raped under a new freeway overpass, "not one driver from all those cars zooming on the new freeway . . . not one stopped to protest, scream."[54]

The official work of the Quarantine Authority and the Division of Highways is essentially the same: to isolate and contain the East L.A. barrio from the rest of the city, to sequester racialized bodies within the fortified parameters of a community bounded by highways and under surveillance by police helicopters. This is how Viramontes registers her protest against the incursion of freeways on East Los Angeles, drawing stark parallels between the violence of urban America in the 1960s and the violence inflicted on minority communities by infrastructural development. Her critique of modernization, like much of the work explored in this chapter, singles out the experiences of women and the psychic challenges posed by new spatial regimes. In one of the more memorable scenes from the book, Viramontes portrays a homeless woman, dumbfounded by the upheaval in her midst:

> The bridge she crossed didn't have the familiar flamboyant arches of the Third Street Bridge. In fact, it resembled an ugly bandage of cement suturing together two boulevards. She turned a whole circle compass around, then placed her bag down and pressed her parchment hands and face against the metal grids of the foreign bridge. Her scaly fingers hooked the grids tightly. Instead of the slow-moving rackety rock of the railroad cars, the woman felt the wind-blast speed of freeway traffic vibrating the metal grids. The velocity traveled right through the marrow conduit of her fingers, straight through the thick veil of her onion skin and down to the glass bottles in her bag. All this

new construction altered the city into a beast alien to her and she castigated herself for standing on the wrong bridge.[55]

Yet this scene of confrontation plays out within a much broader history of Western modernity and its cultural response. Compare, for example, the plight of this woman to that of Gervaise Macquart, the working-class heroine of Émile Zola's 1876 novel, *L'Assommoir*. Battered by poverty, abuse, and alcohol, Gervaise stumbles through the rubble of Haussmann's Paris:

> The whole district was being turned topsy-turvy, the Boulevard Magenta and the Boulevard Ornano were being driven through what had been the Barriere Poissonniere and made a gap through the outer boulevard. You hardly knew where you were. The whole of one side of the rue des Poissonniers was down, and from the rue de la Goutte d'Or you could see a huge open space of sun and air, and instead of the slums which had blocked the view . . . there had been erected . . . a real monument, a six-storey block of flats with carvings on it like a church, giving an impression of opulence. Gervaise was annoyed by these improvements, for they upset this dingy corner of Paris where she felt at home. Her annoyance came from the fact that the district was going up in the world exactly when she was going down.[56]

Thus we have two literary portraits of two lonely women in cities, standing on either side of an ocean of time and space, left to their own ragged devices to make sense of the upheaval around them. Chicanas of the urban southwest, like Viramontes, Baca, and Cervantes, have asserted their own critique of modernization, a critique based on memory and experience and inflected by the unique contingencies of Chicana subjectivity. Yet these are not isolated flashes of rage and resentment. Instead, they resonate within an ongoing critique of Western modernity and its consequences for diverse city people. In the 130 years between *L'Assommoir* and *Their Dogs Came with Them,* the ongoing convulsions of the modern city continue to fuel a common basis for these disparate visions. Zola fleshes out the birth of modern alienation; Viramontes traces the legacy of this experience in very different sociospatial contexts. Separated by intangible chasms, Zola and Viramontes home in on the portrait of a woman's isolation, emphasizing the gendered spaces of difference and exclusion built into the landscape of the modern city.

Viramontes's indictment of modernization and its consequences for working-class women of color gestures toward a broader critique of modernity in the West, but it also spurs new modes of political mobilization in East Los Angeles, where women demonstrate a growing determination to halt historic patterns of spatial injustice. Thus the legacy of mothers and housewives who organized against highway construction during the interstate era continues in East Los Angeles, where the heavy-handed placement of freeways has spurred mothers into action, into taking a public stand against the placement of more unwanted infrastructure. In the early 1980s, in response to a proposal by Governor George Deukmejian to build a state prison in East Los Angeles, a large group of women whose children attended the same schools organized themselves in opposition to this project. Out of this struggle was born the Mothers of East Los Angeles (MELA), which has since become a model for grassroots organizing against efforts to build unwanted infrastructure near schools and homes. Explaining their involvement with MELA, many East L.A. women recall the disruptions of the interstate era. One of MELA's founding members, Juana Gutierrez, who grew up in East Los Angeles, remembers her family having to move twice because of highway construction. Gutierrez contrasts the activism of East L.A. mothers with the local apathy of the interstate era: "The people accepted it [freeways] because the government ordered it. I remember that I was angry and wanted the others to back me up but nobody else wanted to do anything."[57]

Viramontes and Cervantes home in on this sense of resignation, writing about people in the community not wanting "to do anything" against the state highway project. Yet their writing, like Baca's murals, demonstrates that someone wants to do something, if only to raise awareness, challenge received wisdom, and serve collective memory. Their words and images leveled a gendered critique of highway construction, emphasizing the freeway's constriction of women's lives and the toll it took on the barrio. Their struggle ensued in the very shadow of the freeway, asserting the dignity and indignation of a community ravaged by a flurry of highway construction during the 1950s and 1960s. Their work also inspires new forms of collective action such as MELA, which inherited the charge of the East Tremont Housewives by embracing the politics of motherhood.

Toward a Feminist Critique of the Modernist City

The interstate highway program, like the modernist city itself, was largely a male enterprise. With but rare exceptions, men planned, designed, and built freeways in cities, paving the way for a resurgent automobile culture in postwar America. This work entailed its own set of gendered assumptions and meanings. Throughout its history, the automobile has retained its associations with male power, privilege, and prestige, and by solidifying its role as the primary mode of transportation in urban America, the interstate highway program helped reinforce the masculinization of public space. In this light, interstate-highway construction could be seen as a sort of gender subsidy, favoring male patterns of movement and mobility and the vast majority of men who made a living building, selling, insuring, driving, or fixing automobiles and highways.[58]

The women who helped mobilize public opinion against the freeway cast the gendered premises of the modernist city into sharp relief. They called men out for their blind pursuit of movement and mobility, their infringement on the spatial freedom of women, their prioritization of traffic flow over the daily routines of children and families, and their narrow-minded pursuit of material progress. Across metropolitan space, in both cities and suburbs, across political ideology, and across the socioeconomic divide, women of diverse racial and ethnic backgrounds issued a sharp rebuke to the men who planned and built freeways, casting the freeway revolt as a gendered struggle between men and women.

Yet those many differences structured different outcomes within diverse communities. On the front lines of the visible freeway revolt, Jane Jacobs and other women from white middle-class and working-class communities had the wherewithal to organize, speak, write, meet, correspond, and stage outlandish forms of political theater. Some women publicly invoked their responsibilities as mothers and housewives to defend their families and communities against highway-building bulldozers. Their struggle reflected a broader maternal charge to protect the spaces of home, family, and community. Motherhood provided an entry for some women into the public fight against the freeway, but it was not the sole motivation. Other women fought freeways, not so much on behalf of future generations but, rather, for their immigrant forebears, who deserved to remain within the cohesive neighborhoods built through hard work and perseverance. Defying gendered stereotypes of the 1950s, white women like Jane Jacobs and Barbara Mikulski earned political clout in the postwar politics of fighting freeways. They brought their unique voices to this battle, while forcefully articulating common values shared by men and women alike within particular neighborhoods and communities.

Yet even more hidden within this "hidden history" of women in the freeway revolt are women of color, who expressed their community's resentment in the very shadow of the freeway itself. For Graciela Valenzuela, the lack of English proficiency and formal education, the journey across the border, and the struggle to raise a family suggest the reasons Mexican immigrants and Mexican Americans of the interstate era were reluctant to confront a state that had proved hostile to their interests. Their children, however, raised in the dust of highway construction, were more willing to speak out. By the 1970s, a politicized generation of Chicanas, their loyalties split between feminism and the Chicano movement, registered their protest through written and visual forms of cultural expression. They did not savor the victories that came to Lower Manhattan or suburban Seattle, but their voices articulate a far more holistic critique of the highway enterprise, a critique that went beyond specific communities and identities, emphasizing the racial, class, *and* gendered consequences of urban highway construction. Their creative efforts inspire new modes of political organization, helping mobilize barrio communities against subsequent incursions of unwanted infrastructure like prisons, waste incinerators, and recycling plants.

In their fight against the freeway, diverse women drew on their own experiences and perspectives to assert a gendered critique of progress. Despite their many differences in strategy, timing, and outcome, white and nonwhite women alike also invoked a common discourse of memory, heritage, and tradition in their fight against the freeway. Whether it was Lucretia Fisher staking her claim to the colonial heritage of Baltimore's waterfront or Lorna Dee Cervantes invoking collective memories of conquest and colonization, the past played a powerful role in shaping the discourse of the freeway revolt. Chapter 3 takes up this discursive strand, exploring its role in shaping the physical geography of the freeway metropolis.

3   Communities Lost and Found

The Politics of Historical Memory

The endless freeway paved over his sacred ruins, his secrets, his graves, his fertile soil in which all memories were seeded and waiting for the right time to flower, and he could do nothing.

Helena Maria Viramontes, "Neighbors," 1995

Memory is about self interest.

Maxim Billinger

In 1995 the Sacred Heart Catholic Church in the Eight-Mile district of Detroit sponsored a play for its parishioners that dramatized the vibrant history of the black neighborhood it once served. The construction of the Chrysler Freeway in the mid-1950s wiped out this neighborhood, but the sponsors of the play nonetheless staged a dramatic reenactment of its history some forty years later. The all-black cast, dressed as characters from Detroit's Jazz Age, performed the music and dance embedded in Detroit's black cultural history, acting out the struggles of their forebears to forge a thriving community against the odds of poverty and discrimination. The play ended with the entire cast on the stage, in full historical costume, enjoining its audience to "Remember Us!" The name of the play was *Before I-75.*[1]

Interstate 75 leveled the Black Bottom neighborhood of Detroit, but the few remaining residents called on ties to their local church to invent a creative and collaborative way to perform the memory of their lost neighborhood, to reenact the social world of black Detroit before the coming of the freeway. The play and its title suggest that highway construction impaired not only a community's experience of space but also its sense of time. It marks our entry into this chapter's exploration of the role of historical memory in a community's struggle against the freeway. In their opposition to highway construction, diverse Americans have organized to preserve the landmarks of their local past and to insist on the historical significance of those landmarks. Some communities have succeeded in that effort; others have failed.

Before I-75 reflects the way a community strove to remember its past, even after its evisceration during the interstate era. It marks a group's unwillingness to settle for the hand it had been dealt and its attempt to make its own fight against the forced erasure of its history. A play at a local church does not compensate for the loss of community, but it does signal the persistence of that community, even in the sporadic gatherings of a few hundred people. It is also part of broader memory culture that took shape in the wreckage of other communities bulldozed by the freeway.

This chapter considers how an insurgent sensitivity to a community's history inflected past and current struggles against the freeway. The discourse of the freeway revolt was shaped not only by feminism and civil rights but also by historic preservation—a cause that gained much traction during the 1960s, especially with passage of the National Historic Preservation Act in 1966. At the height of the interstate era, the federal government did something of an about-face, restraining its bulldozers in some communities, bowing to local demands to preserve a neighborhood landscape suddenly invested with historic meaning and significance. In the face of the freeway, a community clung to its past to preserve its cohesion, but during the interstate era, this strategy only worked in those communities built by Europeans and their American descendants.

Once again, this chapter presents a story of winners and losers. It looks first at the freeway revolts of New Orleans and New York, which illustrate the way the preservationist impulse bolstered local victories against the freeway. In both examples, white affluent communities with strong connections to government and media defeated highway proposals by asserting the historical significance of their neighborhoods. The chapter then fast-forwards to what is left of two urban black communities after their pummeling by the freeway, to consider contemporary efforts to remember the past through community organization and cooperation. St. Paul, Minnesota, and Miami, Florida, were hotspots of black culture and community before the interstate; both communities were gutted by interstate freeways in the early 1960s, and both sustain current efforts to recuperate the memory of what was lost. The disparate outcomes of these struggles suggest that although people of various cities mobilized against the freeway through a common appreciation of local history and its landmarks in the built environment, the contours of racial and class privilege structured sharp discrepancies in the experience of highway construction and of historical time itself.

History with a Vengeance: New York and New Orleans

The authors of *Toll Roads and Free Roads* (1939) articulated their contempt for the city's remnants of its past:

> An old city, growing by the coalescence of numerous ancestor villages, the irregular and discontinuous street plan of [the old city] is the despair of the stranger and the daily inconvenience of its own citizens.

Laced with aerial sketches of future freeways slicing into the urban fabric, *Toll Roads and Free Roads* emphasized a visual antagonism between the old city and the new. It articulated a long-standing bias within the highway-planning profession against the "decadent" areas of the metropolis and against the "countless impediments that embarrass the movement of twentieth-century traffic."[2] Popular exhibits like Futurama corroborated this suspicion of history by showcasing a shiny vision of a utopian future built around the automobile. In the planning discourse of the midcentury planning profession, a stark contrast took shape between the old city and the new; between the rational, modernized city as the wave of the future, and the old city couched in a negative discourse of disorder, decay, and chaos. Even Lewis Mumford, who upheld a view of the city as a repository of history, adopted this outlook in *The Culture of Cities,* arguing that regional highway networks could help "break up the functionless, overgrown urban masses of the past."[3] Perhaps because the midcentury generation of urban professionals and thinkers were closer in time to the nineteenth-century industrial city and to even older fragments of the urban fabric still surviving, they saw that fabric as expendable— old enough to seem obsolete, but not old enough to count as historic.[4]

Their disregard for the physical remnants of the city's past conformed to a broader culture of architecture and planning in the early decades of the twentieth century. History found itself at odds with this culture, which embraced the machine and its emancipatory potential to propel humanity toward the final stages of material progress. Rejecting all figments of historicism in the built environment, modernist design espoused a teleological view of historical time and demanded a complete break with the past. Utopia would come, but only through a break with the past and its traditions. This perspective found powerful expression in Le Corbusier's stark renderings of the modernist city, particularly through his sketches for "A Contemporary City for Three Million People" (1922), "The Radiant City" (1924), and "Plan Voisin" (1925). These bold visions reflected the architect's contempt for the city street, which to him symbolized an antiquated setting for an outmoded social order. He advocated the "death of the street" by designing elevated superhighways that cut incisively into the heart of the old city, repudiating pedestrian traditions of public life and underscoring modernism's total antagonism between old and new.[5]

With their narrow view of roadwork, American highway planners lacked the ambition and the license to implement the clean-slate approach of Le Corbusier. Yet some within the profession suspected the potential effects of their heavy tread into the historic tissue of the old city. Robert Moses, maybe the man closest to being an American Corbusier, expressed his understanding of antiquarian concerns. The proposal for the Riverfront Expressway in New Orleans, which he drafted in 1946, sparked a "particularly sentimental issue" in the mid-1960s, prompting national debate about the historical significance of the urban built environment. The master planner recognized the audacity of building a six-lane elevated expressway along the southern edge of the French Quarter between Jackson Square and the Mississippi River. Seeking to appease local concerns, Moses argued that construction of the freeway would actually help preserve the integrity of the Vieux Carré by removing traffic from its narrow cobblestone streets. He even professed to re-spect the unique heritage of New Orleans, albeit with limits:

> There is no need to do violence to history or tradition in this process. It is only necessary to give sufficient attention to progress, or if you prefer change, to prevent the Vieux Carré from becoming a sterile museum without vital associations with the stream of life around it.[6]

What might have emboldened Moses in this provocative scheme was his re-vulsion toward the idea of New Orleans, or any city for that matter, becom-ing "a sterile museum." Yet what he probably did not know was that the city maintained a long history of historic preservation, which dated back to the 1918 restoration of the St. Louis Cathedral in the heart of Jackson Square. During the 1920s, the Vieux Carré experienced something of a cultural re-naissance as artists and writers settled in the district. In this bohemian mi-lieu, Le Petit Salon, a French Quarter preservation group, drafted a proposal in 1925 to preserve the Vieux Carré. The following year, New Orleans's City Council established the Vieux Carré Commission (VCC) to protect the old colonial city. By midcentury, this commission had the power to designate historical landmarks within the French Quarter to preserve the area's "quaint and distinctive character."[7]

The VCC played a forceful role in the so-called second battle of New Orleans, a protracted struggle over the construction of the Riverfront Ex-pressway that erupted in the early 1960s. Despite Moses's early admonition that "the antiquarian and the city planner must work together," the proposed expressway drew sharp divisions within the city's establishment.[8]

The "city planner" side of this conflict represented the city's most power-ful leaders in business and government; they pushed the expressway as a vital linchpin in the city's new tourist economy. Pro-highway supporters included downtown clubs, labor unions, two mayoral administrations, the City Coun-cil, the New Orleans Dock Board, the Jewish Merchants Association, the *Times-Picayune,* and New Orleans Public Service, Inc., the city's utility com-pany. The Central Area Committee of the city's chamber of commerce, which sponsored the original drafting of the Riverfront Expressway, remained the driving force behind the push to build the highway. This committee worked closely with the New Orleans Central Planning Committee, which supervised the execution of the project. This powerful alliance of public and private interests considered no alternatives to the twenty-year-old plan drafted by Moses; in their eyes, this was the best and only possibility for modernizing the city's transportation infrastructure.[9]

On the "antiquarian" side of this debate stood the residents of the Vieux Carré, who stuck to their neighborhood through the ebbs and flows of its prosperity. Expressway opponents deplored the incursion of an elevated highway onto their turf, arguing that it blocked historic access to the riverfront and destroyed the unique and special charm of the French Quarter. They organized themselves through such powerful community organizations as the Vieux Carré Commission and the Vieux Carré Property Owners Association, which mounted extensive legal challenges to the state highway department (Figure 3.1). At the forefront of the opposition were upper-crust southern women, such as Martha Gilmore Robinson and Mary Morrison, who worked passionately to preserve the architectural legacy of the Vieux Carré. It also included scions of the city's first families, such as Bill Borah, Dick Baumbach, and Edgar Bloom Stern Jr., who used their family's fortunes to hire researchers, attorneys, and consultants to challenge the city's establishment and to fly across the country to study the dynamics of freeway revolts in other cities. These crusaders carried the mantle of historic preservation in New Orleans, adding muscle and money to the movement. They shrewdly took their cause to the national stage, capitalizing on the French Quarter's reputation in the city's bustling tourist trade.[10]

Ultimately, these freeway fighters fought to preserve a nostalgic idealization of a white southern order, a position that failed to unite a city still grappling with local demands for civil rights. For their part, African Americans stood on the sidelines of the fight to save the Vieux Carré. They had little connection to the French Quarter, except in its historic exploitation of their labor and culture for white consumption. Moreover, while white residents of the Vieux Carré were up in arms over the Riverfront Expressway, black New Orleanians were witnessing the ravaging of their neighborhood by the construction of Interstate 10, an elevated expressway that tore into the heart of Faubourg Tremé, the oldest community of free blacks in the United States and

FIGURE 3.1. Protestors at a public hearing on the proposed Riverside Expressway in the New Orleans City Council chambers, March 25, 1965. Copyright *Times-Picayune*; all rights reserved; reprinted with permission.

the symbolic center of black New Orleans. This meant uprooting a stand of live oaks that grew along a median strip of North Claiborne Avenue. White New Orleans, even the staunchest opponents of the Riverfront Expressway, remained silent as Tremé fell victim to highway-building bulldozers, underscoring the whiteness of the city's freeway revolt.[11]

Tremé lost, but the Vieux Carré won. After a long and protracted battle, U.S. Secretary of Transportation John Volpe, once a highwayman himself, canceled federal funds for the Vieux Carré Expressway on July 1, 1969, conceding that "the Riverfront Expressway would have seriously impaired the historic quality of New Orleans' famed French Quarter."[12] This stunning defeat of the New Orleans business establishment made the French Quarter the symbol of a budding preservation movement and signaled the new weight of historic preservation in highway routing policy. Amendments to the 1966 Federal Highway Act and Department of Transportation Act secured the protected status of historic sites, in addition to parks, recreation areas, and wildlife refuges. That same year, Congress passed the National Historic Preservation Act, which established a National Register of Historic Places and the National Advisory Council on Historic Preservation.[13] This legislation gave further ammunition to opponents of the expressway and marked a major turning point in highway administration. Ultimately, it tipped the scales in favor of the French Quarter and fueled the fight against the freeway in other cities, where well-heeled and well-connected citizens, like Lucretia Fisher in Baltimore, turned to their city's oldest buildings as bulwarks against the freeway.

A similar dynamic played out in New York City, where the residents of Lower Manhattan expressed their attachment to the landmarks of local history as a strategy against Moses's audacious scheme for the Lower Manhattan Expressway. As the southernmost extension of a tripartite system of crosstown highways that would speed car traffic across Manhattan, linking New Jersey with Brooklyn, Queens, and Long Island, LOMEX threatened to sweep through an all-but-abandoned industrial loft district. With 90 percent federal support for its construction, LOMEX, or the Broome Street Expressway, as it was also known, was projected to cost $100 million and threatened to displace some 2,000 families and 1,000 businesses.[14]

LOMEX drew immediate opposition from congressmen, state assemblymen, city councilmen, and such prominent community activists as Jane Jacobs, fresh off her celebrity from *Death and Life*. It also spurred opposition from a hive of artists, who began occupying SoHo's loft spaces during the late 1960s. Through such organizations as the South Houston Artist Tenant Association and Artists against the Expressway, founded in 1969, "the loftsmenschen"—so dubbed by the *Village Voice*—made up a forceful lobbying group that surfaced from SoHo's abandoned loft spaces to oppose the city's plans for expressway construction.[15] The controversy raged throughout 1968 and 1969, as the administration of Mayor John Lindsay sought ways to minimize the expressway's impact on the neighborhoods of Lower Manhattan. Finally, in August 1969, the city's Board of Estimate sided with the opponents of the expressway, unanimously voting to wipe the project off city maps, scrapping what would have been the grand finale in the storied career of Robert Moses.[16]

As in New Orleans, Lower Manhattan's expressway controversy generated an outpouring of historical sentiment. As Barbara Mikulski fought the freeway in Baltimore with an impassioned defense of the built legacy of the city's Polish and German immigrants, local opposition to LOMEX reiterated the threat to Lower Manhattan's established ethnic communities. The potential demise of Little Italy, for example, the cradle of Italian American culture, provoked local expressions of ethnic heritage and pride. The *Village Voice* cast the battle against LOMEX as "the fight for Little Italy," insisting that this was "everybody's fight." Signs held up at anti-LOMEX rallies read "Little Italy Killed by Progress," while the Thirty-Sixth Annual Festa of San Gennaro in 1962 included a booth with a sign that read, "Kill the Xpressway, Down with Moses."[17] The *Voice* gave extensive coverage to the Festa and its neighborhood throughout the mid-1960s, invoking the specter of doom. Its caption for a 1965 photo of the parade read, "This may be the last time the descendants of New York's Italian immigrants can celebrate this tradition in their old neighborhood. Demolition is close at hand."[18]

The threat of LOMEX also heightened the city's sensitivity to the landmarks of its storied past. In 1965 Mayor Robert Wagner and the New York City Council established the New York City Landmarks Preservation Commission (LPC) to register historic districts and individual landmarks. Shortly after its creation, community activists in Greenwich Village created a local version of this body, the Greenwich Village Historic District Council, which asked the LPC for official designation as a "historic district." Facing the destructive work of highway building and urban renewal programs, the council quickly established the historical significance of structures like the Old Merchant's House on East Fourth Street, the cobblestone alley of the Washington Mews, St. John Lutheran Church on Christopher Street, and the Cherry Lane Theater on Commerce Street. In March 1967, as opposition to LOMEX reached a fevered pitch, the LPC announced the designation of Greenwich Village as a single historic district.[19]

The threat of LOMEX provoked a budding appreciation of local history in Greenwich Village, and it also aroused a similar outlook in the adjacent area south of Houston Street, or "SoHo," an area once known as "Hell's Hundred Acres." As a locus for anti-expressway activism and as a burgeoning center of artistic creativity, SoHo drew increasing attention in the late 1960s, especially from historic preservationists such as James Marston Fitch and Margot Gayle. Gayle founded the Friends of Cast-Iron Architecture, which lobbied the LPC to bestow landmark status on SoHo's cast-iron district. The five- to six-story cast-iron-frame buildings of SoHo appeared in the 1860s to house New York's manufacturing district. Made quickly and cheaply from prefabricated, disassembled parts, they were in use until the decline and abandonment of the manufacturing district in the mid-twentieth century. SoHo did not model the canonical styles of architecture that inspired early preservation movements in places like the French Quarter, Beacon Hill, Georgetown, and Greenwich Village, but its repetitive use of glass and cast-iron framing for manufacturing anticipated the emergence of the modern skyscraper, at least according to architectural critics such as Ada Louise Huxtable, who emerged as an early advocate for SoHo's designation as a historic landmark district. To Huxtable, SoHo belonged in the company of the Vieux Carré—a "living museum" of urban history and a bulwark against an audacious highway scheme. As early as 1961, during the initial phases of the LOMEX controversy, Huxtable upheld SoHo as "the richest strand of Victorian commercial architecture and one of the best survivals of 'The Iron Age' in the country," and she deplored its potential sacrifice for the expressway. These "nineteenth century palaces of trade," Huxtable wrote, symbolize a heritage "not worth losing to the impending invasion of the Lower Manhattan Expressway."[20]

SoHo did not become a historic landmark district until 1973, four years after the final defeat of LOMEX, but even by the early 1960s, the growing awareness of SoHo's historical significance proved potent in the battle against New York's highway builders, illustrating the strategic awareness of history in local struggles against interstate highway construction. This preservationist strategy worked in the spatial struggles of New Orleans and Lower Manhattan, two communities that mustered the connections and the resources to wage a long and expensive campaign against two audacious highway schemes. Thus, in a decisive blow to Moses and the highway-building juggernaut, the residents of Lower Manhattan and New Orleans won the right to maintain their brick-and-mortar (and cast-iron) connection to the past.

This narrative is embedded in the discourse of the organized freeway revolt; it flares with emotional tension, climaxing in an assured confidence that history matters and the landmarks of the past deserve legal protection from bureaucratic ruthlessness. There are the usual villains: the historically mindless technocrats obsessed with progress and development. And there are the usual heroes: the neighbors who organized a grassroots campaign to preserve the remnants of the city's past, enlarging national appreciation for local history and its physical place in the built environment.

This is a compelling narrative indeed, but it usually fails to acknowledge the decisive role of class privilege. The preservationists of New York and New Orleans were underdogs in the sense that they fought powerful political and economic forces, but they too maximized wealth and power to pursue their self-interest. Jacobs's appreciation for the architectural remnants of the city's past furthered the gentrification of a distinguished neighborhood that had a rich literary and creative tradition. And as the scions of New Orleans's first families, Bill Borah and Dick Baumbach had every advantage in their battle against the highwaymen, milking their social connections and the financial resources afforded by political alliances, business circles, tennis clubs, fraternities, alumni associations, and debutante balls. The freeway-fighting preservationists of New York and New Orleans also enjoyed the support of powerful city councilmen with loyal constituencies, journalists and editors from the *Washington Post* and the *New York Times,* well-connected lawyers with wealthy clients, and well-organized networks of like-minded professionals who shared a particular vision of the city's past and its place in the city's future.

In short, that vision was rooted in racial and class privilege, which enabled the early victories of historic preservation in the city. Recent critiques of that movement emphasize its limited view of history and its obliviousness to the contributions of workers, women, gays, immigrants, and people of color in making the historic landscape.[21] In this light, it is unsurprising that preservationists in New Orleans stressed the European heritage of the built environment. In their mind, the Vieux Carré was not the site of slave markets and race riots but, rather, a genteel and "special combination of mossy court-yards and narrow streets cobwebbed with time."[22] The architecture of the endangered U.S. Mint, lauded by Vieux Carré preservationists as "one of the finest examples of Greek Revival architecture in the South," now invites more critical interpretations that situate its antebellum popularity within a racial-ized civic order that housed white mastery over nonwhite subjects—a design template for the courtrooms, prisons, and plantations that enforced the sub-jugation of African Americans. The multiracial history of New Orleans, as well as the expanding concentration of racial poverty in the inner city since the 1960s, compels a more critical and less exclusive understanding of the historical significance of the city's built environment, enabling a greater di-versity of perspectives and interpretations.

By contrast, urban communities of color, only recently recognized for their "historic" elements, succumbed to highway construction, relinquish-ing the architectural connection to their community's past. For many urban African Americans in particular, whose very communities were targeted as "blight," highway construction brought an abrupt end to this microcosmic world and imposed another break in the lived experience of historical time, which began with the arrival of armed Europeans on the African continent. Nonetheless, the memories of this world persist, and they find individual ex-amples in literature, poetry, and art and collective expression in a post facto preservation movement that enlists former residents to recover the memo-ries of lost neighborhoods. We turn now to two contemporary examples of this effort. The former residents of Miami's Overtown and St. Paul's Rondo neighborhoods did not have the resources, connections, or chutzpah that en-abled the citizens of SoHo and the French Quarter to defeat daunting highway schemes, but current efforts to remember their past are nonetheless galvaniz-ing a renewed sense of heritage and tradition.

From the Wreckage of the Past

The Rondo Days Festival is a weekend festival held every summer in St. Paul. The organizers of the festival are committed to "preserving, conserving, and accurately interpreting the contributions of African Americans" to the city of St. Paul and to the upper Midwest. On this weekend of black pride, Rondo Days includes parades, demonstrations, political speeches, dances, performances, a drill team competition, a 5K walk and run, and a bike ride. Since its inception in 1982, the Rondo Days Festival has come to be the largest black public celebration in the upper Midwest and an economic asset to the city of St. Paul.[23]

The festival is the direct and lasting consequence of routing a freeway through the heart of St. Paul's oldest African American community. The Rondo–St. Anthony neighborhood, named after its principal streets, dates back to the early twentieth century, when it housed African American railroad workers and their families, in addition to other immigrant ethnic groups. In the mid-1960s, despite years of determined opposition by community leaders and neighborhood activists, Interstate 94 bisected the neighborhood, destroying the commercial and cultural heart of the Twin Cities' oldest African American neighborhood and displacing thousands.

Rondo lives in the determined memories of its former residents, but before its destruction, the Rondo–St. Anthony neighborhood was not exclusively black. It actually began as an ethnically and racially diverse neighborhood, where African Americans lived alongside Russian, Polish, German, Italian, and Irish immigrants. James Griffin, whose autobiography, *Son of Rondo,* remembers that Rondo during the 1930s and 1940s "was not a black ghetto, as some seem to think, but it was truly a melting pot of races and nationalities."[24]

Yet, typical of many urban neighborhoods before World War II, the mere presence of African Americans in a racially and ethnically heterogeneous working-class neighborhood qualified Rondo–St. Anthony as "black" in public discourse and policy. Even within the African American community, of course, there was internal diversity, as people marked class differences within the neighborhood. Thus, "upper Rondo" belonged to African

American professionals and their families, and "lower Rondo" housed black service workers. Yet the two Rondos were not mutually exclusive. One former resident recalled the relationship between the two Rondos as "symbiotic," comparing the neighborhood to State Street in Chicago or Lenox Avenue in Harlem.[25]

A variety of social and cultural institutions supported the Rondo–St. Anthony community. St. James's Church and the Pilgrim Baptist Church served the spiritual needs of the neighborhood's residents. Community centers such as the Neighborhood House, the Hallie Q. Brown Community Center, and a so-called colored chapter of the YWCA provided community services and sponsored a variety of social gatherings. Along Rondo Avenue there emerged a small but thriving commercial strip that included grocery stores, barber and beauty shops, and union halls, all of which served as important social centers for African American families. The dance hall in particular became a cultural focal point within the neighborhood. In Rondo it was known as Stem Hall, and it hosted acts by such top performers as Ella Fitzgerald, Etta James, and Chuck Berry. By the 1940s, Rondo Avenue was simply known by locals as "the Strip" or the "main drag," underscoring the central role of streets and sidewalks in the community's social life.[26]

Talk of freeways began in the mid-1950s, when the federal government licensed Minnesota's highway engineers to begin work on the "central route," which would run through the heart of the Rondo neighborhood. Local community leaders organized immediate opposition to the highway plan. They first pressed for the adoption of the "northern route," an alternate path generated within the planning department that would have spared the Rondo neighborhood. The city denied that request. After accepting the inevitable coming of the freeway, community leaders insisted on relocation assistance and the institution of antidiscriminatory measures in the local housing market. That request was also denied. The only concession the Minnesota Highway Department made to the people of Rondo was the construction of a depressed freeway that minimized the "visual disturbances" of new state infrastructure.[27]

Local residents were not unified in their opposition to construction of a freeway. Many played by the rules, abiding by legal notices to accept compensation and relocate. Some saw the new freeway as an opportunity to press for political and economic rights, such as the passage of open-housing legislation and increased relocation assistance. Others took "fair market value" to improve their living conditions, moving beyond the boundaries of the old neighborhood to "move up the housing ladder."[28] Still others took a more defiant stance, refusing to move. When the bulldozers came in 1959, for example, Reverend George Davis of the Mount Olive Mission, a longtime Rondo resident, remained with his family in his home, holding a shotgun to the door when sheriffs arrived.[29]

Despite flares of opposition, the segment of I-94 through St. Paul and Minneapolis opened in 1961, and it reshaped the geography of race in the Twin Cities area. In 1962, the St. Paul City Housing Authority commissioned a sociological study from Hamline University. Surveying the residents displaced from the Rondo–St. Anthony neighborhood, F. James Davis interviewed 433 households forced to relocate by the freeway, 311 of whom reported as nonwhite. Approximately 90 percent of the white residents who had to relocate found new quarters outside the old Rondo neighborhood, whereas only 15 percent of black residents did so. The majority of black respondents indicated that they did not try to find new housing outside the Rondo neighborhood, citing the higher prices of property in other neighborhoods and "their fear of discrimination." Of those African Americans who did seek housing in new neighborhoods, about half reported that they had trouble relocating, citing evasive real estate agents and uncooperative mortgage lenders. Finding that the overwhelming majority of displaced African Americans resettled in neighborhoods with diminished housing supplies, the report confirmed the initial concerns of Rondo's black leadership: that "the clearance . . . increased the concentration of non-whites in the area."[30]

For longtime residents of the neighborhood, the destruction of Rondo Avenue forced a break with the past. "Leave behind Memories," ran a headline of the *St. Paul Recorder,* reporting on the 1958 clearance of the Rondo–St. Anthony area, a community "stretching back nearly 80 years."[31] Timothy Howard, president of the Rondo–St. Anthony Freeway Organization, which provided relocation information and assistance for displaced families, recognized the broken timeline enforced on evictees: "Many of these families have a lot of history here and now they're being forced to leave the place where they remember the good old days."[32] Mrs. George Davis, the wife of the belligerent pastor who refused to abandon his home, summoned the memories of raising her family in the home that lay in the path of a freeway: "My children and grandchildren were raised in this house. How can I leave?"[33] On the eve of destruction, some Rondo residents invoked their ties to the past to express their reluctance to relocate.

Yet thanks to the determination of a few displaced residents, the story of Rondo does not end with destruction. The past thirty years have witnessed individual and collective efforts to construct a culture of memory around the history of "old Rondo." For example, the Rondo Oral History Project began in 2002, when Hand in Hand Productions, a nonprofit organization established in 1996 to document the history of the Twin Cities' diverse neighborhoods, established a Rondo community advisory group to collect oral history interviews. After collecting the oral histories of thirty-three former residents of the old neighborhood, this group assembled a traveling exhibit of twenty-three storyboards, which circulated throughout the metropolitan area. From this exhibit came the 2005 book *Voices of Rondo: Oral Histories of Saint Paul's Historic Black Community,* which added photographs of life in Rondo before the interstate to oral history transcripts.[34]

These stories register sentimental longings for the "good old days." They include humorous reminiscences about characters who lived in the neighborhood, descriptions of the routine interactions that transpired on the streets and sidewalks of Rondo, warm recollections of church services and holiday celebrations, and quite often memories of the struggle to make ends meet. Most of those interviewed share a common conviction that I-94 destroyed the basis of a vital black community. Some, like Marvin Roger Anderson, a former resident, contend that building the freeway was a crime against African Americans in Saint Paul; says Anderson, "It didn't have to be that way. . . . It was a cruel decision to route it the way they did it, and that's what people felt. They were being ignored."[35] Similarly, Yusef Mgeni, who grew up in Rondo as Charlie Anderson, attributed the growing absence of leadership in St. Paul's black community directly to the freeway crisis: "People who had the means, people who led the community—spiritually, politically, intellectually—were leaving the community. That led to a time when there were more bulldozers in the neighborhood than cockroaches."[36]

The oral histories also indicate a common perception that white highway builders deliberately targeted black people and their neighborhoods in their plans for the freeway. Many within the community knew, for example, that an alternate route had been proposed, one that would have spared Rondo and other neighborhoods. Why then, did Minnesota's highway builders insist on routing I-94 through an African American community that enjoyed a modicum of prosperity? Rondo's leaders posed this exact question publicly, but many within the community already had an answer to this question, which drew on shared experiences of racism in St. Paul and Minneapolis. Constance Raye Jones, a participant in the oral history project, recalls a white highway worker telling her father, "We're getting rid of niggers."[37] Raye's conviction that I-94 was built to destroy a black community also resonated within the broader context of African American history. After the nightmare of slavery, the fiasco of Reconstruction, the indignity of Jim Crow, and the legacy of white violence against black Americans, it is hard to imagine how African Americans could *not* believe that their communities were the deliberate targets of highway construction. Small wonder, then, that one former resident of Rondo branded I-94 a "white man's freeway."[38]

These interviews and the memories they document are part of a broader memory culture that took shape around Rondo's destruction. The memory of destruction is sharp among many former residents, but it takes a back seat to the vivified historical portrait of old Rondo built through an organized outpouring of oral histories, memoirs, autobiographies, and community festivals. It took time for this culture to surface, but by the turn of the twentieth century, Rondo had reemerged in local discourse as a vibrant African American community that once sustained the unique perils and pleasures of being black in the upper Midwest.

Some former residents published autobiographies to preserve their memoirs. In 1990, at the age of seventy, Evelyn Fairbanks wrote *The Days of Rondo*. Her goal was "to live and relive the days of Rondo," a community that she remembers as the kind of place where people knew each other on a first-name basis and where neighbors looked after each other. She tells of the importance of the Hallie Q. Brown Community Center for black youths in the neighborhood, of the big-city sophistication of boys from Minneapolis versus the smaller-town simplicity of St. Paul's young men, and of the role of the Urban League and the NAACP in supporting St. Paul's black community in the age of civil rights. Fairbanks also describes the anxiety that gripped her and her neighborhood in the years leading up to the construction of I-94. Fairbanks's memories are significant not because they account for life in Rondo as it really happened but because they signal the local impulse to record the memories of a lost community for future generations.[39]

As Fairbanks herself put it: "I don't want to leave readers with the impression that I have been sitting on the sidelines, observing, all my life." And so, by writing her memoirs, Fairbanks jumps onto the playing field of history, adding her own experiences to the broader narrative of a neighborhood plowed under by a freeway:

> The community I wrote about is gone. It was erased by the highway department and "progress"—The neighborhood storefronts . . . suffered and closed when the corner became a high crime area. The black population has grown so large that we don't all know each other. The hunger for the old days is so great. . . . I share that hunger. It makes me write stories.[40]

A broader community of black men and women in St. Paul share this "hunger of memory," gathering once a year to celebrate a lost neighborhood. The Rondo Days Festival began as a conversation between two former members of the Rondo community, Marvin Roger Anderson, librarian of the Minnesota Law Library, and Floyd George Smaller, a teacher in St. Paul's school district. The people they knew from their experiences growing up in Rondo, "who did not want to let go of the memories," inspired both men. Both were teenagers when their families were forced to abandon their homes, but they returned to St. Paul after college. At the first planning meeting on July 4, 1982, attended by over fifty former residents of the Rondo neighborhood, Smaller and Anderson spelled out their vision of a four-day festival, kicking off on Thursday and ending on Sunday, which would include a parade, a community picnic, games for kids, writing and poetry contests, a Saturday-night dance, and an interfaith church service on Sunday.[41]

To facilitate the planning process, Smaller and Anderson established the Remember Rondo Committee and launched a membership drive. Their fund-raising efforts garnered $5,000, culminating in the first Rondo Days Festival on the July 4 weekend in 1983. It drew an initial attendance of about eight hundred people, including three hundred former Rondo residents, and convened at Oxford Park, nicknamed People's Park, which edged just above the depressed route of I-94. The irony of the park's location was not lost on Floyd Smaller, who noted that although the roar of traffic could be heard from any given point in the park, it was "overpowered by the pure joy of the occasion." Alexs Pate, a former Rondo resident and the author of *Amistad*, a novelized adaptation of Steven Spielberg's 1997 film of the same title, for Rondo Days wrote "The Days of Rondo," a play that dramatized the history of St. Paul's black community before I-94. St. Paul's Metropolitan Transit Authority granted use of an old bus that once ran up and down Rondo Avenue. The refurbished Rondo Stryker, as it was known, debuted in Saturday's parade, a reminder of the public mode of transport that had served the Rondo community before the age of the freeway.[42]

The publicists and promoters of the first Rondo Days Festival took measures to address the diversity of the Twin Cities' public and to create an inclusive atmosphere that welcomed people of all racial and ethnic backgrounds. Nonetheless, it was clear from the festival's publicity materials, programs, and featured entertainment that the festival was a decidedly black affair, dedicated to the vitality of St. Paul's black community, past and present. A historical exhibit, *A Tradition of Excellence,* housed at the Hallie Q. Brown Community Center, was created specifically for the festival. It documented the lives of St. Paul's most prominent black citizens and recounted the local struggles of the Urban League, the NAACP, and unions such as the Dining Car Union and the Sleeping Car Porters Union. The adjacent Martin Luther King Center hosted the Black Arts Festival, sponsored by the Afro-American Cultural Arts Center. In 2003 the festival was switched from the Fourth of July to the second weekend in June, roughly coinciding with June 19, or Juneteenth, a holiday in many states, which celebrates the day in 1865 that slavery officially ended in Texas, the last Confederate holdout of the American slave system. The symbolism of that shift underscored the

FIGURE 3.2. A poster commemorating the fourth anniversary of the Rondo Days Festival in St. Paul, Minnesota, 1987. Courtesy of the Minnesota Historical Society.

efforts of the sponsors of Rondo Days to affiliate the festival with a local sense of black pride (Figure 3.2).[43]

Since 1983, the Rondo Days Festival has become a highlight of St. Paul's cultural scene and has grown considerably. In 2005, the festival recorded an attendance of over 30,000 people, generating over half a million dollars in revenue.[44] The festival generates revenue, but it also promotes social and political awareness, hosting prominent black officials and activists. Over the years, African American representatives in government and media have made appearances at Rondo Days, lending their names to the festival.

The Rondo Days Festival belongs to a memory culture created through individual and collective efforts. This culture surfaced *after* Rondo's destruction, wrought from a local effort to maintain a sense of continuity with the past and to keep a community's traditions alive. For many African Americans in St. Paul, Rondo has become a sacred space, a cultural touchstone through which former residents of the neighborhood remember the struggles of their forebears and the world they created. Though a modern interstate highway has displaced the physical remnants of that world, former members of the community marshal local resources to remember old Rondo and to restore some of the social bonds it once sustained. Through such efforts, "Rondo" now connotes black pride and identity in the upper Midwest in a way that it had not before. Whereas the neighborhood had been racially and ethnically diverse, its memory is black.

Rondo's former residents used festival, memoirs, and autobiography to preserve the memory of a community lost to the freeway; Miami's black leaders strive to rebuild remnants of a vital black community plowed over by Interstate 95. The template for this "new town" was Miami's first ghetto, named Overtown, which lay on the northwestern fringes of Miami's central business district before the arrival of I-95 in the mid-1960s. Overtown began in the final decades of the nineteenth century as an encampment for black railroad and construction workers. The Supreme Court's *Plessy v. Ferguson* decision of 1896, upholding the constitutionality of the "separate but equal" doctrine, opened the door for Jim Crow laws that segregated African Americans. Overtown, known as "Colored Town" in its early years, was one of the few areas in Miami that allowed black settlement, drawing people from all trades and classes. By the 1930s, Overtown's population had reached about 25,000, making it the center of black culture in southern Florida.[45]

Formal and informal regimes of segregation helped foster a cohesive community in Overtown, as the neighborhood experienced an era of prosperity between the 1920s and the 1950s. The stately homes of African American professionals clustered around Overtown's churches, schools, and businesses, and more modest, wooden-framed shotgun houses (a typical housing type in southern cities) anchored the neighborhood's working-class areas. The Lyric Theater, established by a black entrepreneur in the 1920s, sponsored the lively cultural scene of Ninth Street, which earned the distinctions of being "Little Broadway," the "Harlem of the South," or the "Great Black Way." As tourists flocked to Miami's bustling sports and entertainment venues, Overtown featured black America's brightest stars and was the one place they could find accommodation in a heavily segregated city. Thus, Ella Fitzgerald, Sammy Davis Jr., Billie Holiday, and Nat King Cole performed in the after-hours clubs of Overtown, drawing integrated audiences.[46]

A capital of black culture in the mid-twentieth century, Overtown sustained a diverse mix of Afro-Americans and Afro-Caribbeans. The district served as a gateway for recent Afro-Caribbean immigrants to south Florida, where they learned the racial codes, mores, and protocols of their new home. Thus "Cubans, Jamaicans, Bahamians, and American blacks shared fruit trees and family trees, clotheslines and bloodlines," creating cross-cultural and cross-class ties under the aegis of Jim Crow segregation. Overtown's bustle had become renowned, as the neighborhood overflowed with businesses and services that catered to Miami's diverse black community. As one former Overtown resident put it:

> There were so many businesses in Overtown that you really didn't need to go to downtown Miami, as we called the Flagler Street section, because everything that you really needed was in Overtown. You had the Man's Ship that made the men's clothing, there was a furniture store right on Second Avenue, there was Shanang's restaurant, and there was Manerver's beauty shop. The doctors were there; the dentists were there. Any need that you had could be met in Overtown because the businesses were there.[47]

Yet this was not the Promised Land. Though Overtown's population was pushing 50,000 by the mid-1950s, the community's expansion drew sharp resistance from local whites, who sought to defend Miami's racial barriers, sometimes with violence. Such resistance helped keep Overtown's expansion in check. Like many urban black neighborhoods in the United States up to the 1950s, Overtown embodied a paradox. It contained the best of black American culture yet sustained the worst of conditions. It was an area low on public services and short on housing; as one of the few areas where blacks could settle, Overtown suffered inflated rents and taxes; it lacked the resources of Miami's whites-only schools and hospitals; and its residents endured repeated instances of police brutality, including early curfews and restrictive ordinances. Despite the cultural vitality and socioeconomic diversity of Overtown, it endured the inequalities and indignities leveled at black Americans throughout much of their history.[48]

Ultimately, Overtown surrendered to the path of "progress." The neighborhood met its demise in the early 1960s with the construction of Interstate 95 and its major interchange with Interstate 395. Overtown was Miami's first ghetto, but its destruction intensified existing patterns of racial segregation. I-95 displaced some 30,000 African American residents of Overtown, who had few options for relocation save Miami's satellite concentrations of African Americans in the northwestern section of the metropolitan area. Thus Liberty City, Brownsville, and Opa-Locka witnessed an influx of Overtown refugees, reproducing existing patterns of racial succession and placing greater strain on available housing.[49] Miami's civic establishment welcomed this transition, as they had long viewed Overtown as an obstacle to downtown expansion. The construction of I-95 made their dream a reality, signaling new commercial opportunities in the vicinity of downtown while exerting tighter control over the expansion of the city's black community. This process effectively created a "vast second ghetto" that made Miami one of the most racially segregated cities in the nation as late as 1980.

As for Overtown itself, the neighborhood lost much of its vitality; its population declined precipitously from 45,000 to 10,000 in the course of a decade.[50] I-95 and its intersection with I-395 destroyed some eighty-seven acres of housing and commercial property at the heart of Overtown. During construction, the *Miami Times* described the scene: "A drive through the downtown negro section gives one the idea that something like a king-sized tornado had hit the place." The historian Raymond Mohl described the aftermath as an "urban wasteland": vacant lots strewn with trash, boarded up stores, welfare hotels, abandoned buildings, and homeless encampments under the elevated portions of the expressway.[51] One 2002 study confirms this assessment, noting that 22 percent of land in what used to be Overtown is now a no-man's-land beneath elevated expressway structures.[52] And yet, as anticipated by an earlier generation of civic elites, certain functions of Miami's central business district have crept into the former precincts of Overtown: city, county, and state government offices; a police station; transit facilities; parking lots; a modern basketball arena; and condominiums.

Through all this change, however, the vibrant community created by the oppressed descendants of slaves had become a relic of Miami's past.

Like St. Paul, black Miami has its own answers to the question of what happened to their neighborhood. Since its destruction, Overtown symbolizes environmental injustice. M. Athalie Range, Miami's first black city commissioner, deplored the destruction of Overtown, calling it a "classic example of the transportation planners' disregard of the inner-city populace." "After conducting not one single public hearing in the City of Miami," Range told an audience at a 1971 planning conference, "5,000 housing units were destroyed between 1960 and 1969 in the all-black downtown area of Miami to make room for the North–South Expressway."[53] Similarly, Robert Ingram, police chief of Opa-locka and Overtown native, told the *Miami Herald* in 1982 that "the expressway I-95 ran right down the middle [of Overtown]. It split the community and displaced people."[54]

Others share this sentiment yet strive to preserve what is left and to remember what is gone. Former school teacher Dorothy Jenkins Fields, founder and director of the Black Archives, History, and Research Foundation of South Florida, echoes the sentiments of many African Americans in Miami. The destruction of Overtown was "by design," she says, as the expressway "divided Colored Town and destroyed the community."[55] This conviction, however, prompted Jenkins to begin work on historic preservation in the mid-1970s, establishing a black photographic archive for the 1976 Bicentennial celebration. This led to the establishment of the Black Archives, History, and Research Foundation (BAF), which since 1977 has been collecting, preserving, and disseminating the history and culture of black Miami from 1896 to the present. With its extensive collection of manuscripts, photographs, oral histories, and other source materials, the BAF has become a repository for the history of Overtown before its destruction and sponsors community programs and events, such as tours of historic black communities in South Florida.

In addition to collecting archival materials, the BAF also collects buildings, at least those spared by the expressway. Thus it owns and maintains three historic sites in Miami, restoring two of them for the National Register of Historic Places: the Dorsey House, built in 1920, home of Miami's first black millionaire, and the Lyric Theater, built by black businessman Geder Walker, who was inspired to build the theater by trips to opera houses in Paris, France. Built in 1913, the Lyric Theater became the centerpiece of Miami's Great Black Way and staged performances of gospel, jazz, vaudeville, and the literary arts of Harlem.

These two buildings anchor the proposed Historic Overtown Folklife Village, a new cultural district dedicated to the memory of Miami's largest black community. Fields drew inspiration for the Folklife Village from her 1977 visit to the Foxfire Oral History Program in Rabun Gap, Georgia, which demonstrated success in the preservation and dissemination of Appalachian heritage, culture, foodways, and music through several linked programs in oral history, public education, musical recording, book publishing, and architectural preservation. In the vocabulary of postmodernism, the creators of this "new town" emphasize "historic," "folk," and "village," sharing a vision of urban diversity that Jacobs celebrated in *Death and Life*. They also take their cue from the 1995 White House Conference on Travel and Tourism, which asserted in a position paper, "The 'real America' can best be done through its historic sites and monuments, its folk and traditional artists, its architecture, landscape museums and other cultural institutions."[56] Their vision also has parallels to the scope and ambitions of new urbanism, the urban design movement that embraces local history and architectural heritage to re-create pedestrian- and transit-friendly cities. Yet this is *black* new urbanism. As Fields put it: "I thought that if a black man built this, he built it for us. I think of those buildings as footprints that connect generations of the past, whom we shall never see, with generations of the future, whom we shall never see."[57]

To draft a master plan for the village, the BAF contracted Duany Plater-Zyberk and Company (DPZ), the architectural and planning firm that designed the new urbanist community of Seaside, Florida. Overtown's *Master Plan* begins with a subtle jab at the planners of I-95: "This is a plan of building up, not taking down." It outlines a proposal to rebuild the typical historic fabric of the area to house a variety of uses: dining, shopping, housing, performance, art, and preservations walks. This "heritage entertainment district" includes a museum of local history, a center for genealogical research, a Jazz Walk of Fame, and faithful reproductions of the historic theaters and churches that anchored Overtown in its heyday.[58] With "strong ties to the Black cultural heritage and traditions of South Florida, the Bahamas, the Caribbean and the Harlem Renaissance," the Folklife Village would re-sensitize tourists and locals alike to the history of black Miami while creating opportunities for black community development.[59]

Village designers also made special accommodations for I-95. The *Master Plan* stresses the "primary importance . . . of a dense and tall green edge along I-95." Instead of a setback, however, the planners of the village use the adjacent interstate to distinguish the district's boundaries, creating a "special identity" for the village. The master plan thus calls for sea grape or royal palms, plant species indigenous to southern Florida, to block visual and physical access to the freeway and to create a prominent landscape edge. These design strategies demonstrate that the planners of Folklife Village see the interstate not as an intrusion but as a border that distinguishes the unique character of this "heritage entertainment district."[60]

It sounds suspiciously close to a Disneyfied version of black history, which entails its own set of problems and possibilities. Like Rondo Days or *Before I-75,* the master plan for Overtown Historic Folklife Village faced nagging questions of authenticity. This tourist attraction, despite its claims of historicity, is not the real thing—no theme park or its variations are. It presents a sheen that the open sewers, unpaved roads, and homemade architecture of the real Overtown never had. In the contemporary context of urban development, this polish attracts investment and musters trade, but it also threatens to hijack the real history of human struggle in the name of easy profit. That might happen, but the visionaries behind Folklife Village, people like Dorothy Jenkins Fields, see their effort as *part* of that historic struggle—the struggle to rescue the past from the obliterating forces of progress and to reassert a version of that past squarely in the center of the city fabric. As Fields herself described her efforts behind the Folklife Village: "This project will not bring Overtown back, but it will introduce the legacy of that community for everyone to enjoy."[61]

Whether or not this proposal furthers the contemporary "theming" of the American city, this is not Disneyland's Main Street, USA. Granted, the proposal for Folklife Village is nostalgic, sanitized, and commercial, like Disney's celebrated theme park, but it presents aspects of *black* history that contrast with the generic white history enshrined in Disneyland's Main Street, and it does so while recognizing the historic diversity of Miami's sprawling black community. In this context, the Folklife Village strives to *reracialize* Miami's landscape after its deracination by highway construction in the 1950s. Like many landscapes deemed "historical," the Folklife Village presents an invented tradition in which selected elements of a community's past have been rescued from obscurity and assigned a new set of cultural meanings. It is part of a broader tendency to romanticize the insular world of pre–civil rights black urban communities, but it nonetheless reasserts the visibility of black history in Miami against the erasures of its past. By our twenty-first-century standards, the new social history, which revolutionized the writing of American history by emphasizing the hidden histories of race, class, and gender, might be passé, but its impact on the built environment of the American city is still in blueprint form.[62]

Miami's proposed Folklife Village and St. Paul's Rondo Days festival are among the lingering remains of two black neighborhoods that succumbed to contested highway proposals in the 1950s, both selected in preference to other proposals that would have left these communities intact. Their relationship to the physical reality of the neighborhoods they aim to represent is known through a finite variety of sources—personal recollections, photographs, building permits, insurance maps, property deeds, and other artifacts of the city's past—but as public gestures of remembrance inserted into the contemporary urban fabric, they signal an ongoing resistance to accepting the fate of the old neighborhood. Among the many ways that African Americans remember their past, Rondo Days and the Overtown Folklife Village, despite their commercial gloss, remind us of what interstate highways did to urban black communities during the postwar period. While these memorializing efforts privilege some memories over others and conform, at least in some part, to profit-minded logics of redevelopment, they nonetheless signal a local determination to remember what was lost and to mend a fractured sense of historical time.

Race, Space, and Time

This is not to suggest that *only* black people faced the daunting prospect of rebuilding the past after the devastating effects of highway construction. Chinese Americans in Boston have undertaken similar efforts, convening through community organizations such as the Chinese American Historical Society or the Boston Chinatown Neighborhood Center to remember a neighborhood that was amputated by the 1950s construction of the Central Artery and the Massachusetts Turnpike. Like many of Boston's communities, Chinatown fought to save itself, joining a metropolitan coalition that organized against inner-city highway construction. Yet the construction of Interstate 90 reduced Chinatown by about half its size, destroyed approximately one-third of its housing stock, and displaced some three hundred families living in about 1,200 housing units. In the wake of such destruction, the remaining residents and their descendants who relocated to the suburbs have organized museum exhibits and "heritage trails" to promote the remnants of Chinatown as a local tourist attraction, a cultural landmark just off the freeway that serves to remind Boston of its historic Chinese presence.[63]

In cities throughout the nation, the interstate era sparked a resurgent memory culture, often built from the wreckage of the past. Whether in Baltimore, New Orleans, Miami, St. Paul, or Boston, diverse Americans defended their idealizations of the past against the onslaught of the future. This chapter has shown how this effort took shape in diverse communities, across the lines of race, class, geography, and even those of language, religion, and gender. Even the threat of highway construction strengthened a community's resolve to remember its past and to preserve the landmarks through which it recognized itself and its history.

Yet the outcome of those efforts varied widely. During the interstate era, historic preservationists were limited by their sense of what counted as "historic," privileging the European heritage of the urban built environment. The discovery of "heritage" in the city's landscape coincided with a broader embrace of ethnic roots among white Americans, inspired in no small part by the black civil rights movement. This chapter has shown how a burgeoning preservation movement helped protect certain communities from urban redevelopment schemes, but stubborn questions remain. Why was the fight to save Little Italy in Lower Manhattan described as "everyone's fight," whereas the struggles to preserve Rondo and Overtown were not? What empowered a young Barbara Mikulski to defend the heritage of Baltimore's German and Polish neighborhoods through a heightened sense of ethnic pride, whereas a racial discourse of defense failed in black neighborhoods? What changes in public consciousness enabled a *partial* protection of the city's architectural legacy, one that privileged the heritage of some communities over others?

At its outset in the mid-1960s, the historic preservation movement contributed to the racial splintering of the nation's urban fabric. It denied the freeway's entry into communities deemed historic while granting its passage through communities judged differently. It empowered some communities in their fight against the freeway while putting others at a disadvantage. In the disproportionate number of black communities that bore the brunt of urban highway construction, the preservation strategy had no chance, leaving displaced residents with a meager set of resources to recuperate their connection to the past. This is why we need to pay attention to murals, festivals, autobiographies, oral histories, and archival efforts. In the high-stakes struggles over the fate of the American city, these were the "weapons of the weak," the tools invented by displaced communities to fight the forced erasures of their past. This gives us another way to think about the notion of "colored people's time" (CP time), a term that humorously describes how people of color abstain from allegedly "white" habits of punctuality and time discipline. In the age of the freeway, the experiences of black communities like Rondo and Overtown suggest that CP time also includes a forced sense of historical rupture or a timeline broken by an onslaught of bulldozers.

Whether or not the Rondo Days Festival and the proposed Folklife Village in Miami signal a broadening awareness of black history and its place in the urban built environment, they do reflect the unexpected outcomes of building freeways in black neighborhoods. The injunction to "never forget" compels many social groups to write history and preserve memory, but some groups are better able to *enact* those imperatives than others. Whether through monumental museums or annual public festivals, the effort to combat the erasures of the past among diverse Americans is reshaping the contours of contemporary urban culture. Within the ghostly parameters of what used to be thriving black communities, highway construction eventually paved the way for present-day assertions of black history and black pride. These assertions take shape through the recesses of collective memory and shared struggle, but they are also tied to decisions made within highway-planning departments during the age of the interstate. Herein lies the great paradox of this story: that the modernist city, which bulldozed its way through history and tradition to implement its totalizing vision, actually begot sharply particular expressions of racial memory and pride. Urban highway construction shaped the experience and perception of time, but it also structured new ways of seeing. Chapter 4 shifts from the culture of memory to the culture of vision, exploring disparate visions of the freeway and its place in the city.

4   A Matter of Perspective

The Racial Politics of Seeing the Freeway

There were no paintings of Los Angeles. People then didn't even know what it looked like. And when I was there, they were still finishing up some of the big freeways. I remember seeing, within the first week, a ramp of freeway going into the air and I suddenly thought: "my God, this place needs its Piranesi; Los Angeles could have a Piranesi so here I am!"

David Hockney, 1963

In Europe all roads lead to Rome; in Southern California, all freeways lead to East Los Angeles.

Goez Art Studio, 1975

Though his work defined a marketable image of the suburban good life in 1960s Los Angeles, David Hockney never actually painted an L.A. freeway. The closest he came was his 1980 portrait *Mulholland Drive,* but this is a road, albeit a fabled one, not a freeway. Throughout his artistic career, Hockney painted a lot of palm trees, swimming pools, and naked men, but he never really tackled the new freeways that defined the city's identity in its postwar heyday. He did not have to. A British expat settling in the secluded canyons of the Hollywood Hills, Hockney mostly hung out in the gentrifying precincts of West Hollywood, drawing aesthetic inspiration from its commercial strips, its condominium lifestyle, and its burgeoning gay scene.

Thanks to the success of the freeway revolt in Beverly Hills, there are no free-ways through the adjacent city of West Hollywood.[1]

Beyond the tonier quarters of L.A.'s Westside, however, the freeway earned more prominent recognition in the local art scene. In Boyle Heights, about ten miles east of West Hollywood along Sunset Boulevard, the freeway figures prominently in the visual and literary culture of Chicano Los Angeles, as exemplified in the work of Judith Baca and Helena Maria Viramontes. As this area transitioned from a racially and ethnically diverse working-class neighborhood to an undiverse concentration of working-class Mexican Ameri-cans, six freeways bullied their way into Boyle Heights, converging on two massive highway interchanges that consumed 10 percent of the local hous-ing stock. By the late 1960s, after the California Division of Highways had completed its assault on East Los Angeles, freeways dominated the sensory experience of daily life in the nation's largest barrio: the roar of traffic cours-ing above or below surface streets, the shadows cast by soaring interchanges, the dead ends and circuitous detours, the odor of traffic emissions, and the foreboding maze of concrete walls, piers, and embankments.

Welcome to East Los Angeles, where freeways frame the emerging iden-tity of Mexican America. This chapter focuses on the sight of the new free-ways in Los Angeles and their portrayal in American art and photography since the age of the interstate. Not only did highway construction spark a gendered critique among diverse American women, but it also invited a di-vergent set of racialized perspectives. Although the visual record of American art and photography since the interstate era registers these discrepancies, it says little about their origins in the skewed impact of highway construction during the 1950s and 1960s. To argue for a Chicano perspective or a black perspective of the freeway seems straightforward enough, but to identify a *white* perspective requires seeing the unseen, seeing what has been rendered invisible by historical forces that exempt white artists from a racial point of view. Yet as critical race theory tells us, white perspective and power, like white identity, is most always apparent against the presence and perspective of the Other.[2]

This chapter extends the dialectical analysis of the previous chapters, drawing general comparisons between the work of East L.A. Chicano artists and Westside white artists during the interstate and post-interstate eras. It considers the freeway portraits of other artists as well, but taken as a whole, this body of freeway art reflects a shared impulse to paint the freeway and its relationship to the urban built environment. Despite this common focus, however, these images also leave a visual record of the freeway's disparate impact on the city's socioeconomic geography. There is the "up-close-and-personal" portrait from East Los Angeles—a Chicano perspective steeped in the riotous colors of a Mexican aesthetic and in the political ferment of the Chicano movement. Here we get a fine-grain perspective on the freeway and its underbelly—its columns, embankments, and box girders and their framing of daily visual life. From the whiter Westside, however, a more exacting portrait of the freeway emerges. There, artists homed in on the freeway's fragments, undulations, and precise geometry, as well as on its general abstraction from the urban fabric. Westside artists won the acclaim that came late, if at all, to Eastside artists, and though their work evidenced some of the rebellious strains of the 1960s, it found more obvious parallels in the visual iconography of the highway-planning profession and in the elaborate spectacles of popular culture.

All told, the diverse paintings and photographs explored in this chapter depict the structural disparities of how the freeway is seen. Some, like David Hockney, discovered the freeway; for others, the freeway discovered them. To argue that racial discrimination, class privilege, and public policy frame the freeway's portrait is not to deny the artist the autonomous spark of imagination and creativity but, rather, to affirm the capacity of art to register the dissimilar consequences of modernization and to illustrate how the field of human vision is as charged, politically, as the physical landscape of the city itself.

"White Man's Freeway"

The interstate era of the 1950s and 1960s encompassed a shift in the mainstream world of American art, from the intense visions of the abstract expressionists toward the cool, detached sensibility of pop, which discovered the "stuff" of everyday life in a suburbanizing, consumer-oriented culture.

In this context, the freeway began to insinuate itself into American art, especially on the West Coast, where artists and photographers discovered a new world of aesthetic possibility from the windshields of their cars. On a cross-country trip to California, for example, Andy Warhol, a Pittsburgh native turned New Yorker, noted the new perspective introduced by the freeway: "The further west we drove on the highway, the more Pop everything looked."[3] The freeway's discovery by some L.A. artists produced a decidedly *ungrounded* vision, one rooted not in the particular perspective of a particular community or neighborhood but, rather, in the individual's determination to render the new geometry of postwar consumer culture and to master the aesthetic challenges they posed.

Roger Kuntz, for example, focused on the freeway to paint his way through the shifting currents of mainstream American art. Developing his painting skills in the 1950s, Kuntz struggled between his inherent talent for figurative painting and his ambition to emulate the abstract forms that dominated the postwar art scene. In Southern California, Kuntz discovered the freeway: a structure that invited a straightforward rendering yet also enabled experimentation in the two-dimensional representation of line, form, color, solids, and voids. Kuntz took to painting the image of the freeway in the early 1960s, departing from traditional portraiture into more abstract modes of representation. His 1961 painting *Arches,* for example, is wholly focused on the road environment, with but a pale-blue sliver of sky interrupting his artful composition of solids, shadows, and voids. Kuntz seems to paint from the surface of the road itself, eliminating all signs of human interaction—no people, crowds, cars, traffic, litter, signs, or smog. Color is sparse in his reduced palette of grays, greens, and browns. In a review for *Artforum,* Henry Hopkins expressed his admiration for these spare compositions, praising "the formal grandeur and functional simplicity of the freeway . . . affected by the intensity of the raking sun."[4]

To find the right perspective, Kuntz cruised the L.A. freeways in an Aston Martin convertible. He would drive through an interchange several times, from all directions, and at all levels. Using a 35mm camera and slide film, Kuntz took photographs from his car and posted them in his Laguna Beach studio as source material and studio aids. In most cases, he worked from these photographs to produce a recognizable, three-dimensional image of a freeway environment and to further develop his skills for abstraction.[5]

With a nod toward pop art's enthusiasm for machine-made signs and objects, Kuntz also depicted the bold graphics of freeway signs (Plate 2). Though these large paintings, on the order of five feet by six feet, come close to the real thing in size, the apparent brushwork and cropped framing divulge the hand of the artist. This work belongs in the company of works portraying the "stuff" of popular culture—Jasper Johns's maps and flags, Roy Lichtenstein's comic strips, Warhol's soup cans and detergent boxes, Edward Ruscha's gas stations and supermarkets. We find the same air of detachment that characterizes much of the pop aesthetic. As the first generation of freeway drivers struggled to navigate their way through a high-speed environment of signs, interchanges, lane dividers, on-ramps, and off-ramps, Kuntz delivered a cool abstraction of this kinetic environment—a spare portrait of empty and static arteries. Some critics saw a noble tradition of representing the American West in art, like the one who claimed that Kuntz "romanticized the freeway much in the way that Frederic Remington represented the purple canyons of the West years ago."[6]

Kuntz's paintings might have reinforced stereotypical associations between Los Angeles and its freeways, but in other cities, other artists also confronted the freeway as an aesthetic problem to solve. In the mid-1970s, Los Angeles surpassed Chicago as the nation's second city, provoking San Franciscans to brand their city as the opposite of Los Angeles: an enduring (and endearing) landmark of Victorian urbanism, a cosmopolitan assortment of quirky neighborhoods, from the stately to the seedy, nestled at the hilly tip of a foggy peninsula, beholden to the few cable cars left over from the heyday of American cities before Henry Ford. The relative absence of freeways reinforced local distinctions from Los Angeles, as San Franciscans had denied state and federal highway-building authorities entry into their neighborhoods. Thanks to the success of that city's freeway revolt in the 1950s, San Franciscans proudly shared Harvey Milk's conviction that "people are more important than highways."[7]

The few freeways that were built, however, nonetheless found representation in the acclaimed corpus of Bay Area art. Wayne Thiebaud, for example, had earned national recognition for painting cakes, gumballs, and other staples in the diet of blue-collar America. In the early 1970s, this graphic artist turned figurative painter bought a small house as an extra residence and studio in the Potrero Hill neighborhood of San Francisco, a gentrifying neighborhood in the steep hills south of the city's financial district. There he began painting the San Francisco cityscape, with its precipitous streets, perch-like intersections, and rows of blocky architecture. Some critics branded Thiebaud's work as pop, though the bulk of this work emerged before pop's heyday. With formal training in advertising, poster art, and layout design, Thiebaud balanced his interest in the work of Jan Vermeer, Piet Mondrian, Edgar Degas, Richard Diebenkorn, Edward Hopper, and others with his fondness for the vernacular objects that impressed him with character and presence.[8]

The same visual delight that Thiebaud took from neckties, pies, toys, and hot dogs, he found in the form of the freeway. By the mid-1970s, the city's two major freeways flanked the Potrero Hill neighborhood: State Highway 101, which connected to Interstate 80 at the Oakland Bay Bridge, and Interstate 280, which emptied traffic into the nearby South of Market neighborhood. From his hillside vantage point, Thiebaud saw the San Francisco freeway not as an environmental problem—as did most of his fellow San Franciscans— but as a problem in formal composition, making it a subtheme in his render-ing of the cityscape. His inspiration from the freeway traces back to his early experiences on family road trips between Southern California and southern Utah, where his Uncle Lowell, a road builder himself, taught Thiebaud how to drive. Later in his life, Thiebaud made extensive road trips across the nation, often between Los Angeles and New York, or between San Francisco and Los Angeles, straight down Interstate 5, to Laguna Beach, where Thiebaud shared a home with his family. The visual experience of freeway driving introduced new perspectives and images, problems to be worked out on canvas. He took special notice of the symbolic markings on the freeway, such as the paint ap-plied to make lines, arrows, and words on the road surface. The long black marks of tires skidding on pavement also impressed Thiebaud. This is what he called the "patina of travel"—the traces of human activity encoded on the surface of the road.[9]

With his love of cartooning and commercial art, Thiebaud searched for "the push of things like the caricature of proportion, the caricature of light, the caricature of color where you overstress or understress certain aspects of, for instance, the freeway."[10] Indeed, such caricature shapes Thiebaud's portraits of the freeway: the exaggerated contortions of the road (*Freeways, 1975–79*), the improbable inclines (*Diagonal Freeways, 1995*), the long and heavy brushstrokes that dramatize movement and direction (*Heavy Traffic, 1988; Towards 280, 1999–2000*). Thiebaud also modified his vision to realize this effect. Looking at San Francisco's freeways through the lens of a telescope, Thiebaud sketched the lines of his flattened and slightly distorted view. He brought these sketches into his studio, producing an image on canvas that was mostly the product of his imagination, with some reliance on memory and technology. Thiebaud's freeways are of his imagination, not of the city in which he lived. Their line, shape, and color suit only the aesthetic imperatives of the picture itself and the artist's lifelong determination to meet the challenges of representation.

Thiebaud was not known for being shy in his use of color, but his freeway portraits exhibit restraint. Concrete and asphalt left Thiebaud with a more subdued palette, banishing the bold colors that defined his early work. His 1979 etching *Freeway Curve* rejects the exuberant pigments that colored his famous portraits of America's favorite foods (Plate 3).

Freeway Curve, like most of Thiebaud's freeway paintings, adopts a privileged vantage point. This is what Jacobs criticized as "the Olympian view": a lofty perspective of the city favored by the mandarin architects and planners of high modernism. In *Seeing Like a State*, the anthropologist James Scott argues that this has been the perspective of power, a perspective detached from the on-the-ground experience of daily life yet, in its clean symmetry and stark geometry, compelling on paper. It is not necessarily a modern way of seeing the city, as kings and emperors since at least the Renaissance saw the world from this angle, but it acquired a particular force during the twentieth century, when modern bureaucracies of both totalitarian regimes and liberal democracies utilized new technologies—airplanes, helicopters, and satellites—to render the city's complexity in legible terms and to justify bold interventions on the urban fabric.[11]

In the United States, highway planners deployed this perspective not only for the determination of vehicular paths but for other applications as well, including highway research, design, planning, maintenance, inventory, and project review. During the 1920s and 1930s, in order to affirm their plans for construction, architects and planners drafted top-down perspectives of proposed highways, such as Robert Whitten's sketch of Boston's Central Artery in the 1930 *Report on a Thoroughfare Plan for Boston* (Figure 4.1).[12] During the interstate era, however, state highway departments used more advanced technologies, such as "photogrammetric mapping" to aid traffic engineering, contracting photographers and pilots to produce large-scale aerial photographs of designated traffic paths or existing highway facilities on a scale of 1 foot to 200 inches. Ultimately, these images provided highway engineers with an effective and efficient means of communication, both with each other and with the public at large, yet like many of the paintings surveyed in this chapter, the aerial photograph also represented a form of caricature, exaggerating the legibility of urban form and the freeway's compatibility with the city.[13]

Even as opposition to highway construction mounted on the ground during the 1960s, American artists continued their fascination with the God's-eye view. Thiebaud takes this perspective again in *Urban Freeways* (1979), hovering over the city to explore the visual qualities of a highway interchange (Plate 4). Here the layered curves of intersecting freeways pose a seemingly organic contrast to the right-angle geometry of the built environment, with but a narrow stretch of grass and a perfect row of upright palm trees adding a modicum of color and flora to this otherwise man-made landscape. The freeway's contortions define the composition, much as in the rare image of a freeway produced by the nature-loving photographer Ansel Adams. For *Interchange, Los Angeles Freeway* (1967), Adams hovered over Los Angeles in a helicopter to capture the sinuous lines of a highway interchange. Although the possibilities for caricature seem less available to the photographer than to the artist or architect, Adams nonetheless delivers his own abstraction of the freeway environment through a cropped framing of a looping highway interchange, denying the freeway its technical aspects and making it conform to the passion for organic form that inspired his prodigious output of creative work and environmental activism (Figure 4.2).[14]

FIGURE 4.1. The Olympian view. In *Report on the Thoroughfare Plan for Boston,* prepared by the Boston City Planning Board, Robert Whitten, consultant, 1930.

Adams was not the only California photographer of the interstate era to take notice of the emerging freeway system. Julius Shulman, the visual poet of midcentury modernism, ventured out of the poshest enclaves of Los Angeles (where he photographed the residential architecture of Richard Neutra and other mandarins of midcentury modernism) to take a few incidental shots of the city's new freeways. In a way, the very construction of those freeways forced Shulman to discover that world, as he had left his childhood neighborhood of Boyle Heights just as it yielded to the onslaught of six major freeways. This was precisely where Graciela Valenzuela arrived with her family to stake a claim to the spaces abandoned by a prior generation of Jewish immigrants. In his youth, in fact, Shulman had lived in a house on North Cummings Street, which had been truncated by the construction of I-5 in the 1950s. Eventually, Shulman settled in Laurel Canyon, taking

FIGURE 4.2. Ansel Adams, *Interchange, Los Angeles Freeway,* 1967. Collection of the Center for Creative Photography, University of Arizona. Copyright 2013 the Ansel Adams Publishing Rights Trust.

a home designed by the Case Study architect Raphael Soriano. His migration from Eastside to Westside, from Boyle Heights to the Hollywood Hills, follows the general trajectory of the city's Jewry, who left the working-class precincts of East Los Angeles for the Westside. As construction of two massive highway interchanges began in Boyle Heights, the Eastside Jews packed up and left, taking their shops, synagogues, and cameras with them. In their place, a generation of Mexican immigrants stepped in, confronting a dearth of socioeconomic opportunity and a surfeit of new freeways.[15]

On the Westside, where the freeway revolt claimed a few victories, Shulman discovered the photogenic world of Southern California's good life, built in the modernist idiom of glass and steel. His voluminous corpus of work is a catalog of Southern California's distinctive brand of architectural modernism, proving that the region was fertile ground for design innovation as well as for progressive nouveux riches who housed themselves in steel-framed glass boxes. Though Shulman took few photographs of L.A. freeways, he noticed their seductive lines and sleek form. He climbed freeway embankments to photograph the layered tiers of a new highway interchange, and he shot the freeway at night, slowing shutter speed and increasing exposure to create light trails on the freeway (Figure 4.3).

By dramatizing the flow of commuter traffic and creating a dazzling effect that found recurring expression in the pages of *California Highways and Public Works* and other official trade journals, Shulman brought a distinct glamour to the freeway, blurring the boundaries between art, fashion, architecture, and photography. Leaving the wreckage of East Los Angeles in the 1950s, Shulman emerged as the freeway's fashion stylist, making it fit into the iconography of midcentury modernism and Southern California's suburban good life.[16]

Another photographer who has captured the iconography of L.A. freeways in more recent years is Catherine Opie. Opie first emerged on the city's art scene in 1993 with *Portraits*, a controversial set of studio portraits of gay, lesbian, and transgendered men and women, many of them associated with the drag and S and M subcultures of San Francisco and Los Angeles. As a "queer out dyke artist," Opie included herself in these portraits, many of

FIGURE 4.3. Julius Shulman, *City at Night (Los Angeles, Calif.)*, 1956. Copyright
    J. Paul Getty Trust. Julius Shulman Photography Archive, Research Library
    at the Getty Research Institute, 2004.R.10. Reprinted with permission.

which included backdrops of intense color.[17] In 1994, Opie produced *Self-
Portrait/Pervert,* depicting the photographer bare-chested, her head encased
in a tight, eyeless black leather mask. Needles piercing her skin at precise in-
tervals run down the length of her arms, and the word "pervert" is inscribed
in decorative lettering on her chest, like a bloody tattoo etched by a razor.
As Opie herself stated, "I thought it was important, if I was going to document my community, to document myself within that community."[18] From
the fringes of California's gay and lesbian community, this was the visual
expression of identity politics to the max, waged at the height of the culture
wars in the 1990s to lambast settled notions of normalcy.[19]

After such provocative work had thrust Opie and her world into the spotlight of fame and notoriety, her fans in the queer community might have been puzzled, if not disappointed, by what came next. In 1994, Opie produced a series of platinum prints of L.A. freeways, inspired by her daily commute on I-5 between Irvine and Los Angeles. The series *Freeways* (1994–95) marked a sharp break from her previous work. These were images of freeway interchanges and overpasses, shot early on weekend mornings, rendered without people, cars, or signs. The undulating lines of these compositions veer toward abstraction, denying the freeway its function in the lived reality of suburban life. Reviewing Opie's midcareer retrospective at the Guggenheim Museum in 2008, *New York Times* art critic Holland Cotter wrote that her freeways acquired the "chill, glamorous monumentality of spaceships . . . as if viewed through the mists of a distant planet."[20] To produce this effect, Opie used a panoramic camera to produce negatives that she developed as small contact prints, on the order of 2¼ inches by 6¾ inches. The small scale of the photographs versus the expansive images of freeways built a tension that, at least according to one critic, imparts a "beauty and tenderness" to the freeway and "hints at a certain collective appreciation."[21]

It dawned on Opie in her commute between Los Angeles and Irvine that freeways belonged to Southern California's sprawling suburban areas. "The freeways separate communities," she claimed, "but I would say that the biggest thing they do is separate the city from the suburb."[22] Opie seems unfamiliar with East Los Angeles and its quarantine by freeways during the interstate era, but her freeway portraits are neither urban nor suburban; they depict structural fragments, eschewing signs of social and spatial context. How liberating it might have been to shift from *Portraits* to *Freeways*: from her own community to no one's community, to an inhuman landscape of concrete and sky. The absence of color reinforces the identitylessness of these images, which are far from the studio portraits that scream personal flare, grit, and spirit. In this figment of postapocalypse Los Angeles, Opie's freeways are of no particular race, gender, class, or sexual orientation—they do not even belong to any particular locale, for their names and numbers are left unspecified. These social markings are absent altogether, assigning to the freeways a timeless quality that transcends the particulars of culture and identity.

It seems that we have come full circle, back to the iconography of the highway-planning profession at the height of its power during the interstate era. Like Shulman and other celebrated artists working in a visual medium, Opie canonized the image of the freeway in a series of photographs that made their way into the Whitney Museum of American Art and other prestigious exhibition spaces. In its formal attributes and its stylistic innovations, her work demonstrates a rigor and a mastery of the landscape that matches the commanding vision of highway builders and engineers during the interstate era, who deployed sketches, renderings, photographs, and other visual materials to justify the technical perfection of their endeavor. If *Freeways* carries a political message, it is one that pales in comparison to that of previous work, or, as Opie claims, "the most political thing about these photographs" is their exclusion of people and automobiles.[23]

Opie credits her vision of the freeway to early photographers like Maxime Du Camp, the son of a wealthy Parisian family who indulged his desire for travel to distant and exotic lands on his father's assets. Arriving in Egypt with a panoramic camera in 1849, Du Camp photographed the ruins of antiquity, creating a visual imprint of "the Orient" on the Western imagination. This self-taught photographer and man of adventure introduced a new scope and scale of Western vision, shaping the way twentieth-century artists and photographers saw the monuments of their day.[24] This could include the most famous L.A. expats, David Hockney, who pronounced himself a West Coast Giovanni Piranesi before the building of the L.A. freeways, and Reyner Banham, who also came to Los Angeles in the 1960s to write his ode to the beach and the Sunset Strip. Giddy with adventure in Southern California, Hockney and Banham came to Los Angeles like the poets of Britain's Romantic age, who wandered through Greece and Turkey in a binge of aristocratic excess to poeticize the ruins of an ancient civilization.

Yet Opie takes a cooler, more distanced view of these structures, not unlike James Doolin, a landscape painter from Connecticut who came to Los Angeles by way of Philadelphia, New York, and Australia. The farther west Doolin moved, the less abstract his work became. By the time he got to Los Angeles, Doolin had mastered a kind of hyperrealism, more in tune with mapmaking than with figurative painting. For his acclaimed painting

PLATE 1. The freeway as fun: Autopia Ride in Tomorrowland, Disneyland, 1955.

PLATE 2. Roger Kuntz, *San Diego,* 1962–63. Oil on canvas, 60 inches × 72 inches. Laguna Art Museum Collection, gift of Mary M. Kuntz-Coté, 1991.214. Photograph by Christopher Bliss Photography, Laguna Beach, California. Courtesy of the Estate of Roger Kuntz; reproduced by permission.

PLATE 3. Wayne Thiebaud, *Freeway Curve,* 1979. Etching, 18¹³⁄₁₆ inches × 21⅞ inches. Faulconer Gallery, Grinnell College Art Collection. Copyright Wayne Thiebaud. Licensed by VAGA, New York, N.Y.

PLATE 4. Wayne Thiebaud, *Urban Freeways,* 1979. Oil on canvas, 44⅜ inches × 36⅛ inches. Lebaron's Fine Art, Sacramento, California. Copyright Wayne Thiebaud. Licensed by VAGA, New York, N.Y.

PLATE 5. James Doolin, *Los Angeles After 2000,* 1995–96. Oil on canvas, 120 inches × 240 inches. Metropolitan Transit Authority, Los Angeles. Courtesy of Estate of James Doolin.

PLATE 6. Frank Romero, *Pink Landscape,* 1984. Oil on canvas, 36 inches ×
60¼ inches. Courtesy of the artist.

PLATE 7. Hollenbeck Park, Los Angeles. Postcard, circa 1930s.

PLATE 8. David Botello, *Wedding Photos—Hollenbeck Park*, 1990. Acrylic on canvas, 36 inches × 48 inches. Courtesy of the artist.

PLATE 9. Carlos Almaraz, *Crash in Phthalo Green,* 1984. Oil on canvas, 42 inches × 72 inches. Gift of the 1992 Collectors Committee (AC1992.136.1), Los Angeles County Museum of Art. Digital image copyright 2014 Museum Associates / LACMA. Licensed by Art Resource, N.Y.

PLATE 10. Frank Romero, *Freeway Wars,* 1995. Serigraph,
31½ inches × 38 inches. Courtesy of the artist.

PLATE 11. Frank Romero, *East on the 10,* 1993. Oil on canvas,
46 inches × 54½ inches. Courtesy of the artist.

PLATE 12. Wayne Thiebaud, *Heavy Traffic*, 1988. Oil on wood, 15⅞ inches × 19¾ inches. Lebaron's Fine Art, Sacramento, California. Copyright Wayne Thiebaud. Licensed by VAGA, New York, N.Y.

PLATE 13. David Botello, *Alone and Together under the Freeway*, 1992. Acrylic on canvas, 25 inches × 34 inches. Courtesy of the artist.

PLATE 14. Carlotta Hernandez (artist) and Rico Bueno (designer), *Parque Chicano*, 1974. Photograph by the author.

PLATE 15. Esteban Villa and Ricardo Favela, Aztec warrior mural on Chicano Park concrete pier, 1975. Photograph by Nathan Gibbs.

PLATE 16. Victor Ochoa and team, *Varrio Logan*, 1978. Photograph by the author.

Shopping Mall (1973–77), an eight-square-foot canvas portraying an aerial view of four street corners in Santa Monica, Doolin sketched and photographed the streets from every angle, climbing onto rooftops and studying blueprints, digging for maps in archives, and making watercolor and oil studies of light and color changes for all the shadows, buildings, cars, and pedestrians. The result is an omnipotent, God's-eye view of a minute fraction of the city grid, obsessively detailed down to the oil spots on the road.[25]

Doolin went to the same extraordinary lengths to portray L.A. freeways. For *Bridges* (1998), Doolin camped out at the site of I-5–I-110 interchange, making sketches and taking photographs to capture the expansive vista before him. He also hired someone to man his campsite while he explored every nook and crevice of this elaborate structure, where two freeways cross paths with the Los Angeles River and the city's principal railroad line. A solitary figure stands alone in the center of the canvas, almost a dot in a monstrous landscape of concrete, steel, and rushing traffic. This might be Doolin himself, wandering over tracks and under freeways to find the soul of this inhuman environment. The residue of drainage pipes on the retaining wall that supports the freeway, the graffiti, the erosion of the soil—Doolin captures the fine-grain details of this landscape, discerned through rigorous observation and careful study.[26]

Doolin's almost scientific approach to portraying L.A. freeways complemented his dogged quest to find the extreme perspective. For *Highway Patrol* (1986), Doolin secured permission from the Los Angeles Police Department to ride in the back seat of a patrol car to see the freeway through the eyes of law enforcement. For *Crossroads* (1999), Doolin's wife, Lauren, drove the artist on the freeway so that he could take photographs from which to craft the freeway's image. On several occasions, Doolin hired a helicopter and pilot so that he could photograph the city's freeways from the sky. For Doolin, portraying the freeway on canvas was not about going to the structure and setting up his easel. Rather, the artist employed a variety of source materials—photographs, sketches, maps, city plans, archival materials, engineering maps—to convey the physical reality of the urban landscape, but imbued with a spectral quality that conveys an underlying sense of menace, unease, or alienation. Doolin's freeways appear to be tied to reality, but his play with perspective unhinges that connection, forcing the viewer into an inhuman vantage point that could come only at great peril. Thus, *Crossroads* plunks the viewer right onto the roadway itself, in the stream of rushing traffic; *Twilight* (1999) suspends the viewer's perspective at an impossibly high angle over a congested freeway intersection.[27]

These gestures can make the viewer feel like a God. This might explain why city officials in Los Angeles chose Doolin to adorn the expansive lobby of the lavish new headquarters of the city's Metropolitan Transit Authority (MTA), which opened in 1995. On its opening, the $300-million-dollar structure—garbed in Italian granite and English brick, replete with a $300,000 aquarium—was the most expensive transit headquarters in the nation, dubbed by one critic as the Taj Mahal of public transit. Winning a national competition to paint the walls of its soaring lobby, Doolin enlisted the help of two assistants to create four murals depicting Southern California's evolving transportation infrastructure. On the ground floor, *Los Angeles circa 1870* delivers a preindustrial view of open pastures stitched by a single railroad line. To its left, *Los Angeles circa 1910* depicts three railroad lines and a trolley network crisscrossing orchards and a cluster of high-rise buildings in the city's historic core.[28]

The last two murals highlight the prominence of freeways in the evolving urban landscape. *Los Angeles circa 1960* shows the new four-level freeway interchange, built in 1959, adjacent to a nascent downtown. Buses have replaced streetcars and a bluish-orange haze filters the dots of light that punctuate the sprawling landscape. But taking the glass escalators to the mezzanine level reveals the pièce de résistance. Above a wall of closed-circuit TVs that monitor traffic flow on the city's sprawling freeway system, one finds *Los Angeles after 2000,* an expansive vista of the L.A. basin at twilight, painted on a half-circle measuring ten feet high and twenty feet across (Plate 5). The sun sinks beneath the curving horizon line, heightening the illusion of infinite sprawl. Trails of jet exhaust streak across the sunset sky, mimicking the intersecting lines of freeways on the urban surface. Technology, infrastructure, and transit lines highlight the circuit-board metropolis of twenty-first-century Los Angeles—the arresting image in the headquarters of the nation's largest metropolitan transit authority.

The corridors of public power in Los Angeles thus enshrine a privileged perspective of the freeway. Exacting, restrained, top-down, even tense and alienating, this perspective abstains from expressive form and color. The view faces west, toward the prosperous Westside and the sun dipping into Pacific Ocean, cropping the byzantine interchanges that dominate the vast barrio that stretches east of the downtown core. Instead, we are given the soaring angle, unhinged from the landscape of daily life, divorced from the social context of homes, streets, markets, sidewalks, pedestrians, and even cars—a perspective that aggrandizes the freeway, even while inviting questions about its place in society. This is the image of power, guided by the thrill of discovery and mastery over space—an image fit for the palatial headquarters of transit authority in the freeway metropolis.

Eastside Stories

Moving east about a mile from the MTA headquarters, we come to Boyle Heights, the historic center of East Los Angeles and a community knitted in freeways. Walking south on Euclid Street from Seventh to Eighth Avenue involves crossing over and under twenty-seven lanes of four separate freeways: the Santa Monica, Hollywood, Santa Ana, and Pomona Freeways. Less than a mile northwest of that site, walking east on Fourth Street from the Aliso Pico Housing Project to Hollenbeck Park requires passing twenty-four freeway lanes: over the Hollywood Freeway, across its on-ramp and off-ramp, and under the Golden State and San Bernardino Freeways. And about one mile north from there, walking south on State Street from the University of Southern California (USC) Medical Center, one traverses twenty lanes of typically sluggish freeway traffic: past three carpool lanes of the San Bernardino Freeway, across an entrance to the Hollywood Freeway, then an exit from the Santa Monica Freeway, and over the combined width of the Golden State and San Bernardino Freeways. This scene is repeated in other East L.A. neighborhoods. The Long Beach Freeway makes a cloverleaf interchange with the San Bernardino Freeway in City Terrace, the eastern neighbor of Boyle Heights, and tangles once again with the Pomona Freeway in the adjacent community of Belvedere.[29] In East Los Angeles, home to the second largest concentration

FIGURE 4.4. East Los Angeles interchange, circa 1963. UCLA Department of
Geography, Benjamin and Gladys Thomas Air Photo Archives, the Spence
Collection.

of Mexican-origin peoples in the world, the concrete walls and columns
of seven freeways provide a ubiquitous backdrop for the local bricolage of
murals, graffiti, and Spanish-language advertising (Figure 4.4).[30]

For most of the 1950s and throughout the 1960s, seven freeways gouged
their way into East Los Angeles. I-5 from the south, also called the Santa Ana
Freeway, reached East Los Angeles from Orange County in 1956. It met a
portion of Interstate 10, running east to San Bernardino, the following year.
In 1958, the California Division of Highways finished the northward segment of I-5, the Golden State Freeway. Three years later, the western portion
of I-10, the Santa Monica Freeway, finally met the San Bernardino Freeway

segment. Also in 1961, Interstate 710, the Long Beach Freeway, opened at the eastern end of East Los Angeles, and the following year, U.S. Highway 101, or the Hollywood Freeway, ran through Boyle Heights. And finally, in 1965, State Highway 60, or the Pomona Freeway, linked up with the 5, 101, and 10 freeways, all converging in the East L.A. Interchange, one of three massive interchanges that dominate the East L.A. landscape.[31]

This is the turf of Frank Romero, Carlos Almaraz, and David Botello, three East L.A. artists whose work stands out in the field of Chicano art and who spent much their careers depicting scenes of daily life in the barrio. As children, they witnessed the invasion of interstate highways, as well as the explosion of the Chicano civil rights movement during the late 1960s. In unique ways, each artist embraced the politics of *Chicanismo,* but they maintained a shared commitment to the search for an aesthetic of social justice and community empowerment. By the 1980s, in the aftermath of the movement, these artists returned to the solitary work of studio painting, yet they continued to draw inspiration from the barrio.[32]

Born in 1941 in Whittier, a community of East Los Angeles, Frank Romero recalls Los Angeles "being more rural than it obviously is now." Such recollections inform his 1984 painting *Pink Landscape,* which situates symbols of the artist's personal history among the more prominent features of the urban landscape. Distinguished by its ziggurat crown, the Los Angeles City Hall, which reigned as the tallest building in Los Angeles between 1928 and 1964, stands in the center of the canvas between two symbols of Romero's youth: a church and a home that bears some resemblance to the artist's home in East Los Angeles. The image also conjures the city's youth, when orange groves had not yet given way to housing developments and when smog had not yet blocked the sight of not-so-distant mountains. Other elements suggest Los Angeles as well: the twin-engine airplane, maybe a reference to the local aircraft industry that employed Romero's father, and the 1950s pickup truck, long admired by Chicano car enthusiasts (Plate 6).[33]

This scene could be anywhere in the L.A. area, but the presence of the freeway in the foreground distinguishes an Eastsider's perspective—post 1956. It frames the urban scene, partitioning the view of the landscape. Two freeways, actually, the Golden State Freeway (I-5), completed in 1958, and the Hollywood Freeway (U.S. 101), completed in 1962, follow a parallel path that divides East Los Angeles from the downtown core. As Romero himself said, "I always do paintings looking towards downtown," and though *Pink Landscape* does not specify a particular vantage point, the view is looking west from Boyle Heights, where the horizontal line of the freeway provides a visual contrast to the verticality of the downtown core. Like the U.S.–Mexican border, the freeway attempts to distinguish one social world from another, dividing the barrio from the urban core.[34]

A similar view of the freeway informs from the work of David Botello, another East L.A. artist who, like Romero, rendered radical changes in the local landscape. Botello emerged within the Chicana/o art scene in Los Angeles by opening the Goez Art Studio and Gallery in 1969, and he later collaborated with fellow East Angelino David Wayne Healy in the early 1970s to establish the East Los Streetscapers, a public murals program committed to neighborhood beautification. By the 1980s, however, as the thrust of a unified Chicano movement flickered, Botello returned to canvas painting, rendering scenes of everyday life in the barrio. For much of his artistic career, Botello lived within a few blocks of Hollenbeck Park, established in 1892 by John E. Hollenbeck, founder of First National Bank. In its early years, Hollenbeck Park was a tourist destination, a "city park renowned for its lush greenery and tranquil harmony," nestled amid a few proud blocks of upstanding Victorian homes.[35] Postcards from the 1930s underscore the park's role as a tourist destination, a popular setting for weekend picnics, horticultural expositions, and carriage rides. A lake in the center of the park provided a visual focal point and a tranquil respite from the grind of city life (Plate 7).[36]

In the 1950s, however, the California Division of Highways, following the directives spelled out by the BPR in *Toll Roads and Free Roads,* stitched an elevated highway along the western edge of Hollenbeck Park, obliterating a one-mile stretch of Victorian houses that stood on North Cummings Street, where Julius Shulman lived before his exodus to the Westside (Figure 4.5). In protest, a handful of Boyle Heights residents staged a local version of the freeway revolt with signs that read, "SAVE THE PARK!" As bulldozers broke ground for construction, the editor of the *Eastside Sun,* Joseph Eli Kovner,

FIGURE 4.5. Hollenbeck Park, Hollenbeck Lake, and Interstate 5 (under construction), circa 1957. UCLA Department of Geography, Benjamin and Gladys Thomas Air Photo Archives, the Spence Collection.

condemned the Division of Highways for "destroying what little green space we have in this community."[37] Only after the freeway's completion did the Division of Highways issue its rationale:

> Where the Golden State Freeway passes through the Boyle Heights district of East Los Angeles, an encroachment of the freeway into Hollenbeck Park was unavoidable. In order to disturb the existing park facilities as little as possible, the freeway carried over the most westerly portion of the lake on an attractively designed box girder reinforced concrete bridge with specially designed slender columns.[38]

As an East L.A. native, Botello witnessed the concrete encasement of Hollenbeck Park and rendered a portrait of the park's unwanted future. His 1990 painting *Wedding Photos—Hollenbeck Park* (Plate 8) shows a pastoral scene in the postmodern city: a photographer framing his shot of a wedding party against a willow tree. The freeway in the background, carrying trucks and vans, fulfills the Division of Highway's 1958 prophecy: "This freeway is expected to carry large volumes of truck traffic whose origins and destination are the industrial area lying south of the Santa Monica and Santa Ana Freeways."[39] And by plainly rendering what the photographer tries to hide, Botello not only disputes photography's claim to exacting visual truth but also takes a subtle jab at the nature of nature in the barrio. In a redlined neighborhood riddled with freeways and their interchanges, short on front lawns and backyards, the working-class residents of the barrio stake their claim to a park built originally for the city's Victorian bourgeoisie. Today, Hollenbeck Park is not only for wedding parties, families, artists, and street vendors, but as mandated by the California Division of Highways, it is also for freeways and car traffic.

Like *Pink Landscape*, *Wedding Photos* orients the viewer toward the structure of the freeway. Again, the freeway delimits the boundaries of the barrio. The skyscrapers in the background seem part of another city, close in physical terms yet far in the city's socioeconomic geography. The trucks belching exhaust signal the environmental consequences of routing freeways through East Los Angeles, demonstrating a local knowledge of what researchers are just beginning to confirm. A 2007 report from USC's Department of Preventative Medicine, for example, found that children between the ages of ten and eighteen who live within five hundred yards of a freeway exhibit pronounced deficits in lung function, often leading to a lifetime of respiratory illnesses. More recent studies paint an even bleaker picture: a 2010 study sponsored by the National Institutes of Health concluded that children born to mothers living within approximately 1,000 feet of a freeway had twice the risk of autism.[40]

Science is beginning to tell us that freeways are toxic, but this knowledge is already made plain in the art of the barrio. This oil-on-canvas expression of critical awareness is part of what Raul Homero Villa describes as *barrio-logos*, a local form of knowledge grounded in the physical and cultural space of the barrio.[41] Through his involvement with the Goez Art Studio and Gallery in East Los Angeles in the early 1970s, David Botello helped establish a community-based arts organization that incorporated critical pedagogy into local art production, creating new art strategies to assist, empower, and educate Chicano artists and youth. Botello extended this emphasis on art in the service of the barrio's empowerment and education through his involvement with the East Los Streetscapers, emphasizing muralism in the local transmission of critical knowledge. Botello returned to his studio to resume canvas painting in the 1980s, but even there, as the painting *Wedding Photos* suggests, he continued his commitment to critical education through artistic expression.

Botello and Romero present the Eastside point of view, grounded in individual inspiration and imagination but also in the historical coordinates of community formation, displacement and relocation, infrastructural development, and planning policy. Both artists emphasize the quotidian presence of the freeway and its prominence in the foreground or background of daily life. Through their own relationship to the East L.A. landscape and to its convulsive transformation during the 1950s and 1960s, Botello and Romero found aesthetic inspiration in the freeways that encroached on their field of vision, emphasizing freeways' prominence in the surrounding urban scene. They might foul the air or block the sun, or they might follow the symmetry of the urban environment and its natural setting, but the freeways are always there, in the barrio but not of the barrio: monoliths built only to serve traffic and to guide it above, through, and around East Los Angeles.

If Botello and Romero rendered up-close portraits of the freeway, Carlos Almaraz took that perspective to unsettling extremes. Born in Mexico in 1941, Almaraz came to East Los Angeles at age nine, graduating from Garfield High School in 1959, just as three major freeways were carving their way around the school. Like Romero, Almaraz studied painting at the Otis College of Art and Design after high school, studying under the Italian artist and illustrator Joseph Mugnaini. In 1966, Almaraz moved to New York City, a guest in the SoHo loft of artists Richard Serra and Nancy Graves, but he returned to Los

Angeles in 1969, disillusioned with the reigning emphasis on minimalism and conceptual art. By the early 1970s, Almaraz had immersed himself in the Chicano movement, collaborating with Frank Romero, Gilbert Luján, and Roberto de la Rocha to establish Los Four, a Chicano art collective that emphasized art as a communal enterprise, seeking to bring further recognition to Chicano art in East Los Angeles. Almaraz read deeply in Mexican history during this time and worked with Cesar Chavez to help organize farmworkers in California's San Joaquin Valley. But by the early 1980s, Almaraz was ready for a change. As he recounted shortly before his death from AIDS-related illness in 1989, "I had had it, I needed to return to the studio to do some very personal work that was my own . . . that reflected my more introverted aspect, and to develop ideas that were nonpolitical, that were totally my ideas."[42] Almaraz thus turned to the freeway.

In 1985, Almaraz showed a series of tiny canvas paintings at San Francisco's Fuller Goldeen Gallery. These were oil paintings, on the order of five inches by seven inches, of car wrecks on freeways. These images also appeared on larger canvases, such as *Sunset Crash* (1982), *Flipover* (1983), and *Crash in Phthalo Green* (1984; Plate 9). There are no people in these images, only freeways, cars, and fiery destruction. It is tempting to interpret these violent scenes as the subliminal expression of a personal struggle with mental and physical health, but Almaraz credited this vision to a matter of physical proximity. After living in the Boyle Heights home of Frank Romero during the years of Los Four, Almaraz moved to a studio apartment in nearby Echo Park, a dilapidated barrio community on the northwestern edge of the downtown core. His studio sat on Echo Park Lake, whose southerly rim was grazed by the construction of the Hollywood Freeway in the late 1950s. There Almaraz developed a sense of "the limits of my life," finding inspiration from the unique predicament of living between a "very serene lake" and "the Hollywood Freeway, which literally has crashes going on every few hours. . . . I used to wake up to the sound of metal crunching."[43]

Almaraz lavished paint on the canvas to convey the tension between beauty and violence, delivering spectacular scenes of color, light, motion, and death. And while the serial repetition of the image of a car crash on small canvases might trivialize such dreadful events, the larger portraits invite sublime awe. Writ large or small, this morbid spectacle takes place on the freeway, which stands impervious to the deadly combustion of fuel. Though highway engineers could take a furtive delight in this portrait of sturdy freeways, it is hard to imagine these paintings hanging in the public corridors of highway administration. These images subvert the earnest ambitions of highway planners and engineers to implement rigorous standards of safety and efficiency. The length of on-ramps and off-ramps, the curvature of freeway connectors, the design of center dividers, the demarcation of lane boundaries, the regulation of speed, even the orchestration of signage and the composition of asphalt—these rudimentary aspects of highway construction follow a standardized set of precise measurements, calibrated across three generations of freeway builders, all in the name of moving traffic through the city, safely and efficiently. And yet *Crash in Phthalo Green* invites viewers to forego their expectations of safe infrastructure to bask in the dreadful glow of a most modern nightmare.[44]

Frank Romero also recognized the ironic interchange of freeways and violence in his 1995 painting *Freeway Wars,* which depicts an exchange of gunfire from the windows of cars speeding on the freeway (Plate 10). This style of murder has become commonplace on L.A. freeways, either as isolated incidents of violence or as the serial rampages of murderous psychopaths, who prey on unwitting drivers in the anonymous and fluid space of the freeway. This is a portrait of how freeways are *not* supposed to work. Like Almaraz's crash series, the painting *Freeway Wars* depicts death at high-speed extremes, illustrating a lethal discrepancy between the civil intent of the technocrats who built freeways and their felonious use by savvy criminals.

As Chicano artists steeped in the politics and culture of East Los Angeles during the late 1960s and early 1970s, Romero, Almaraz, and Botello committed themselves to the search for a Chicano aesthetic. They looked within their own community to find that aesthetic, which took shape not only through the excitement of a thriving Chicano art scene in the 1970s but also through the built environment of East Los Angeles. Their work takes up its streets, sidewalks, markets, parks, houses, and automobiles, showing a uniquely Chicano understanding of place, identity, and representation. The freeway is there as well, present on canvas as it is in the barrio. Romero, for his part, once described his work as "stories about where I grew up—where we all grew up—which was on the Eastside. So they were Eastside stories."[45] Similarly, Almaraz, who left New York fed up with white people ogling white canvases floating on white walls, realized, "It was okay to paint the world around you" and to explore "the landscape of your past and present."[46] Coming back to Los Angeles, Almaraz set up his studio in Echo Park, alongside the Hollywood Freeway, then barely eight years old.

In other words, these East L.A. artists embraced context in their pursuit of a Chicano aesthetic—not just the physical context of the barrio landscape, but also the cultural context of *Chicanismo,* which emphasized affinity with the aesthetic traditions of Mexico and its indigenous people. Their use of intense color, for example, echoes the traditional palette of Mexican art and culture, generating new interpretations of a structure built without color. Romero, for example, says that even though "it confused and angered the establishment," he realized, "It was okay to do emotionalism in your work, to use bright, vibrant color." And for someone who defines Chicano art as "not cold, not about hard edges," Romero's insertion of a sinuous freeway into a pink landscape dismisses, perhaps defies, the gray surfaces, hard edges, and straight lines of the freeway structure.[47] So do Almaraz's freeways, which are green, yellow, and purple. Botello's freeways are dark, by contrast, but they heighten the intense color of Hollenbeck Park and the surrounding barrio landscape.

To acquire a sense of how color distinguishes a Chicano perspective of the freeway, compare Romero's *East on the 10* (1993; Plate 11) with Thiebaud's *Heavy Traffic* (1988; Plate 12), painted some five years apart. The two California artists adopt similar vantage points from which to see the freeway. Yet Romero, steeped in the palette of Mexican and Chicano culture, delivers a scene awash in riotous color, whereas Thiebaud abstains from bright color to depict an almost wintery scene of freeway traffic. The imposition of hot color by Romero and other East L.A. artists brings a working-class aesthetic of Mexican origin to the freeway, what the Chicano art historian Tomás Ybarra Frausto calls *rasquachismo,* which bears some likeness to kitsch in Western culture. Like kitsch, the *rasquache* style is resourceful, ironic, playful, and metaphoric, aestheticizing, or at times sanctifying, otherwise utilitarian ob-

jects. It prefers "bright colors to somber, high intensity to low,"[48] and according to art historian Amalia Mesa Bains, it "has a stance that is both defiant
and inventive."[49]

Born of the Chicano arts movement in the 1970s, these images defy the
aesthetic conventions of their time and question the freeway's presence in
the local scene. Romero and Almaraz alike expressed their conscious de-
parture from the movements that defined American art during the postwar
period, looking within their own communities to generate a new aesthetic
that ignored the expectations of the art establishment in New York and Los
Angeles. The freeway insinuated itself into their canvases, just as it broke into
the precincts of the barrio. Viewed from the sidelines of pedestrian life, from
the streets, sidewalks, and parks of the neighborhoods that bore the brunt of
interstate highway construction, the freeway assumes an overbearing posture, diminishing local quality of life. We might call this way of seeing the
freeway the grounded perspective—grounded in the intertwined histories
of community formation and highway construction in East Los Angeles,
grounded in the built environment of the neighborhood, and grounded in
the political culture of *Chicanismo,* which developed its own aesthetic rooted
in the interstices of Mexican and U.S. American cultural traditions.

Romero, Almaraz, and Botello earned national and international acclaim for their work. Romero's paintings, for example, have earned inclusion in the permanent collections of the Los Angeles County Museum of Art
and the National Gallery of Art in Washington, D.C. Success brings great
recognition, but also a second home in the south of France, where Romero
has turned his canvas toward the rustic countryside. Yet as a native of East
Los Angeles, his imagination retains the visual imprint of the freeway.
Throughout the 1990s and into the first decade of the twenty-first century,
Romero continued his focus on the freeway's iconography, delving into a
more abstract vision of looping interchanges, rendered in pink and green,
yellow and purple, or other bold pairings of intense color. After his early portraits of the freeway's indomitable presence in the barrio, Romero ultimately
moved toward the abstraction mastered by Kuntz and Opie, yet these images
still retain the palette of Mexican aesthetic traditions and the wry outlook
of an Eastsider who seems to have made peace with the freeways in his face.

In the sprawling art scene of contemporary Los Angeles, a younger generation of Mexican American artists continues to focus on the freeway. Ruben Ochoa, for example, a native Southern Californian and the son of Mexican immigrants, explores the freeway's place in the urban landscape, making art that unsettles its relationship to the city's diverse communities.[50] In 2006, for example, Ochoa built *Freeway Wall Next to a . . .* , a scale model of a concrete freeway wall in a gallery space, a massive installation that forced on viewers the kind of intimacy with freeways familiar to many urban people of color. For *Extracted* (2006), Ochoa secured permission from the California Department of Transportation for a site-specific work in which a specialized wallpaper was applied to a section of a freeway retaining wall, simulating the partial extraction of the wall, as if to reveal layers of rock sediment and natural growth. After the Chicano generation of artists visualized the freeway's domination of the barrio, the "post-Chicano" generation makes it disappear altogether.[51]

It is hard to think of any part of any American city as hard hit by highway construction as East Los Angeles in the 1950s and 1960s. Although a handful of residents expressed early opposition to highway construction, their protests fizzled, leaving East Los Angeles to emerge, simultaneously, as the nation's largest Spanish-speaking barrio and the heart of Southern California's sprawling freeway system. By the 1970s, the Chicano movement had exploded beneath and between the ubiquitous freeways of East Los Angeles, inspiring a new aesthetic in the service of social justice and community empowerment. Helping invent a new Chicano style, Romero, Almaraz, and Botello turned their eyes on the barrio and its scenes of beauty and injustice. The freeway, did not—could not—escape their aesthetic vision. By portraying the freeway's infraction on the local landscape, as well as its unsightliness, violence, shadows, toxicity, and even rare beauty, East L.A. artists of the Chicano generation visualized a Chicano critique of the freeway, emphasizing its unwanted imposition on the barrio and its people.

The grounded view from the barrio found its antithesis in the detached perspective of European American artists like Kuntz, Thiebaud, Shulman, Opie, and Doolin. These artists saw the freeway through the racial prerogatives of whiteness, claiming the right to see this structure from whatever vantage point suited their aesthetic inclinations. If this meant daring to stand on the roadway itself, or hovering above it in a helicopter, or procuring maps and photos from an archive, then it included a privileged access to public space that distinguished a privileged point of view. These images create a sense of discovery and wonder, akin to the awe of previous generations toward the monuments of the past, but they also lack the sense of intimacy and familiarity that characterizes a barrio point of view.

These disparate perspectives took shape not only through the human gifts of creativity and inspiration but also through racially biased policies that brought freeways to the barrio in the first place. These were the paths of least resistance, where property values were low, opposition was weak, and "blight" prevailed, at least in civic discourse. As the interstate era entailed different consequences for different communities in the city, it also structured different ways of seeing the freeway, different means for their expression, and different access to the public's attention. Race, essentially a hierarchy of human difference, underpins all these differences, especially as it shaped public discourse in powerful ways during the 1960s and 1970s. White and nonwhite artists racialized the image of the freeway, some from the sky, and some from the shadows. Chapter 5 delves back into those shadows to discover how some communities have racialized the structure of the freeway itself.

Taking Back the Freeway

Strategies of Adaptation and Improvisation

By any measure, the Interstate 93 corridor that cuts through the Ten Hills section of Somerville ranks as one of the meanest and most disagreeable portions of highway in America. At this point, the highway squats on heavy, gray concrete supports about a story above the ground. Few souls venture on foot to the land of perpetual shadow beneath the roadway, a place one person described as a "Muggers Mall." Those who do, want to get out as fast as they possibly can. On the ground at the base of the graffiti-scarred supports are pieces of cars and trucks that have floated down from above: a bit of muffler or catalytic converter; a piece of chrome trim or side mirror; and the dirt and trash that perpetually moving cars and trucks inevitably spawn.

Tom Lewis, *Divided Highways*

There she was, suddenly and unexpectedly, appearing on the walls of a dark freeway underpass of Chicago's John F. Kennedy Expressway on a cold morning in April 2005. In what Chicago highway officials confirmed was the yellowish residue of salt runoff on the concrete wall of an expressway underpass at Fullerton Avenue, Elbia Tello saw the image of the Virgin Mary. Others affirmed her vision, and soon a makeshift shrine to the Virgin had been assembled in this forbidding space, a shrine replete with candles, flowers, and rosaries. Hundreds of worshippers reached across police barricades to touch the sacred image. Kneeling before Our Lady of the Underpass on a wet, dreary day, the residents of Bucktown demonstrated their capacity to make something out of nothing.[1]

This is not unlike the homemade shrines that accent the fractured landscape of East Los Angeles. At the many dead ends of its streets, where the California Division of Highways built walls to separate pedestrian space from vehicular space, local residents have assembled shrines, painting images of the Virgin Mary or Jesus Christ, leaving flowers or rosaries at their feet, often with photos of the deceased (Figure 5.1). These symbolic acts illustrate the way residents living in the vicinity of unwanted infrastructure invent ways to create meaning and significance in even the most banal urban spaces. Freeways, after all, serve no role in their architectural context. They support the flow of through traffic, but not the quality of life in their immediate vicinity. Yet even the deadest spaces created by highway infrastructure sometimes find redemption though local efforts to create a sense of place, transforming segments of freeway architecture into sites vested with spiritual meaning and cultural pride.

This chapter considers various urban sites where local artists, architects, and musicians strive to transform freeway infrastructure into cultural assets, making it relevant to the people living in it. The primary focus is on San Diego's Chicano Park, a neighborhood park and an outdoor gallery of murals established, through stringent community activism, beneath the canopy of a massive highway interchange. Chicano Park demonstrates one community's struggle to reclaim the space beneath the freeway and reintegrate it into the cultural fabric of one of California's largest barrios, but this struggle goes on in other cities as well, with varying degrees of success. Some efforts remain figments of the local imagination, drawing-board proposals for community transformation; others reflect spontaneous yet recurring interventions on highway infrastructure. Whether ephemeral, permanent, or, like Miami's Folklife Village, still on the drawing board, these interventions reflect an important yet overlooked process by which communities claim the right of self-representation through cultural production, reclaiming the freeway and its architecture in the process, making it their own. The folklore of the freeway includes these strategies, which signal a stubborn refusal to accept the place-

FIGURE 5.1. A homemade shrine built at a retaining wall of State Route 60, East Los Angeles. Photograph by the author.

ment of unwanted infrastructure on state terms and an opportunistic claim to the freeway as a canvas for expressing distinctive cultural traditions, aesthetic tastes, and the memory of historical experience.

This chapter's focus is on those communities on the losing end of the struggle to avert the placement of unwanted infrastructure—the communities unable to muster the political or economic resources to successfully fight the coming of the freeway. Unlike the previous chapters, this is not a story of winners and losers. It is a story of making do, of using cultural resources to dip deep into the well of history, heritage, and tradition, weaving the alien architecture of highway infrastructure into the distinctive cultural fabric of the modern ghetto and barrio.

Under the Freeway

Grove Shafter Park is what the people of West Oakland got in exchange for the placement of a massive highway interchange in their neighborhood. Completed by the city of Oakland in 1972, this 5.5-acre park is segmented into three areas, separated by the elevated and sunken roadways of the "Macarthur Maze," or the "Distribution Center," as the interchange of Interstate 580, Interstate 980, and Route 24 is known among CalTrans officials. Prodded by a neighborhood group, the California Division of Highways and the U.S. Department of Housing and Urban Development sponsored the construction of a park that includes a playground, a basketball court, benches, picnic tables, barbecues, bathrooms, chain-link fences that prevent people from falling onto the freeway, and a cavernous overpass that covers two sidewalks and a four-lane surface street.[2] Yet the park's relationship to its surrounding community is tenuous. Today, it supports homeless encampments, abandoned cars, and the illicit exchange of sex and drugs. Among the few signs of life in the park is the rush of traffic above and below, holding the senses hostage. Despite the best intentions of civic groups and public agencies, the promise of Grove Shafter Park remains unfulfilled.

In a metropolitan region teeming with wealth from Internet startups and hi-tech companies, this lifeless park lies at the heart of a poor black neighborhood that has seen better times. Between 1920 and 1950, West Oakland supported a cohesive community of black working-class families who created a vibrant commercial and cultural scene. World War II, however, sparked drastic changes to West Oakland's socioeconomic profile and to its physical landscape. Suburbanization led to a depletion of the area's jobs and wealth and to the loss of its black middle class, while highway construction furthered West Oakland's decline, displacing residents and businesses and isolating the area from the rest of the city. Grove Shafter Park appeared in the wake of this transformation, a post–civil rights token of redress for the changes that ravaged this community during the 1950s and 1960s.[3]

A few local residents recognize the troubling paradox of this park and have proposed ways to improve its relationship to the surrounding community. Walter Hood, a professor of landscape architecture at the University of California, Berkeley, and a resident of West Oakland, sketched a new vision for the park in *Urban Diaries,* a design for community revitalization based on his observations of the neighborhood during the early 1990s. Hood recognized that the Macarthur Maze created what he calls "medieval fortress walls" that effectively quarantined West Oakland, after destroying its cohesive communities. In *Urban Diaries,* he proposes building structures around the Maze that would bring to the area not only jobs but also fresh produce, fresh air, health care, nightlife, music, education, and spiritual leadership: the very things that historically anchor urban black communities. What is more striking about Hood's design, however, is its verticality: its use of ramps, columns, piers, and high-rise towers to *elevate* the community above the freeway—to cast shadows over a structure that has cast its own shadows for too long. Hood accepts the freeway as a fact of life in West Oakland, but he aims to subordinate it to the building up of local infrastructure. Hood concludes *Urban Diaries* with a question that confronts all city people living near a freeway: "The gigantic scale of the freeway will never come down to serve the community, but can the community rise up beyond the limitations that the freeway imposes?"[4]

The plan proposed in *Urban Diaries* remains on the drawing board, still a figment of one resident's imagination, but it nonetheless signals a local awareness of what freeways do to their surroundings and is an effort to undo the damage. In *Death and Life,* Jane Jacobs argued that building expressways in cities creates "border vacuums" that deplete a neighborhood of its social life, imposing barriers that impede pedestrian circulation and induce disorientation. As single-use spaces, border vacuums—created not just by expressways, but also by hospitals, civic centers, and universities—deaden urban space, discouraging economic activity and creating opportunities for crime and vagrancy. To underscore her point, Jacobs singles out the Cross Bronx Expressway for creating a border vacuum that deprived local businesses of the pedestrian traffic that ensured their livelihood, forcing vacancies in the area and inducing a spike in violent crime.[5]

A more graphic example of a border vacuum comes from Boyle Heights in East Los Angeles, where local observers find imaginative ways to convey the menace lurking beneath the freeway. David Botello's 1992 painting *Alone and Together under the Freeway* (Plate 13), for example, takes us to the underbelly of the Interstate 5 freeway in Hollenbeck Park, the heart of Boyle Heights. The viewer stands with the painter in the shadow of the freeway overpass, looking toward a sunlit park in the distance. The contrast between the bright colors of a sunlit park and the dark shadows of a freeway overpass underscore the unsightly paradox of routing a freeway through a popular and long-treasured public park.[6] The painting takes us to the very kind of border vacuum that troubled Jacobs, rendering her criticism on canvas some three decades after publication of *Death and Life*. A homeless person appears in the foreground of the painting, taking refuge in the shadow of the freeway, and a couple finds romantic solitude in this space as well. There is intimacy, but also isolation. It corroborates Jacobs's diagnosis of the freeway as a menace to city life: this is a space that invites derelicts and transients and the illicit exchange of sex and drugs.[7] The image underscores the absence of social life in this space, suggesting that freeways discourage the kind of social contact that architects and planners once encouraged through their designs for parks, plazas, sidewalks, fountains, boulevards, and shopping districts. In Los Angeles, where the city's nouveaux riches command sweeping views of city sprawl from their hillside perches, *Alone and Together* illustrates the diminished perspective of an urban underclass buried beneath layers of highway infrastructure. It offers a frank criticism of the way freeways impair certain urban communities, rendering that predicament plainly for broader contemplation.

Urban Improvisations

Botello brings the freeway to his art; others bring their art to the freeway. In March 1978, on the northern fringes of South Central Los Angeles, the performance artist Senga Nengudi staged *Ceremony for Freeway Fets*, an improvisational dance performance under the overpass of the Harbor Freeway. Nengudi emerged within the art scene of black Los Angeles in the aftermath of the Watts riots, which unleashed a prolonged phase of artistic, intellectual, and activist work in South Central Los Angeles In the late 1960s, after formal training in dance and art at California State University, Los Angeles, Nengudi worked at the Watts Towers Art Center, collaborating with other black artists, such as Noah Purifoy, known for his junk assemblage sculptures made from the rubble of the Watts Rebellion. In this creative environment, Nengudi began sculpting nylon panty hose—stretching, filling, knotting, tying, twisting, and pulling the material to create biomorphic forms that playfully delivered a gendered critique of modern consumer culture. Yet by using worn, discarded stockings, Nengudi situated her work in the socioeconomic conditions of black Los Angeles, emphasizing the material limits and aesthetic possibilities of creating art in the ghetto.[8]

Making art in the deracinated landscape of South Central Los Angeles post-Watts, Nengudi made do with the materials and structures at hand, which helps explain why Nengudi chose to stage her later work in a site beneath the overpass of the Harbor Freeway, in between the massive concrete columns that undergird one of the largest volumes of traffic in the city. With permission from CalTrans, Nengudi invited her colleagues from Studio Z, a local art collective that included such notable black artists as David Hammons, Maren Hassinger, and Barbara McCullough, to gather beneath the Harbor Freeway overpass at Pico Boulevard. For Nengudi, this site, with its dirt, shrubs, and tiny palms, "had the sense of Africa." To create the installation piece *Freeway Fets,* Nengudi borrowed a crane from CalTrans to wrap a thin circle of panty hose fabric around the top of the concrete columns, from which she dangled appendages that suggested the forms of male and female anatomy, swaying in the wind "like a grass skirt."[9]

In March 1978, Nengudi and the members of Studio Z then staged *Ceremony for Freeway Fets,* an improvisational dance exercise, to inaugurate *Freeway Fets.* Two studio members played the part of masculine and feminine spirits, and Nengudi herself donned a white painter's tarp and a mask to play the unifying spirit between the opposing genders (Figure 5.2). Other members provided musical accompaniment, playing flute, saxophone, clarinet, conga drum, and cowbell in rhythmic syncopation. The players wore costumes designed by Nengudi, including headdresses made from panty hose fabric, her signature material. Dancing through the costumed congregation of musicians and performers, Nengudi described this rapturous moment beneath the freeway as "something positive and . . . worthwhile."[10]

Nengudi used "fets" as shorthand for "fetish," and just as her art fetishized

FIGURE 5.2. Senga Nengudi, *Ceremony for Freeway Fets,* Los Angeles, March 1978. Photograph by Rodney "Kwaku" Young. Courtesy of the artist and Thomas Erben Gallery, New York City.

an ordinary object like panty hose, it also fetishized the freeway, investing its spaces with spiritual meaning and cultural significance. On this shelf of barren earth that never sees the light of day, under a concrete canopy anchored by massive concrete columns, Nengudi performed an improvisational and collaborative ritual. Here she recognized a magical potency, linking *Freeway Fets* and *Ceremony for Freeway Fets* within broader traditions of ritual performance from Africa, Europe, and North America. Staking a fleeting claim on this shadowy nook of South Central Los Angeles for one afternoon in 1978, Nengudi explored the transformative power of music, costume, and dance under the freeway, infusing the banal spaces of urban infrastructure with black cultural sensibilities.

Such spontaneous flares of black creativity are manifest with greater frequency beneath the freeways of other American cities. In Faubourg Tremé of New Orleans, an epicenter of black social and cultural life since the late eighteenth century, Interstate 10 cleaves the historic precincts of black New Orleans from the white tourist district of the French Quarter. At the height of the civil rights movement, just after the city integrated its public schools, I-10 installed a concrete wall between the races, inaugurating a prolonged period of decline in Tremé, fueling white flight, depleting the local tax base, and stoking a local conviction that highway planners were the conspiratorial agents of the white power structure in New Orleans.[11]

Yet the shadowy space beneath this elevated expressway cultivates a cultural tradition central to the identity of black New Orleans. The jazz parade, or second-line parade, emerged as an outgrowth of an indigenous rite of mourning that included a brass band playing songs of mourning and celebration, a ritual bearing diverse cultural influences from West Africa, the Caribbean, Europe, and the American South. Guiding a coffin hoisted on the shoulders of pallbearers, the brass band walks the streets of Tremé, past the landmarks of the deceased's life, leading a procession of mourners ready to say their final good-byes and to "cut the body loose." The band, the deceased, the pallbearers, funeral directors, family, and friends make up the first line; the second line includes those who follow the band just to enjoy the music. At some point in the late nineteenth century, the second line detached from the first line, assuming its own identity as a neighborhood parade sponsored by mutual aid and benevolent societies. Today, the Olympia, the Dirty Dozen, New Birth, and Rebirth are just a few of the second-line brass bands that create a "moving block party," coaxing local residents out of their homes to join a procession driven by the rhythmic sounds of trombones, trumpets, horns, saxophones, tuba, bass drums, and snare drums.[12]

In both the first line and the second line, a musician's ability to move the crowd depends on an acute sensitivity to space and place. Knowing what to play *where,* where to take it down and where to turn it up, where to play dirges and hymns and where to play jazz and funk—traditionally, this knowledge depended on the geography of the deceased's life, but it also depends on intimate knowledge of the local acoustics. For the musicians in post-interstate-era Tremé, brass bands sound best under I-10. Its concrete canopy contains the sound, heaving it back on the crowd. The noise of traffic above heightens

FIGURE 5.3. A brass band float and second line under Interstate 10, Tremé, New Orleans, 2010. Photograph by Derek Bridges.

rather than diminishes the music's intensity, forcing the band to assert its rhythm over the sound of roaring engines. Second-line participants play along with whistles, cowbells, and tambourines, enjoining the band to "take it to the bridge"—under the I-10 overpass—where the crowd doubles in size, bodies move closer, the volume rises, the tempo peaks, and the band unleashes its power for maximum sonic effect (Figure 5.3).[13]

Some ethnomusicologists would identify this space as a "soundmark," a gathering spot for a community that expresses itself through music and dance, through which people orient themselves to one another and to their shared environment. In this instance, the musicians of Tremé occupy a space born of racial and class inequality to carry on the cultural traditions of black New Orleans. Just as African slaves defied the strictures of slavery and racial segregation by dancing in Congo Square (now Armstrong Park) on Sundays in the late eighteenth century, second-line celebrations challenge the racial barriers imposed during the interstate era by reclaiming the space beneath I-10 with sonic expressions of pride and solidarity. The uncontainable sounds of the brass band signal the "rebirth" of black New Orleans, not only after its decline during the interstate era but also after the devastating impact of Hurricane Katrina, which took a particularly vicious toll on the city's black community. But instead of marches, banners, speeches, and other conventional forms of political expression, the residents of Tremé "speak" their claim on this fragment of urban landscape through a politics of pleasure, conveyed improvisationally and collectively, through music and dance.

The musicians of Tremé thus saw the same invitation that Nengudi recognized beneath the freeway. For creative work in communities marginalized by highway construction, the freeway overpass, built of resources rarely seen in the modern ghetto, creates an intimate space that provides an enclosure for performance and ritual. The concrete enhances the site's acoustics, amplifying and multiplying the participatory sound, which asserts itself over the din of nearby traffic. Lacking the cultural infrastructure that supports the arts in American cities, creative work in the ghetto makes do with the spatial status quo. Despite the opposition the freeway encountered during its construction, and despite its isolation of black neighborhoods, it inspires new uses among people living in its shadow, people who occupy its spaces to maintain social rituals and cultural traditions.

Los Angeles and New Orleans provide two examples of the way the freeway invites spontaneous assertions of black culture and identity from the surrounding community. As creators of improvisational work, artists like Nengudi or the second-line musicians of Tremé use the spaces beneath the freeway to perform their interpretations of black cultural traditions, rooted in both Africa and America. Whereas European traditions of dance and music rely on black-box theaters and proscenium-arch stages to enforce a separation between performer and audience, African performative traditions emphasize a collaborative relationship between the two, not only by using such oral traditions as call and response, but also by integrating performances into the urban built environment, utilizing ordinary spaces like sidewalks, streets, bars, trolleys, buses, subways, and even freeways as a makeshift setting for ritual and performance. These improvisatory performances demand a heightened, in-the-moment awareness of the surrounding environment, and they summon a community's creative ability to reappropriate the freeway's form, even while rejecting its primary function.

A Park under a Freeway

In addition to its musical possibilities, the I-10 overpass in Tremé also features murals that depict the neighborhood's storied history (Figure 5.4). In 2002, a city arts program invited community-based artists to paint murals on the columns that support the I-10 overpass. The inner columns depict people and places from the neighborhood's past, and the outer columns are painted to resemble the rows of ancient oak trees that were uprooted for the construction of I-10. Many of the murals reference the history of the civil rights struggle in New Orleans, and others portray notable figures in Tremé's history. The elaborate murals, standing out against the cold concrete surfaces of the freeway overpass, include colorful portraits of Mardi Gras Indians and local institutions that once served the community.[14]

The murals of the I-10 overpass in Tremé reflect another strategy by which urban communities of color struggle to recover a cohesive sense of community and history after the spatial trauma of highway construction. A more spectacular example of this effort comes from the barrio of San Diego. Chicano Park, located in the heart of Barrio Logan, just south of downtown, at the foot of the San Diego–Coronado Bay Bridge, features elaborate murals painted on the concrete columns that support the interchange of the bridge and I-5, completed by CalTrans in the early 1970s. Although this parcel of land was initially intended to be the site for a proposed highway patrol station, community activists, fed up with the incursions of highways and junkyards, seized control of the site in 1970, demanding a neighborhood park instead of a highway patrol station and claiming the right to paint murals on the concrete columns supporting the elevated interchange. San Diego's Chicano Park is now the symbolic heart of San Diego's barrio, a spectacular example of how a community improvises a new relationship to the freeway, taking advantage of its immediate proximity to inspire a *Chicano* sense of place (Plate 14).

FIGURE 5.4. Beneath I-10, Tremé, New Orleans, 2010. Photograph by Linda Pfeiffer.

The neighborhood that now boasts Chicano Park bore the brunt of the structural transformation of the American city at midcentury. It began as a racially and ethnically diverse working-class community, anchored by local manufacturing, without the racial restrictions that ensured white homogeneity in most of San Diego. Its proximity to two expanding naval stations on San Diego Bay—the Thirty-Second Street Naval Station and the North Island Naval Air Station on the nearby island of Coronado—made the neighborhood vulnerable to mega projects, especially during the war years, and its subsequent rezoning by the San Diego City Council in 1957 from a residential to an industrial district brought further unwelcome changes, including a number of scrap yards where refuse from nearby shipbuilding plants piled up. During this time, whites fled the neighborhood for newer suburban neighborhoods, and Mexican immigrants and Mexican Americans moved in, making Logan Heights the nation's second-largest urban concentration of Mexican-origin peoples by the mid-1960s.[15]

The interstate era brought further changes to the neighborhood land-scape. The California Division of Highways, aggressive in its effort to build a state-of-the-art highway infrastructure, especially in the cities, noted that the "industrial and military character" of Logan Heights was "well suited for a new transportation" corridor. With a master plan for some three hundred miles of new freeways in the San Diego urban region, the Division of Highways began in the early 1950s with the construction of I-5, the city's primary traffic artery that ran north from the Mexican border, through the heart of Logan Heights, and skirting downtown San Diego on its way to Los Angeles, Sacramento, Portland, and Seattle.[16]

A second highway project also had an impact on the neighborhood. As the North Island Naval Air Station expanded its operations, state and city officials recognized the need for a bridge connecting it and the island resort community of Coronado to the mainland. Division engineers considered various bridge designs, settling on a four-lane, box-girder structure built on thirty concrete arches, anchored by piles submerged one hundred feet below the surface. This design suited aesthetic considerations, it minimized ob-struction to naval operations, and it permitted easy extension of utility lines to Coronado Island. In 1970, the American Institute of Steel Construction bestowed its Most Beautiful Bridge award on the San Diego–Coronado Bay Bridge, praising its sturdy construction and its "graceful mission style arches that echo San Diego's colorful past."[17]

This bridge that made architectural nods to California's mission past tore into the heart of San Diego's barrio. Highway planners studied nine proposals to connect the San Diego–Coronado Bay Bridge, or State Route 75, to I-5, six of which terminated along Crosby Street, between Tenth and Eleventh Avenues, right in the heart of Barrio Logan. Because that neighbor-hood had been rezoned as industrial and because it met "a new cross town freeway skirting northerly and easterly of the San Diego downtown business district," the Division of Highways settled on that site for the bridge's San Diego end (Figure 5.5).[18]

The completion of the San Diego–Coronado Bay Bridge invited a well-publicized round of self-congratulations among Division of Highways repre-sentatives and San Diego civic officials, but it met a less enthusiastic reception

FIGURE 5.5. San Diego–Coronado Bay Bridge/I-5 interchange, Logan Heights, circa 1967. Department of Public Works, *Annual Report, 1968–1969* (State of California, 1969), 112.

in Barrio Logan, which was giving way to junkyards, bridges, utility companies, power stations, and freeway traffic.[19] The bridge now cast a long shadow over the neighborhood, blocking access to the waterfront and views of the bay, bringing the noise and smell of traffic to the area. These developments precipitated a substantial decline in the local population—from 20,000 to 5,000 between 1950 and 1970—leaving the residents of a fledgling barrio to contend with these incursions on the local landscape.[20]

Amid these incursions on Barrio Logan, dictated by city, state, and federal authorities, a few assertive citizens began to speak out. Up to this point, few had expressed opposition: population shifts and rapid urban growth undermined the kind of communal cohesion that fosters political organization. No petitions were made to the City Council, and no forums were held to discuss what was happening to the neighborhood. Yet in 1967, community leaders from Logan Heights demanded the placement of a community park beneath the concrete pylons that supported the freeway–bridge interchange, signaling renewed concern for the neighborhood's quality of life. Two years later, in June 1969, the state of California agreed to lease a 1.8-acre parcel of land to the city of San Diego to be used for a community park in Logan Heights. The lease would run for twenty years, and the state would prepare the site before handing it over to the city for supervision and maintenance.[21]

Yet when it seemed that the city would renege on the state's promise to place a park beneath the highway–bridge interchange, the community organized into action. On April 22, 1970, a handful of local residents, joined by some 250 high school and college students, mostly from Chicano Studies classes, descended on the site, having learned that the city was grading the soil to construct a highway patrol station beneath the freeway interchange, not a park as promised. Forming a human chain around the bulldozers on the site, the demonstrators occupied the parcel for twelve consecutive days and nights, demanding the establishment of a neighborhood park (Figure 5.6). "We're ready to die for this park," one protestor told the *San Diego Union,* and as the demonstration garnered local media attention, it drew broader public support, especially among the residents of Barrio Logan. During the occupation, demonstrators began creating their own makeshift park, planting cacti, magueys, and flowers; local residents provided food and other supplies.

FIGURE 5.6. Protestors in Chicano Park, *San Diego Union*, 1970. Copyright San Diego History Center.

Bearing the eagle insignia that symbolized the struggle of Cesar Chavez and the United Farm Workers, a Chicano flag was hoisted on the site, affiliating the demonstration with the broader aims of the Chicano movement, which demanded community empowerment and self-determination.[22]

This was the climax of San Diego's Chicano movement, spurred by Mexican American civil rights and labor activism, but also by the city's attempt to appropriate land that many felt belonged to the community. During the demonstration, a local community center hosted a public hearing where demonstrators took the opportunity to voice their demands to San Diego city councilmen and officials from the Division of Highways and the California Highway Patrol. These officials reiterated the state's ownership of the land, but they agreed to halt construction on the highway patrol station. They also promised to consider alternative sites for that project and to reconsider the community's demand for a neighborhood park. If the city and the state could agree on an alternative site, the city would lease the land from the state to build a park.

Present at the meeting was local resident and artist Salvador Torres, who gave an impassioned speech outlining his vision of Chicano Park, a vision in which Chicano painters and sculptors would turn the bridge and freeway pylons "into things of beauty, reflecting Mexican American culture." Born and raised in Barrio Logan, Torres studied art at the California College of Arts and Crafts in Oakland and then returned to San Diego to immerse himself in the city's burgeoning art scene. In the late 1960s, he participated in two local Chicano art groups, Artistas de los Barrios and Toltecas en Aztlán, and in 1971 he established El Congreso de Artistas Chicanos en Aztlán, an organization committed to creating art in the service of consciousness-raising and community empowerment. He articulated a community vision of murals painted on the concrete pylons upholding the freeway–bridge interchange. "They sent this freeway down the heart of our community and nearly killed it," Torres stated. "We did not want it. We hated the bridge and the freeway. But now that we have them, we have to deal with them creatively." Rebecca Castro, a Mesa College student and a demonstrator at the site, told a *San Diego Union* reporter of the plan to paint murals and place mosaics on the pillars: "This will make a great park. . . . When the sun is right [under the freeway] it looks like a cathedral." Another resident saw the pylons as a kind of urban forest: "The area is cement, so the pillars are our trees."[23]

On May 1, 1970, San Diego's assistant city manager announced that the city would work with state officials to convert the site into a neighborhood park. After twelve days of occupation, the demonstrators declared victory, vacating the site and allowing negotiations to begin. On July 1, 1970, the San Diego City Council authorized a $21,814.96 contract for development of a 1.8-acre parcel of land for a park in Barrio Logan. City workers would grade and landscape the site and install sidewalks, a sprinkler system, and a drinking fountain. Months later, after the California Highway Patrol transferred its deed for the land to the city, all bureaucratic hurdles had been crossed. The U.S. Department of Housing and Urban Development approved a grant that covered the costs of building a community center on the site, and on April 26, 1971, during the one-year anniversary of the site's occupation, the California State Legislature voted unanimously in an emergency session to approve the deal between the city and the state. On May 23, 1971, Governor Ronald Reagan signed the bill into law, perhaps in atonement for his heavily criticized response to the People's Park conflict in Berkeley, which had left one person dead and injured scores of others. Shortly afterward, the residents of Barrio Logan held the first Chicano Park Day to commemorate the park takeover; more than a thousand people participated by attending cultural events and listening to political speeches.[24]

Although the murals had been an integral part of the Chicano Park vision from its inception, the first ones did not appear until 1973. Enlisting the support of Victor Ochoa, a local artist who had attended the arts program at San Diego City College with Torres, and José Montoya, a graduate of the California College of Arts and Crafts and the founder of the art collective Royal Chicano Air Force, Torres finally obtained legal permission to begin painting. Torres was particularly inspired by a recent trip to Mexico City, where he had attended the inaugural ceremonies for the opening of the Polyforum Siqueiros, a hexagonal building containing a 50,000-square-foot mural by David Alfaro Siqueiros, the last surviving member of Los Tres, Mexico's master muralists of the twentieth century (Siqueiros, Diego Rivera, and José Clemente Orozco). Torres saw structural similarities between this structure, designed by architects and Joaquin Alvarez Ordoñez and Guillermo Rossell de la Lama, and the underbelly of the bridge–highway interchange and recognized the local potential for a similar compatibility between Mexican mural traditions and modernist concrete architecture. By mid-1973, the San Diego Coronado Bridge Authority granted Torres and other artists permission to prepare and paint the surfaces of the freeway abutments and pylons. First, mural crews brushed and sandblasted the concrete. Next they applied muriatic acid to the concrete surfaces to kill bacteria, and then put on a white primer. The National Steel and Shipbuilding Company and San Diego Gas and Electric donated wire brushes and hard hats for the artists.[25]

Murals held a distinct significance within the Chicano civil rights culture. As an art form indigenous to the Americas, dating back to pre-Columbian civilizations, murals represented a Mexican tradition of cultural expression. In the heyday of the Chicano movement, Chicano and Chicana muralists self-consciously invoked Mexican and indigenous traditions in their work, painting murals in the public spaces of barrios across southwestern cities to depict the struggles of Mexican American people, their indigenous heritage, and their call to revolutionary ideals.[26]

The geography of muralism, moreover, held a political significance for Chicano artists and activists. Art historian Shifra Goldman writes, "Street muralism became a national movement" in the 1970s and "a major form of public communication for Chicanos in the Midwest and the Southwest, for Puerto Ricans on the East Coast, and for some Latin Americans."[27] Whereas Los Tres usually showcased their works in grand, interior spaces, often through the largesse of private patrons, street muralists of the Chicano generation targeted quotidian outdoor spaces. On the streets, Spanish-speaking people with limited access to schools, colleges, and universities could learn about Mexican American history and working-class struggle, which had been omitted from dominant narratives of American history. Thus community centers and public parks were ideal locales for painting murals, as they were valued spaces in the barrio, attracting large numbers of people daily and expanding a tradition of using public space found in Latin American cities. In these everyday spaces, Chicano muralism offered a means of neighborhood

beautification, but it also asserted a new *barrio-logos,* an alternative epistemology grounded in the experience and identity of Mexican Americans.[28]

The muralists of Chicano Park recognized their indebtedness to a tradition of Mexican muralism, but they also wanted to make Chicano Park a
collaborative endeavor, inviting community members who were not trained
artists to help in the process of making the park. In May 1973, the Chicano
art group Toltecas en Aztlán enlisted approximately three hundred barrio
residents to color the walls abutting the I-5 on Logan Avenue. Although
this endeavor involved the community in creating what eventually became
Chicano Park, it did not match the stated vision of trained artists and community activists. According to Torres, "The paints were all laid out . . . and
we attacked the wall with our rollers. We put color everywhere. There were at
least two or three hundred people there that all of a sudden were all over the
walls. It was done spontaneously. We exploded on the walls."[29] Some trained
artists bristled at this level of amateur input, but the following year, the core
artistic group returned to execute their more studied vision, decorating the
concrete pylons with images that reflected the stated ideals and aspirations
of the Chicano movement.[30]

After local residents had their chance to decorate one corner of the
highway–bridge interchange, a group of eleven artists, including Torres and
Ochoa, began work in 1973 on the first mural of Chicano Park, *Quetzalcoatl,*
which depicts the feathered serpent of Aztec mythology. That same year, a
subsequent group of Chicano artists executed the *Historical Mural,* which
depicts portraits of such Mexican revolutionaries as Miguel Hidalgo and
José Maria Morelos, early leaders in the Mexican War of Independence from
Spain; the leaders of the Mexican Revolution, Emiliano Zapata and Pancho
Villa; and the modern-day Chicano activists Cesar Chavez, Reies Tijerina,
and Rodolfo "Corky" Gonzales. These two murals marked the inauguration
of the artists' vision of Chicano Park, which emphasized the images associated with the Chicano civil rights movement during the late 1960s and early
1970s: scenes of Aztec deities that conveyed Chicano pride in their indigenous past, scenes of Mexican history that emphasized the revolutionary
struggle for national sovereignty, and scenes from Mexican American civil
rights activism, especially the labor struggles of Chavez and the United Farm

Workers. All these images played a conspicuous role in the Chicano movement throughout the Southwest, which emphasized the heroic struggles of Indians, Mexicans, workers, and Chicanos/as to generate communal pride and solidarity (Plates 15 and 16).

Since the 1970s and throughout the 1980s, Chicano and non-Chicano muralists alike have come to Chicano Park to enhance the murals program by decorating more pylons supporting the freeway–bridge interchange. In addition to iconic references to Aztec and Toltec mythology and to Mexican revolutionary struggle, the murals of Chicano Park feature portraits of the Virgin Mary, Frida Kahlo, and Che Guevara. One prominent pylon, adjacent to a central kiosk decorated as a Mayan temple, features a scene from the Chicano Park takeover, depicting the residents' struggle to establish Chicano Park. Today, Chicano Park stands as an iconic pantheon of Chicano history, identity, and culture. In 1980 it was recognized by the city of San Diego as an official historic site and as "a significant representation of an era in the development of San Diego."[31] It is the largest outdoor display of murals in the world, and it marks one community's struggle to place itself within the convulsive landscape of the American city.

The success of Chicano Park goes beyond its rich collection of murals. It remains a recurring site for communal festivity, family celebrations, and political expression. On any given day, particularly on weekends, it is not uncommon to find families gathering for birthdays, *quinceañeras,* and wedding celebrations, often using the park's barbecues for *carne asada.* A farmers market supplies fresh produce and the culinary staples of Mexican cuisine. Local children use the playground frequently, and one can usually find a game on the basketball court. The community center built by the city regularly offers art classes for children and adults, and it houses the Chicano Park Steering Committee, responsible for organizing the Chicano Park Day celebration, an annual gathering featuring speakers, performances, and dancing to commemorate the establishment of Chicano Park, which marked its fortieth anniversary in April 2010. Chicano Park is also the site of the annual Low Rider Car Show, where local car enthusiasts proudly display tricked-out Impalas, Malibus, and El Caminos.

Chicano Park thrives on the willingness of local residents to maintain the vibrant character of the space. As local residents of the community, Chicano Park's designers took every measure to ensure that their neighbors would use the park. In addition to barbecues, a playground, skateboard ramps, and a basketball court, the park also features parking lots, a bus stop, lighted paths, and drinking fountains. To these amenities, however, local residents have added their own flourishes, personalizing the park and enhancing its homemade character. A community garden borders the eastern edge of the park, bordered by a chain link fence that separates the park from the onramp to the I-5. There are the typical rosebushes, but there are also chilis, yuccas, cacti, and other botanical reminders of *Mexico Lindo* (beautiful Mexico). Each planting is encircled by a ring of small rocks, painted in the colors of the Mexican national flag. A cactus is usually decorated with tinsel and ornaments, like a Christmas tree. For the faithful there is a homemade shrine, a concrete pier painted with the image of the Virgin Mary, much like the homemade shrines of East Los Angeles, also adorned with candles, flowers, incense, cards, and rosaries.

Some forty years after its initial establishment, Chicano Park remains a cherished space. Its murals remain in good condition, unmarked by graffiti or tagging, and a new generation of muralists follows the original vision of the park's founders, painting new murals on the columns extending west toward the waterfront. These new additions reflect the concerns of a younger generation of community activists, moving beyond the clichéd icons of the Chicano movement. Particularly striking in this setting is the contrast of scale: overhead, the monumental span of the highway's box girders and T-columns, and on the ground, the intimate spaces of homemade shrines and gardens. The murals negotiate the tension between the monumental and the intimate, or between the civic and the communal: while their scale heightens their visual impact, their content insists on the cultural particularity of this space, telling us that this is San Diego's barrio, a capital of Mexican America.

Much like Chicano identity itself, Chicano Park is a hybrid space, a synthesis of tradition and modernity—of structure and culture—rooted in the liminal spaces of U.S.–Mexican borderlands. Chicano Park has inspired other Chicano artists in other barrios to take symbolic ownership of unwanted infrastructure. In El Paso, Texas, for example, another epicenter of the Chicano civil rights movement, "the Spaghetti Bowl" is the local nickname for the interchange of I-10, U.S. Route 54, and U.S. Route 180. It was built on the eastern edge of El Paso's Second Ward, which, since World War II, has become synonymous with the city's predominant Mexican American barrio, lying directly north of the U.S.–Mexican border. Segundo Barrio, as local residents call the area, is home to Lincoln Park, which lies directly beneath the Spaghetti Bowl. Like Chicano Park, Lincoln Park is another forest of concrete pylons that uphold a highway interchange. But the pylons, painted with murals that convey the broader aims and ideals of the Chicano movement, also support community expressions of Chicano history and identity.[32]

As in San Diego and Los Angeles, there is a lingering distrust of state highway builders among El Paso's Chicano community. A mural painted by Alfredo Morales on the 200 block of Seventh Avenue, about three blocks from the U.S.–Mexican border, records this suspicion. *Lágrimas; or, Tribute to Joe Battle,* delivers a pointed jab at Joe Battle, a forty-five-year veteran of the Texas Department of Transportation who was director of that agency during the early 1970s, a period of intensive highway construction in the El Paso area. In 1973, Battle executed plans to build the Border Highway (Loop 375) through Chihuahuita, a neighborhood of Segundo Barrio directly north of the border. The focus of the mural is the piercing stare of Victorio, the Apache chieftain said to have been the last Apache on Texas soil, whose tears flow into Rio Grande River. In the left background are scenes of urban industry and a large red stop sign that signals community demands to stop the Border Highway project. To the right are automobiles and the green-and-white signs of the highway that runs along the border and through Segundo Barrio. Visible to drivers along the Border Highway as it follows the contours of the Rio Grande, *Lágrimas* documents a community's vigilance against the unwanted incursions of industry, urban renewal, and highway construction (Figure 5.7).[33]

Yet the residents of El Paso's Segundo Barrio have channeled their grievances into a park that now stands as a centerpiece of neighborhood pride and cohesion. Like San Diego's Chicano Park, Lincoln Park stands beneath an elaborate highway interchange, built in the late 1960s to integrate the arrival of I-10 into El Paso's emerging highway network. The park is named after

FIGURE 5.7. Alfredo Morales, *Lágrimas; or, Tribute to Joe Battle,* 1978, El Paso, Texas. Cynthia Farah Haines Papers, University of Texas–El Paso Library.

the Lincoln School, established in 1912 but relocated in the early 1970s to accommodate the construction of the Spaghetti Bowl interchange. Although the school's buildings survived the construction of the freeway, city officials razed a nearby church, El Santuario, that provided a cultural focal point in the communities of Segundo Barrio. The Lincoln Recreation Center assumed stewardship over the remnants of the Lincoln School, and the surrounding land designated Lincoln Park. After visiting the famed murals of San Diego's Chicano Park in 1980, the center's director, Bobby Adauto, approached the artist Felipe Adame to design and paint murals on the pillars of the Spaghetti Bowl. Adame, who had painted with the muralists of Chicano Park, brought his vision and talent to the barrio of El Paso to create its version of Chicano Park.[34]

After initiating the murals program, Adame pursued other community projects, but work on the murals of Lincoln Park continued into the late 1990s, through the involvement of the Juntos Art Association. To distinguish this park from San Diego's Chicano Park, the association invited art students from local school districts and community colleges to continue the murals program. Under the sponsorship of Juntos and the Private Industry Council in El Paso, local artists supervised and trained students to design and paint the Lincoln Park murals, maximizing community involvement in the process. The El Paso Police Department also got involved by launching the Youth Initiative Program to sponsor student competitions. To further ensure community participation, park officials also invited individuals from the surrounding neighborhoods to serve on a community panel to review and approve proposals for the park's murals (Figure 5.8).[35]

Key to the success of the murals program is the Lincoln Park Conservation Committee (LPCC), which promotes the park as the cultural heart of El Paso's Chicano community. Through advocacy, as well as through the creation and maintenance of community murals, the LPCC insists that Lincoln Park is *el corazón de El Paso* (the heart of El Paso), words painted by Gabriel Gaytan on a column at the entrance of Lincoln Park. The LPCC also sponsors the annual celebration known as Lincoln Park Day, modeled after Chicano Park Day in San Diego. Each summer since 2005, the residents of Segundo Barrio come to Lincoln Park, gathering under the canopy of the Spaghetti Bowl to celebrate the customs and culture of El Paso's barrio. The weekend celebration includes dances, live performances, political rallies and speeches, car shows, and children's programs. It draws the support of local community agencies, which sponsor booths to introduce the public to their services.

With their insistence on Mexican American identity, culture, and history, the murals of Lincoln Park assert the presence of a community pushed aside in the course of urban renewal and highway building projects. Their proximity to the border heightens their significance, as they underscore the ambiguities of national identity in the contested terrain of the borderlands. The Spaghetti Bowl lies just east of the Chamizal region, the site of a long-standing territorial dispute between Mexico and the United States. Because of the shifting course of the Rio Grande, the river designated by the Treaty of Guadalupe Hidalgo as the official line of demarcation between the United

FIGURE 5.8. Ruben Salazar mural, Lincoln Park, El Paso, Texas. Copyright 2013 by Carolyn Rhea Drapes. Printed with permission. http://chacal.us.

States and Mexico, the six hundred acres of land known as the Chamizal region has been both American and Mexican in the course of its history. The dispute between the United States and Mexico over this parcel of land ended in 1963, when President Lyndon Johnson signed the Chamizal Convention Act of 1964, which ceded most of the Chamizal territory to Mexico.[36]

But even if alluvial shifts in the Rio Grande River prolonged geopolitical conflict between the United States and Mexico, highway construction in El Paso helped alleviate these hotly contested ambiguities. Texas Highway 375 tangles with I-10 at the Spaghetti Bowl but then veers south, making a westward turn to follow the U.S.–Mexican border for several miles, slicing through what was once the Chihuahuita neighborhood. Unlike the fickle twists and turns of the Rio Grande River, the Border Highway fixes the boundary between the United States and Mexico in a way that a river could not.

In this context, the murals of El Paso evidence one community's effort to renegotiate the ambiguities of a region riddled with territorial conflict. One mural in Lincoln Park makes this point particularly well, emphasizing the binational attachments of many Mexican Americans in El Paso. In 1999, the muralist Carlos Callejo and a group of high school art students depicted another portrait of the Virgin Mary on a supporting column of El Paso's Spaghetti Bowl. The mural depicts the Virgin emerging from her blue cloak, enshrouded by both the Mexican and U.S. flags. Below this image are inscribed the words *Nuestra Reina de El Paso, Ombligo de Aztlán* (Our Queen of El Paso, Navel of Aztlán).[37]

Chicano Park and Lincoln Park have become unique sites for local celebrations of Chicana/o identity and heritage. As the cultural heart of two Mexican American barrios, these homemade parks evidence the process by which community activists and artists have taken advantage of proximate freeways to create an environment conducive to neighborhood integrity and cultural vitality. Losers, perhaps, in the struggle against the placement of unwanted infrastructure, Mexican Americans of San Diego's Barrio Logan and El Paso's Segundo Barrio summoned the expressive traditions of Mexican American culture to reclaim a degree of control over the physical environment. In this process, the freeway—at once the symbol of civic progress in postwar America and the bane of so many barrios and ghettos—becomes the canvas on which Mexican Americans represent themselves and their history within the broader urban context.

Seen from a certain vantage point, the muralists of Lincoln Park and Chicano Park, and the communities that support them, have reclaimed the freeway and the land it occupies, integrating it back into the barrios of El Paso and San Diego. This recovery included the application of the *rasquache* style to the surfaces of freeway interchanges. Like the paintings of Romero, Botello, and Almaraz, the murals of Chicano Park and Lincoln Park rely on the incorporation of ordinary material artifacts—freeway columns, for example—in making a homemade barrio aesthetic. Such adaptive reuse of freeway architecture underscores what the Chicana art historian Amalia Mesa Bains recognizes as "a combination of resistant and resilient attitudes devised to allow the Chicano to survive and persevere with a sense of dignity. The capacity to hold life together with bits of string, old coffee cans and broken mirrors in a dazzling gesture of aesthetic bravado is at the heart of *rasquachismo*."[38]

Taking a material artifact such as a freeway interchange and painting it in bold colors with vivid scenes of Chicano history and culture reflects a stylistic reappropriation of the freeway landscape, *Chicanoizing* it to suit the cultural contours of the barrio. This might offer a monumental example of Mike Davis's "magical urbanism," in which a local penchant for bright color warms the frigid architecture of the modernist city, but it also reflects a collective unwillingness to accept the spatial status quo. Freeways divide the barrios of San Diego and El Paso, inflicting a lasting scar, but through the creative vision and concerted effort of local artists, such impairments have become improvements, creating new centers of cultural pride and communal cohesion. Spatial justice remains elusive in the barrio, but there remains a steadfast refusal to accept the damage that has been done.

At Home in the Expressway World

How to make the space of the freeway relevant—not to drivers but to the people who live in its shadow—is the goal of artists and designers like Judith Baca and Walter Hood as well as of the muralists of Chicano Park and Lincoln

Park. These examples answer Hood's question, whether a community can rise up, with signs of resistance and affirmation: resisting the imposition of unwanted infrastructure and affirming the vitality of the surrounding culture.

Chicano Park and its counterpart examples, real or envisioned, illustrate how people living in black and Latino communities reconcile themselves with the placement of unwanted infrastructure. The appropriation of these spaces does not solve the problems that afflict these neighborhoods, but it does create more livable environments; these spaces also generate a sense of local pride and command respect from the broader community. This is not the kind of spatial justice that delivers political and economic parity. Rather, it amplifies the demand for spatial justice, using freeways to talk back to their creators, to those who added insult to injury by routing freeways though neighborhoods hemorrhaging jobs and wealth even before the interstate era. For whatever reasons, this back talk has not been heard in the historiography of the freeway revolt, but it is there: thousands of motorists bear witness to it every day in San Diego, Los Angeles, and El Paso, and in Oakland, too, if people like Walter Hood get their way.

The folklore of the freeway thus includes the creative initiatives taken by people living in the border vacuums of barrios and ghettos to turn lemons into lemonade, making do with the injustices accompanying the postwar phase of urban modernization. These initiatives are part of a lasting freeway revolt that continues to play out in American cities. The voices of dissent and the invocations of racial pride have been tattooed on the skin of public infrastructure, and they register the intent of local residents to accept the freeway on their own terms, not on those of transportation authorities.

In postwar America, highway construction cut across geographies of class, race, ethnicity, gender, religion, and geography, but in inner-city neighborhoods, already ravaged by deindustrialization, white flight, abandonment, and violence, it entailed particularly vicious consequences. In this context, the murals of Chicano Park signal a cultural vitality that marks a strategic response to the challenges of modernity. They are both a response to modernity and a product of modernity, but they are also an affront to modernity—a thumb-your-nose insistence on heritage, tradition, and singularity in a rapidly changing world that threatens to destroy all distinct vestiges of diverse cultures, languages, and identities. To the extent that the racially skewed consequences of urban renewal, slum clearance, police brutality, poverty, and unemployment in postwar America provoked both peaceful and violent expressions of racial solidarity among black and brown Americans, highway construction unintentionally sparked sharper expressions of racial difference in the city. Standing in Chicano Park, one wonders whether highway planners know that the fruits of their labor have become lasting monuments to the Chicano movement. Do they know how their highways have been implicated in local struggles for class, racial, and gender equality? The unintended legacy of building the modernist city is still unfolding, but Chicano Park is one place where it begins.

Identity Politics in Post-Interstate America

Haole Highway

Dwarfing the high-rise office and apartment towers of Honolulu, Hawaii, the Koʻolau mountain range presides over the island of Oahu. The range was formed tens of thousands of years ago by volcanic eruptions; it has peaks jutting twice the height of the Empire State Building. These verdant mountains, laced with streams and waterfalls, cradled the civilization of the first Hawaiians.

Driving the sixteen miles of Interstate H-3 from Honolulu to Kaneohe Bay takes one through the Tetsuo Harano Tunnel, bored through the Koʻolaus in the 1980s. To undertake this monumental feat of engineering, construction crews extracted half a million cubic yards of mountain rock and laid 200,000 cubic yards of concrete, 18 million pounds of steel reinforcements, and 30 miles of fiber optic cable. The tunnel's towering concrete portals, over 1,000 feet high, slope slightly backward into the lush mountainside, like sentries guarding passage through the heart of an extinct volcano.

Like many interstate highways, H-3 owes its existence to the Cold War. As the United States deepened its involvement against Communist aggression in Southeast Asia in the early 1960s, state and federal highway engineers planned a direct highway link from Naval Station Pearl Harbor to Marine Corps Base Hawaii at Kaneohe Bay. Despite the absence of state borders in Hawaii, this military rationale qualified H-3 for federal funding under the Interstate Highway Act, completing the final segment of a tripartite system of highways designed to solve traffic demands and connect the island's major military centers. H-3 would also link Honolulu to the windward side of Oahu, a less developed area that supported scattered rural—and dwindling—settlements of indigenous Hawaiians.[1] This project had the backing of Hawaii's establishment: military and transportation officials, business leaders, contractors, labor, and congressional representatives, most notably the late Senator Daniel Inouye, who pushed H-3 through Congress as chairman of the Senate Appropriations Committee.

Drafted in the early 1960s, H-3 finally opened to vehicular traffic in 1997, but the prolonged opposition to its construction illustrates a striking twist in the folklore of the freeway. Throughout the 1970s and into the 1980s, local environmentalists posed determined opposition to the highway's completion. Although the legal challenges they mounted added costly delays to the project, the discourse of opposition to H-3 took a new inflection during the 1980s amid an upsurge of indigenous activism among local Hawaiians claiming ancestral ties to the land. This movement included demands for the creation of ethnic studies programs in Hawaii's state university system to rewrite Hawaii's history from an indigenous perspective, as well as a revival of traditional cultural practices—all founded on a renewed respect for the land that cradled the first Hawaiian civilization.[2]

H-3 galvanized this movement further when construction crews began unearthing ruins in the northern Halawa Valley, a site believed to have been sacred to indigenous Hawaiians. In 1987, to address local opposition, the Hawaii Department of Transportation contracted archaeologists from the Bernice Pauahi Bishop Museum, the oldest museum in Hawaii and repository of the world's largest collection of Polynesian artifacts, for on-site archeological research.[3] These experts corroborated the state's claim that no harm was done—the sites in question were not sacred ruins but, rather, the remnants of a dryland agricultural system. The Bishop Museum archaeologists reached a similar conclusion some five years later, when bulldozers dug up more ruins, even though one of its own archaeologists went on record to state that these ruins were in fact a *Hale O Papa* (House of Papa), a *heiau* (temple) that honored Papahanaumoku, the Mother Earth and female ancestor of all indigenous Hawaiians. According to University of Hawaii historian

Davianna Pomaikaʻi McGregor, this *heiau* served a unique role as a special refuge for women, a site of birthing and healing.[4]

Bishop officials immediately dismissed this outspoken archaeologist from his post, raising a storm of controversy and casting public doubt on the museum's impartiality. Meanwhile, a group of women claiming ancestral ties to the Halawa Valley registered their protest by organizing themselves as Women of Hale O Papa. They occupied the site to worship the goddess to whom they believed the site belonged, blocking further construction in the area. One woman, feeling the spiritual pull of the valley, gave birth to a son on the remains of the *heiau,* in the shadow of H-3, believing that her actions were *pono* (a Hawaiian term for what is right and good for the land). The women attending the birth camped on the site for several months, answering, in the words of one activist, "the call to the women of Hawaii to occupy the *heiau*."[5]

As the construction of H-3 spurred indigenous Hawaiian women into action, it also reignited local superstition. First, there was the story of Daniel Yanagida, who believed that state bulldozers had unearthed the sacred remains of his ancestors. Instilled with respect for ancient burial grounds, Yanagida went to the construction site every day over the course of several months, asking crew members to return the bones to the earth, but with no written proof to substantiate his claim, archaeologists working at the site denied his request. Three months later, before he could oversee the reburial of his ancestors' sacred remains, Yanagida died, stoking local speculation that the gods were exacting revenge for the destruction of sacred land, even on their own faithful servants.[6]

This story garnered much coverage in the local press because it belonged to a broader oral-history tradition on the Hawaiian Islands that emphasizes divine retribution for the desecration of the earth by Europeans and European Americans, known as *haole* among indigenous Hawaiians. When the Libby, McNeill, and Libby Pineapple Company razed the Haluakaiamoana *heiau* to build its cannery in 1910, for example, a mysterious plague destroyed its pineapple crop, forcing the cannery to close. Workers dredging the Ala Wai Canal for the creation of a tourist zone at Waikiki Beach, which destroyed sacred taro patches and fishponds, suffered a staggering number of on-the-job accidents and injuries. Likewise, the construction of H-3 experienced its own set of inexplicable occurrences, reigniting an oral tradition of super-stition and folklore. Once workers ran screaming after reportedly seeing a seven-foot-tall ghost in a *malo* (loincloth) coming straight out of a rock; oth-ers told of seeing bulldozers levitate or of hearing a mysterious sound as of someone blowing a conch shell deep inside the trans-Koʻolau tunnel. H-3's construction workers also suffered a rash of injuries and deaths, caused by falling girders, collapsing walls, car and helicopter crashes, snapping ca-bles, and faulty cranes. Some interpreted these mishaps as the wrath of the gods. "I get so angry when I see the desecration of our sacred grounds," said Lilikala Kameʻeleihiwa, associate professor of Hawaiian Studies at the Uni-versity of Hawaii, Manoa, and staunch critic of H-3; "every time I hear about someone dying in connection with it, I am happy."[7]

Happiness, however, ultimately came to the supporters of H-3, who could celebrate the final completion of the project after long and costly delays. To inaugurate the highway's opening, and to make good with islanders, the Hawaii Department of Transportation sponsored the Trans-Koʻolau Trek, a 10-kilometer "fun run" that drew some 17,000 people on May 11, 1997, co-inciding with Mother's Day. This only spurred further ire among H-3 oppo-nents, especially the Women of Hale O Papa, who took offense at the official celebration of a highway that desecrated a temple to Hawaii's sacred Mother Earth. As one group member put it, "It is a sign of settler racism that the H-3 Freeway, built to connect two bases of illegal occupying American military, will be opened with 100,000 people in a 'fun' run over the ruins of our god-dess ancestors."[8]

Despite such fanfare, Honolulu's civic culture remained divided over H-3. In 1998, the Honolulu Contemporary Museum staged a more som-ber inauguration of H-3 with its exhibition *E Luku Wale E . . . Devastation upon Devastation,* a series of photographs from Mark Hamasaki and Anne Kapulani Landgraf, who together form the art collective Piliāmoʻo. Begin-ning in March 1989, Hamasaki and Landgraf began documenting the con-struction of H-3, forcing the viewer to consider the harsh impact of human technology and engineering on the natural environment. Piliāmoʻo, how-ever, situates its images within a racialized critique that equates the deraci-nation of the land (Hawaiian *ʻaina*) with the destruction of indigenous cul-

FIGURE C.1. Laweau ka hoaka, August 18, 1991. Photograph by Piliamoʻo (Mark
  Hamasaki and Anne Kapulani Landgraf).

ture and tradition. Adding further controversy, the photographers wrote the
captions to their photos in Hawaiian, not English, making a clear statement
about who should have the last word (Figure C.1).

Boring through the remains of an ancient volcano, impinging on sites
sacred to indigenous Hawaiians, the sixteen miles of H-3 were the most
expensive road in human history.[9] At a staggering cost of $1.3 billion, H-3
cost approximately $83 million per mile because of the daunting technical
challenges and the prolonged court battles and public demonstrations that
ensued over the course of some four decades. Yet from the perspective of
some indigenous Hawaiians, the costs were even greater. H-3 was but the latest affront to indigenous sovereignty in Hawaii, a concretization of colonial

relations and another form of territorial subjugation. Against the expert authority of state engineers and archaeologists, local opposition summoned ancient superstition and folkloric tradition to fight the violation of sacred land.

Race, Culture, and Concrete

Is H-3 a conveyor of the public good or an unholy act of desecration? Are interstate highways the conduits of national progress or the instruments of oppression? This book has surveyed the freighted history of building highways since the age of the interstate to show the ways this debate continues through various forms of cultural expression that question the presence of the freeway in the city and the intentions behind its construction. From Seattle to Miami, Boston to Honolulu, the freeway has earned a distinct notoriety in American culture, interpreted through collective memory, lived experience, and social identity. The preceding chapters have explored the disparate expressions of these interpretations to illustrate that the meaning of the freeway is still up for grabs, even as it erodes under the ever-coursing tide of traffic, even as we bury it beneath our cities, as if to right the wrongs of the past.

The burial of the John F. Kennedy Expressway in Boston, known officially as the Central Artery Tunnel Project and colloquially as the Big Dig, began in 1987 and finished in 2003. After costly delays and several construction failures, the project spliced the North End neighborhood back into its metropolitan context, creating a new strip of green space in the heart of the city. To date, the Big Dig remains the most spectacular, and most expensive, example of putting the hubris of the interstate generation of highway planners and engineers in its place.[10]

Other cities have followed suit. After the 1989 Loma Prieta earthquake in the San Francisco Bay Area, local officials took the opportunity to tear down the Embarcadero Freeway that severed the city from its historic waterfront. Although this was one of the few freeways that managed to escape the wrath of San Francisco's freeway revolt in the 1950s, it ultimately came down in 1991, revitalizing the city's waterfront for tourist trade. In 2003, Milwaukee mayor John Norquist took revenge on a one-mile stretch of freeway that he had opposed as a young legislator in the early 1970s. The tearing down of the

Park East Freeway signaled the enduring patience of Milwaukee's freeway revolt. Though it did not completely succeed in its early effort to block the freeway's entry into the city, it waited to strike back, demolishing the few freeways that were built. Norquist, a longtime admirer of Jane Jacobs and president of the Congress for New Urbanism since 2005, succeeded in enacting his own prescription that "the urban superhighway should be relegated to the scrap heap of history."[11]

The hefty task of erasing the freeway from the urban scene, a megaproject for the twenty-first century, enacts the logic of the freeway revolt on the contemporary urban landscape: what highway planners built to eradicate blight has become a sign of blight itself. The freeway revolt, in its organized, visible forms, can take credit for these interventions. It also triggered substantive revisions in federal highway policy. In 1966, Congress approved the creation of the U.S. Department of Transportation to supervise the work of the Federal Highway Administration and the Bureau of Public Roads and to provide new mechanisms for conflict resolution. That year also introduced another Federal Aid Highway Act as well as the National Historic Preservation Act, both of which mandated new measures to protect parks and historic sites. Further reforms ensued in the following years. The Federal Aid Highway Act of 1968 coordinated highway construction with relocation assistance, while the Urban Mass Transportation Act of 1970 and the Federal Aid Highway Act of 1973 diverted funds away from the interstate program and toward the development of mass transit. By decentralizing federal transportation policy—by creating more oversight and more bureaucracy—Congress tightened its leash on the highwaymen.

Today planners and scholars alike pine for the preinterstate metropolis. The new urbanists, for example, crave the more intimate scale of urban life before the freeway and seek to mitigate the bland anonymity of urban sprawl. Their movement tries to implement a Jacobs-style ideal of sidewalk diversity, a concentrated mix of forms and uses, vested with nostalgic pastiche, but often without the socioeconomic mix that continues to define the prospects and possibilities of urban life. Similarly, recent historical scholarship exhibits a new urbanist approach to the American city. This work excavates the prefreeway history of communities like Boyle Heights in East Los

Angeles, discovering not only the smaller scale of neighborhood life but also a multiracial, multiethnic mix of working-class people. With its unparalleled blend of cultures, religions, languages, complexions, skills, and trades, Boyle Heights before the interstate is now touted as a pan-ethnic model of cultural diversity and communal stability, a template from the past for the city of the future—that is, after we have buried the freeways that enforce its isolation from the rest of the city.[12]

For their part, today's generation of highway planners and engineers demonstrate greater sensitivity to the scale of their work and its fit into surrounding neighborhoods. This includes new aesthetic treatments designed to integrate the freeway into its sociospatial context, giving it character, lessening its blunt monotony, and sometimes gesturing toward the cultural identity of surrounding communities. In 2004, for example, the Texas Department of Transportation approved the painting of ninety columns of U.S. Highway 59 between Polk and Capitol Streets in downtown Houston to mark the entrance to Chinatown. Painting these piers vermilion affirms the significance of the color in Chinese culture, denoting an official "entrance" to Houston's Chinatown, which had been sequestered by highway construction in the 1960s. A similar effort guides new freeway projects in Phoenix, Arizona, where a segment of I-10 has been submerged below grade and landscaped with rocks, gravel, palms, cacti, and other semiarid plants. Freeway designers have etched geometric designs that resemble indigenous petroglyphs into the sandstone-colored retaining walls and overpasses. This stretch of I-10 gestures toward its historical and environmental context, imbued with a distinctive pastiche that suggests Arizona's desert climate and its Native American heritage.[13]

Everyone seems to finally agree that context matters, but for communities living in the shadow of the freeway, the application of colors and symbols to contemporary highway architecture delivers too little too late. Such gestures also threaten to hijack the varied historical contexts through which diverse peoples interpret the freeway and its meaning. Indigenous Hawaiians, for example, expressed their opposition to H-3 through a long view of Hawaiian history, stressing the destruction of Native land and culture at the hands of Europeans and European Americans. The barrio intelligentsia of artists and writers in the urban Southwest view the freeways in their midst through a broader history of conquest—another marked instance of displacement and dispossession. In the urban South and in other cities throughout the nation, African Americans have interpreted the freeway through the collective memory of Jim Crow segregation, writ large on the expanding scale of the postwar urban region. Though these histories defy current efforts to reapply context through pastiche and symbolism, they nonetheless illustrate how diverse communities *recontextualize* the structure of the freeway in their own terms—implicating its presence in broader histories of dispossession and disenfranchisement.

There is historical context, but there is also cultural context, which the chapters in this book have emphasized. Chicano Park asserts a spectacular rendering of brown pride in the heart of the city, a Chicano articulation of identity and history, as imagined by a politicized generation of Mexican Americans. In Miami, the Overtown Historic Folklife Village strives to re-create the historic landscape of black enterprise and culture that was wiped out by I-95, struggling to find a middle ground between the cultural ideals of the civil rights movement, on the one hand, and the city's logic of capital investment and land development, on the other. Chicana/o cultural workers in East Los Angeles, feeding off the creative energy of the Chicano movement, continue to speak, write, sketch, and paint the forgotten context of the neighborhood's overlapping freeways, insisting on the uniqueness and singularity of their perceptions and experiences. By bulldozing through the distinctive social and cultural contexts of the city's diverse neighborhoods, highway planners and engineers of the interstate generation sparked local efforts to make sense of the freeway's presence and to integrate its architecture into the city's variegated terrain of language, identity, and place.

The words and images that define the folklore of the freeway illustrate the regenerative capacity of communities to clear the dust, regroup, and create anew. Their collective efforts enhance the cultural vitality of the entire city, not just of specific neighborhoods. Chicano Park, for example, became a state treasure in 1997, when the California legislature voted for its inclusion on the California Register of Historic Resources. In 2013, the National Park Service included Chicano Park on the National Register of Historic Places.

Rondo Days, for its part, has become an economic asset within the cultural infrastructure of the Twin Cities, prompting the national Travel Industry Association to recognize the festival as "a priceless brand association, offering a competitive advantage to St. Paul and its businesses."[14] Barrio Logan and Rondo show us that even those communities hit hardest by highway-building bulldozers can fight back peacefully, through creative forms of cultural expression that garner national and international recognition.

Like the regeneration of new cells over a scar or wound, context creeps back into the deracinated spaces of the city through local effort, talent, and imagination. The folklore of the freeway provides a cultural emollient for the laceration of neighborhoods and communities, helping mend the connections between people and place. These collective efforts, everywhere apparent in the presence of a freeway, from the obscure markings of a tagger to the spectacular murals of Chicano Park, are the unintended and unexpected consequences of the modernist city project. What was a mandate from the top down sparked a retort from the bottom up, from the shadows of the freeway, which cultivated new expressions of community and identity. Do highway planners and builders know that their work provoked stringent articulations of racial identity and difference? Do they know how they helped "make" race in the city? With some egregious exceptions, the interstate generation of highway planners and builders gave indirect consideration to race, yet their work unwittingly sponsored a racialized version of the freeway revolt, embedded within the cultural fabric of the contemporary urban scene. The cultural material explored in the chapters of this book thus insists on a broader and more inclusive understanding of the politics of fighting freeways and ultimately demonstrates the racial consequences of making urban space.

Despite the public discourse of scientific objectivity and rational planning engendered by the interstate highway program, freeways, especially in their metropolitan contexts, were built to serve powerful interests that shared a commitment to eradicating blight from the city. More often than not, this meant that black and brown communities, and other communities of color, working-class and middle-class alike, found themselves in the path of progress. That the bias built into the interstate highway program provoked heightened expressions of racial conflict and pride should not be surprising.

Where there is repression, there is resistance, and this tension has played out in American history along racial lines. We do not have to venture very far back into the past to discern this dynamic. Consider twentieth-century Mexican American history as an example: the deportation campaigns of the 1930s, the Zoot Suit Riots of the 1940s, and the construction of Dodger Stadium in the 1950s all helped codify a racialized sense of solidarity among Chicanos and Chicanas. For African Americans, to single out just one example, establishment repression of the Black Panthers in the 1960s galvanized the broader black community to support the party, which got a lift from the times.[15] These acts of injustice left a residue of racial conflict and consciousness. They played no small part in the historic making of race, and they find parallels in the post–World War II history of highway construction, which drew racial lines around the diverse neighborhoods of the American city, helping to *spatialize* a more cohesive sense of racial difference and identity.

The introduction of the freeway to the city provoked the senses, inciting intense debate between men and women about the importance of streets and sidewalks and, as Marcel Proust would say, about the "remembrance of things past." It brought women to the forefront of political organization and provoked a feminist critique of modernist city planning. It also structured new ways of seeing the city, from the perspectives of both drivers and those driven. Interstate highway construction shaped vision and memory, and it induced new modes of urban experience, channeled through the myriad discourses of identity that surfaced in the 1960s. Such subjective expressions become the stuff of folklore; they challenged the allegedly objective science that legitimized the discourse of highway technocracy in the 1950s, and, from the perspective of hard-edged social science, they threaten the knowability of highway construction and its history in postwar America.

Yet historical truth evades comprehension on both sides. If anything, it is my hope that *The Folklore of the Freeway* illustrates that the urban history of interstate highway construction disallows easy distinctions between science and myth. The planners and engineers who designed the interstate highway program not only maintained their own folklore but also helped create it. Certainly, they drew support from the mass-produced "magic" of world's fairs, photographs, and theme parks, but they also generated the hard data that precluded accountability. Their voluminous compilation of algorithms, flow charts, graphs, and tables enabled easy justification of their preordained conclusions, shaped by the biases and interests of powerful social actors. The maps and renderings they presented to the public were not neutral portraits of objective reality; they had their own rhetorical force, marking strategic points of view. Their data, in other words, embodied a specific form of representation that produced a "scientific mystique," as vital to the efficient implementation of the interstate highway program as the bulldozers that cleared the way.[16]

On the eve of the 1960s, the designers of the interstate highway program stood as men of their time, servants of public need. As more automobiles converged on the historic precincts of the urban core, congestion mandated the interventions of an elite corps of experts trained to build big new roads that could open new suburban frontiers. Their achievement captured the world's imagination, demonstrating the capacity of American technical expertise to build a national transportation infrastructure that served the masses efficiently and expediently. In this moment, they enjoyed an exalted status as experts, confident in their command of the public's trust and imagination. With specialized skill and training, these men embodied a 1950s faith in the power of science to solve the world's problems, to integrate the machine into the rhythms of daily life, and to facilitate national prosperity and material progress.

The 1960s, however, brought an abrupt end to their exalted status. As the decade progressed, the technocrats, for the most part, remained stuck in a dated posture of objective expertise, which seemed increasingly rigid and narrow, or "square," in the language of the time. On almost every front of American professional culture, the 1960s introduced a new hostility to the objective posture, exposing it and its universal claims as "strategic ritual."[17] The combined force of civil rights, feminism, historic preservation, multiculturalism, and environmentalism destabilized the notion of the city as a holistic reality, replacing that useful fiction with a dawning sense of the city as a highly fragmented and wholly unstable hodgepodge of diverse communities, each with its own languages, lifeways, and worldviews.

In this environment, the highway-planning profession underwent a crisis of legitimacy, as did the entirety of the modernist city project, which gave way to new modes of urban experience, laced with new perspectives and new points of view. The protagonists of the freeway revolt fought to preserve the ragged beauty of the city and its history, asserting the rights of pedestrians over automobiles, the pleasures of sidewalk diversity and disorder, and the priority of preserving nature and history in the city. They demonstrated new models of community activism, and the power to strike at master plans from the grassroots level. Their selective embrace of plurality and diversity opened the door to a new chapter in the history of the American city, structured by new programs and new policies designed to bring life to the lifeless order of the modernist city. Perhaps most of all, the organized expressions of the freeway revolt taught us to stand up to the driving force of progress and to block the bulldozers that threatened to tear the city's fragile ecology asunder.

But what is left of these efforts? SoHo, Tribeca, San Francisco's Embarcadero and the Ferry Building, the French Quarter, a revitalized North End in Boston, Cambridge, Princeton, Beverly Hills—all nice communities within their respective urban contexts, but is this the postmodern condition we have been waiting for? For all the grassroots rhetoric, the success of the visible freeway revolt has left us with some of the nation's most exclusive enclaves of wealth and privilege. These communities command top dollar for their real estate, drawing an elite clientele from around the world in their voracious appetite for luxury goods, fine art, and haute cuisine. The freeway casts its shadows elsewhere, beyond the conceptual edges of the bourgeois metropolis. This does not look like the intricate sidewalk ballet that Jacobs brought to our collective imagination, but maybe it is.

Fragments of the postmodern city lurk in the shadows of the freeway. There, new expressions of identity and difference disrupt the master narratives that guided urban design during the age of the interstate. This includes the master narrative of the modernist city, with its push for ordered and disciplined space, but also the master logic of the capitalist city, which creates hierarchies of space around the free market. The folklore of the freeway presents alternative experiences of urban space from the bottom up, often outside the regulatory scope of public policy and the boundaries of the formal economy. It alters our perception of the urban built environment, presenting new models of spatial organization and representation. And it is built through homemade efforts to reinvent the public realm through the appropriation of official space and its meanings. It brings new life to the shadows of the freeway, pluralizing the urban landscape by inserting new voices, new perspectives, and new histories.[18]

Diverse Americans have thus built their own repositories of local knowledge about the freeway and its presence in the city. This knowledge, rooted in lived experience and historical memory, inflected by distinctive cultural traditions and identities, remains beyond the purview of the highway-planning profession and of the scholarly community of urban historians, whose members generally abstain from questions of culture in their assessment of urban structural change. Yet for many communities hidden in the shadows of the freeway, historically bereft of political and economic power, the folklore of the freeway provides an alternative framework for understanding the radical forces unleashed on the postwar American city. The folklore of the freeway can amplify grievances—not just against the highway-building program, but also against the widening fissures of race and class more generally. Through art, literature, poetry, and other forms of cultural representation, people in diverse communities fashioned alternative epistemologies about the structural transformation of urban life after World War II, producing new understandings of urban space and new modes of urban experience.

This is not an invitation for Dr. Pangloss to come back from *Candide* to tell us that "all is for the best in the best of all possible worlds." *The Folklore of the Freeway* eschews false optimism, emphatically rejecting the conclusion that all is well in the inner city. Even while we recognize the creative energies that surge in the shadow of the freeway, we cannot lose sight of the enduring struggles for spatial justice that confront ever more daunting challenges. The cultural expressions explored in this book remain a vital part of that struggle, keeping our collective focus on the road toward a more just and equitable urban future.

Acknowledgments

In the course of writing this book, I had the privilege of working with many bright and talented people: scholars, librarians, archivists, graduate students, and undergraduate students, who provided careful readings, helpful feedback, professional advice, and diligent assistance.

This book really took off during a fellowship year at the Charles Warren Center for Studies in American History at Harvard University, where I joined a seminar of brilliant scholars who share my interest in architecture, urbanism, and the history of the built environment. Alice Friedman, Martha McNamara, Anne Whiston Spirn, Jane Kamensky, Danny Abramson, Paula Lupkin, Paul Groth, and Ellen Stroud created a collegial atmosphere for the pursuit of my research. Lizabeth Cohen and Margaret Crawford held the reins of this seminar, asking provocative questions, sharing their work, and bringing colleagues and graduate students into the fold of our engaging discussions. Two years later, I had another amazing fellowship opportunity at Stanford University, where I joined another distinguished group of scholars at the Center for Comparative Studies in Race and Ethnicity. My profound thanks to Dorothy Steele, Hazel Markus, and Jennifer Eberhardt for convening our seminar year, and to my fellow fellows—Mark Sawyer, Dorothy Roberts, Harvey Young, and Gabriela Arrendondo—for sharing their work and insight. These marvelous opportunities introduced new horizons of discovery in my academic life and new possibilities for interdisciplinary research.

I was also privileged to spend a few weeks at the University of Minnesota, at the invitation of its Quadrant initiative, where I led seminar discussions and presented my work; my thanks to John Archer, Elaine Tyler May, Katherine Solomonson, and Greg Donofrio for their interest, insight, and support. My involvement with Quadrant also brought me into the orbit of the University of Minnesota Press, to which I owe profound thanks for its commitment to this book. I closely followed the advice of executive editor Richard Morrison and of Pieter Martin, a deft editor and a conscientious reader. Thanks also to Pieter's assistant, Kristian Tvedten, for his diligent attention to the manuscript, and to Kathy Delfosse for her editorial skill. I am also grateful to have been able to present my work at Yale University, MIT, the University of Michigan, Mt. Holyoke College, Rutgers University at Newark, and the University of California Santa Barbara; my thanks to my colleagues who sponsored these opportunities, including Iyko Day, Matt Lassiter, George Lipsitz, Robert Fogelson, Chris Cappozola, and Stephen Pitti.

During the cross-country course of my research, I benefited immensely from the professional expertise of librarians and archivists, who introduced me to the collections of printed materials that have been amassed around the history of fighting freeways in fifteen American cities. Much gratitude to the library staffs of the Minnesota Historical Society, the Ramsey County Historical Society (Minnesota), the Princeton Public Library, the State Transportation Library of Massachusetts, the Boston Public Library, the New York Public Library, the Francis Loeb Library at the Harvard Graduate School of Design, the Oakland Public Library, the San Francisco Public Library, the Enoch Pratt Free Library in Baltimore, the Langsdale Library at the University of Baltimore, the San Diego Public Library, the Special Collections Library of the University of Texas at El Paso, the Institute of Transportation Studies at UC Berkeley, the Getty Research Institute, the Air Photo Archives at UCLA (thanks, Charlie Toscano!), the Chicano/Latino Library at San Diego State University, the Hawaii State Archives, the Hawaii State Law Library, the Hawaii and Pacific Room of the Hawaii State Library, the Black Archives History and Research Foundation of South Florida, and the Miami Public Library. I met so many archivists and librarians dedicated to local history and to the specific histories of their neighborhoods and communities; to them I extend my profound thanks. In this capacity, a few names stand out: Richard Weingroff at the U.S. Department of Transportation, Martin Brennan and Angela Riggio at the Charles Young Research Library at UCLA, Gavin Kleepsies at the Cambridge Historical Society, Dore Minatodani at the University of Hawai'i Library, and Kaiwi Nui at the Halawa Luluku Interpretive Development Center. I am also grateful to the many artists who generously shared their work, or to their estate guardians. My sincere thanks to Frank and Sharon Romero, David Botello, Mark Hamasaki, David Fichter, Senga Nengudi, Linda Pfeiffer, Caroline Rhea Drapes, Lauren Doolin, Mary Kuntz-Cole, and to Judy Baca, whose work continues to inspire us all. Thanks also to the late, great poet of Los Angeles, Wanda Coleman.

I thank friends and colleagues who generously read portions of the manuscript. This includes "the road gang" of interstate historians like Mark Rose and Raymond Mohl, who lent generous reading assistance and collegial support. Thanks to Becky Nicolaides, Ramon Gutierrez, Jeff Melnick, Neil Maher, and Robin Kelley, and to Wim De Wit and Christopher Alexander at the Getty Research Institute. Special thanks to Mary Ryan for the driving tour of Baltimore and to Jane Kamensky and Margaret Crawford for much support and encouragement. My deepest expression of gratitude to UCLA and to the University of California; to longtime friends and colleagues Stephen Aron (and his lovely wife, Amy Green) and Abel Valenzuela (and to his parents, Abel and Graciela Valenzuela, who shared their personal experiences with highway construction in East Los Angeles), and to my new friend and colleague in UCLA's School of Engineering, Scott Brandenberg, who introduced the engineer's perspective of building freeways in the city. To UCLA's Center for the Study of Women and its dynamic director, Kathleen McHugh, I extend sincere thanks for the stipend support. Among the most tangible benefits of working at UCLA has been regular contact with bright and engaged students, some of whom lent generous research and reading assistance to this project. Eric Saulnier and Aaron Ziolkowski read drafts and supplied invaluable assistance, and Jean-Paul deGuzman conducted tireless research assistance that shaped the content of this book in profound ways. Thanks also to Tom McKinley, Stacey McCarroll Cutshaw, and Amy Scott for critical support and to Natasha Tuck for sharing her Bernal Heights home during my time at Stanford.

Finally, thanks to friends and family who kept me sane, grounded, and loved throughout the process. To my parents, Edward and Teresa Avila: thanks, Mom, for contributing your newfound indexing skills, and thanks, Dad, for always asking for the next book. To my brother Chris and his sons, Eric and Ryan Avila, who represent what is at stake for the next generation; to my cousin Patrice Winn, for fun and love in Los Angeles; to dear old friends Kirk Ch. Vaughn and Lynn Hoberg, who redefine my meaning of family; and to my dear new friend Ken Sumner III, who brings joy and companionship. These people remind me every day of what matters most in this world: books, yes, and much more.

Notes

INTRODUCTION

1. Richard O. Baumbach and William E. Borah, *The Second Battle of New Orleans: A History of the Vieux Carré Riverfront Expressway Controversy* (Tuscaloosa: University of Alabama Press, 1980); Alan Lupo, *Rites of Way: The Politics of Transportation in Boston and the U.S. City* (New York: Little, Brown, 1971); Helen Leavitt, *Superhighway–Superhoax* (New York: Doubleday, 1970); Ben Kelley, *The Pavers and the Paved: The Real Cost of America's Highway Program* (New York: Donald W. Brown, 1971); Robert Caro, *The Power Broker: Robert Moses and the Fall of New York* (New York: Vintage Books, 1974).

2. Marshall Berman, *All That Is Solid Melts into Air: The Experience of Modernity* (New York: Simon and Schuster, 1982), 312.

3. My thanks to George Lipsitz for sharing this joke with me.

4. Ralph McCartney, interview by Devon Williams, August 14, 1997, *Tell the Story*, Oral History Project, Black Archives Foundation, Miami, Florida; Dr. Constance Raye Jones Price, interview by Kateleen Hope Cavett, February 24, 2003, Rondo Oral History Project, Ramsey County Historical Society, St. Paul, Minnesota; Yusef Mgeni (born and raised in the Rondo neighborhood as Charlie Anderson), interview by Kateleen Hope Cavett, Rondo Oral History Project, March 21, 2003; Rudolfo Acuña, *Occupied America: A History of Chicanos*, 4th ed. (New York: Longman, 2000); Helena Maria Viramontes, interview by Michael Silverblatt, "Bookworm," August 16, 2007, on KCRW, www.kcrw.com/etc/programs/bw/bw070816helena_maria_viramon.

5. James Scott, *Domination and the Arts of Resistance: Hidden Transcripts* (New Haven: Yale University Press, 1990); Robin D. G. Kelley, *Race Rebels: Culture, Politics, and the Black Working Class* (New York: Free Press, 1994), 8.

6. For a discussion of urban infrastructure and social inequality, see David Torres-Rouff, "Water Use, Ethnic Conflict, and Infrastructure in Nineteenth Century Los

Angeles," *Pacific Historical Review* 75, no. 1 (February 2006): 119–40. See also Matthew Gandy, *Concrete and Clay: Reworking Nature in New York City* (Cambridge: MIT Press, 2002); and Thomas Sugrue, *The Origins of the Urban Crisis: Race and Inequality in Post-war Detroit* (Princeton: Princeton University Press, 1996).

7. This point draws on Edward Soja's notions of spatial justice; see Soja, *Seeking Spatial Justice* (Minneapolis: University of Minnesota Press, 2010).

8. James Holston, *The Modernist City: An Anthropological Critique of Brasilia* (Chicago: University of Chicago Press, 1989); Reyner Banham, *Theory and Design in the First Machine Age* (London: Architectural Press, 1960); Kenneth Frampton, *Modern Architecture: A Critical History*, 3rd ed. (London: Thames and Hudson, 1992); Robert Fishman, *Urban Utopias in the Twentieth Century: Ebenezer Howard, Frank Lloyd Wright, and Le Corbusier* (Cambridge: MIT Press, 1992). For a more general cultural history of modernity and postmodernity, see Berman, *All That Is Solid Melts into Air*; and David Harvey, *The Condition of Postmodernity: An Enquiry into the Origins of Cultural Change* (Oxford and Cambridge, Mass.: Basil Blackwell, 1989).

9. Holston, *The Modernist City*, 13.

10. Terry H. Anderson, *The Movement and the Sixties: Protest in America from Greensboro to Wounded Knee* (New York: Oxford University Press, 1996).

11. On the freeway in Los Angeles, in particular, two works stand out: David Brodsly, *L.A. Freeway: An Appreciative Essay* (Berkeley: University of California Press, 1981); Reyner Banham, *Los Angeles: The Architecture of Four Ecologies* (Berkeley: University of California Press, 2009). On Los Angeles generally and its expressive cultures, see Mike Davis, *Magical Urbanism: Latinos Reinvent the US City* (London: Verso Press, 2000); Kelley, *Race Rebels*; Anthony Macías, *Mexican American Mojo: Popular Music, Dance, and Urban Culture in Los Angeles, 1935–1968* (Durham, N.C.: Duke University Press, 2008); Josh Kun, *Audiotopia: Music, Race, and America* (Berkeley: University of California Press, 2005).

12. On the urban history of Mexican Americans in twentieth-century America, see Albert Camarillo, *Chicanos in a Changing Society: From Mexican Pueblos to American Barrios in Santa Barbara and Southern California, 1848–1930* (Cambridge, Mass.: Harvard University Press, 1996); George Sanchez, *Becoming Mexican American: Ethnicity, Culture, and Identity in Chicano Los Angeles, 1900–1945* (New York: Oxford University Press, 1993); Ricardo Romo, *East Los Angeles: History of a Barrio* (Austin: University of Texas Press, 1983); Rudolfo Acuña, *Anything but Mexican: Chicanos in Contemporary Los Angeles* (London: Verso Press, 1995).

13. David H. Pinkney, *Napoleon III and the Rebuilding of Paris* (Princeton: Princeton University Press, 1958); Berman, *All That Is Solid Melts into Air*; David Harvey, *Paris: Capital of Modernity* (New York: Routledge, 2006); see also David P. Jordan, *Transforming Paris: The Life and Labors of Baron Haussmann* (New York: Free Press, 1995);

Michael Carmona, *Haussmann: His Life and Times and the Making of Modern Paris* (Chicago: Ivan R. Dee, 2002).

14. Valette quoted in Robert L. Herbert, *Impressionism: Art, Leisure, and Parisian Society* (New Haven: Yale University Press, 1988), 3.

15. T. J. Clark, *The Painting of Modern Life: Paris in the Art of Manet and His Followers* (Princeton: Princeton University Press, 1999).

16. Robert Moses, "What Happened to Haussmann," *Architectural Forum* 77 (July 1942): 57–66.

17. See *L'Assomoir,* for example, or other novels from Zola's Rougon-Marquart series.

18. Berman, *All That Is Solid Melts into Air,* 142–71.

19. Clark, *The Painting of Modern Life*; Herbert, *Impressionism.*

20. Clark, *The Painting of Modern Life,* 55.

21. The term "second ghetto" comes from Arnold Hirsch, who describes modernist public housing towers as a new form of containment for black racial poverty. See Hirsch, *Making the Second Ghetto: Race and Housing in Chicago, 1940–1960* (Chicago: University of Chicago Press, 1998).

22. *St. Paul Dispatch,* September 28, 1956.

23. To be fair, the Central Artery/Tunnel Project (CAT Project, known as the Big Dig) was also about expanding and retooling Boston's highway system to meet current traffic needs, though many constituencies at both local and national levels wanted to see the tearing down of Interstate 93, the "Green Monster" that cut the city in half, separating it from Boston Harbor. See Dan McNichol, *The Big Dig: The Largest Urban Construction Project in the History of the Modern World* (New York: Silver Lining Books, 2000).

1. THE MASTER'S PLAN

1. Banham, *Theory and Design in the First Machine Age*; Leonardo Benevolo, *The Origins of Modern Town Planning* (Cambridge: MIT Press, 1967); Kenneth Frampton, *Modern Architecture: A Critical History* (New York: Oxford University Press, 1980); Fishman, *Urban Utopias in the Twentieth Century*; Holston, *The Modernist City.*

2. Dan McNichol, *The Roads That Built America: The Incredible Story of the U.S. Interstate System* (New York: Sterling Publishing, 2006); William Kaszynski, *The American Highway: The History and Culture of Roads in the United States* (Jefferson, N.C.: McFarland, 2000); Tom Lewis, *Divided Highways: Building the Interstate Highways, Transforming American Life* (New York: Penguin Books, 1997); John Murphy, *The Eisenhower Interstate System: Building America Then and Now* (New York: Chelsea House, 2009); Felix Rohatyn, *Bold Endeavors: How Our Government Built America and Why It Must Rebuild Now* (New York: Simon and Schuster, 2009); Earl Swift, *The Big Roads: The Untold Story of the Engineers, Visionaries, and Trailblazers Who Created the American Superhighways* (New York: Houghton Mifflin Harcourt, 2011); Harvey, *The Condition of Postmodernity.*

3. Mark H. Rose and Raymond A. Mohl, *Interstate: Highway Politics and Policy since 1939,* 3rd ed. (Knoxville: University of Tennessee Press, 2012); Alan Altshuler and David Luberoff, *Mega Projects: The Changing Politics of Urban Public Investment* (Washington, D.C.: Brookings Institution Press, 2003).

4. Kenneth R. Geiser Jr., *Urban Transportation Decision Making: Political Processes of Urban Freeway Controversies* (Cambridge: Department of Urban Studies and Planning, Urban Systems Laboratory, Massachusetts Institute of Technology, 1970), 464–72. See also Lewis, *Divided Highways,* 131–36.

5. Mark Rose, *Interstate: Express Highway Politics, 1939–1989,* rev. ed. (Knoxville: University of Tennessee Press, 1990); Bruce Seely, "The Beginning of State Highway Administrations, 1893–1921: Engineers Take Control," *TR News* 245 (July–August 2006): 3–9.

6. MacDonald quoted in Bruce E. Seely, *Building the American Highway System: Engineers as Policy Makers* (Philadelphia: Temple University Press, 1987), 106; Lewis, *Divided Highways,* 15.

7. Lewis, *Divided Highways.*

8. Bruce E. Seely, "The Scientific Mystique in Engineering: Highway Research at the Bureau of Public Roads, 1918–1940," *Technology and Culture* 25, no. 4 (October 1984): 798–832; Seely, "How the Interstate System Came to Be: Tracing the Historical Process," *TR News* 244 (May–June 2006): 4–9; see also Alan Altshuler, *The City Planning Process: A Political Analysis* (Ithaca, N.Y.: Cornell University Press, 1964), 24–44.

9. In 1973 AASHO became the American Association of State Highway and Transportation Officials (AASHTO).

10. Kennedy quoted in Rose, *Interstate,* 58.

11. John Teaford, *Rough Road to Renaissance: Urban Revitalization in America, 1940–1985* (Baltimore: The Johns Hopkins University Press, 1990), 162.

12. Altshuler and Luberoff, *Mega Projects,* 82.

13. Eric Avila, *Popular Culture in the Age of White Flight: Fear and Fantasy in Suburban Los Angeles* (Berkeley: University of California Press, 2004), 203.

14. "'Futurama' in Fair Is Viewed in Test," *New York Times,* April 16, 1939; "Fair Visitors 'Fly' over New York of 1960," *New York Times,* April 16, 1939.

15. It also found poignant expression in the designs of Le Corbusier, the Swiss champion of modernist planning and design, who rendered the city from far above and outside. In "A Contemporary City for Three Million People," for example, Le Corbusier represented vehicles as mere dots moving in an orderly fashion along sweeping thoroughfares. Jane Jacobs, *The Death and Life of Great American Cities* (New York: Vintage, 1961), 437.

16. Sheets, quoted in Seely, *Building the American Highway System,* 175.

17. Teaford, *Rough Road to Renaissance,* 95–96; Raymond Mohl, "Stop the Road:

Freeway Revolts in American Cities," *Journal of Urban History* 30, no. 5 (July 2004): 677–78.

18. Raymond Mohl, "Race and Space in the Modern City: Interstate 95 and the Black Community in Miami," in *Urban Policy in Twentieth Century America,* ed. Arnold R. Hirsch and Raymond A. Mohl (New Brunswick, N.J.: Rutgers University Press, 1993), 107–18; Rose, *Interstate,* 42–44; Lewis, *Divided Highways,* 108; Clifton Donald Ellis, "Visions of Urban Freeways, 1930–1970" (PhD diss., University of California, Berkeley, 1990), 64.

19. Lewis, *Divided Highways,* Eisenhower quoted at 105, 112. President John F. Kennedy also played the defense card in boosting the interstate highway program. Ibid., 163.

20. Allan K. Sloan, *Citizen Participation in Transportation Planning: The Boston Experience* (Cambridge, Mass.: Ballinger Publishing, 1974), 16.

21. Jay M. Gould, *The Technical Elite* (New York: Augustus M. Kelley, 1966).

22. Jacobs, *The Death and Life of Great American Cities,* 7.

23. Geiser, *Urban Transportation Decision Making,* 331–33.

24. Gordon Fellman and Barbara Brandt, *The Deceived Majority: Politics and Protest in Middle America* (New Brunswick, N.J.: Transaction Books, 1973); Berman, *All That Is Solid Melts into Air.*

25. Rose and Mohl, *Interstate,* 113–33; Lewis, *Divided Highways,* 191–93.

26. William Issel, "'Land Values, Human Values, and the Preservation of the City's Treasured Appearance': Environmentalism, Preservationism, and San Francisco's Freeway Revolt," *Pacific Historical Review* 68, no. 4 (November 1999): 611–46; Altshuler and Luberoff, *Mega Projects,* 86.

27. Max Page and Randall Mason, *Giving Preservation a History: Histories of Historic Preservation in the United States* (New York: Routledge, 2004); Daniel Bluestone, *Buildings, Landscapes, and Memory: Case Studies in Historic Preservation* (New York: W. W. Norton, 2011).

28. "A Nation of Neighborhoods: Series Explores the 'New Localism,'" *Christian Science Monitor,* September 9, 1977, 1.

29. Jacobs, *The Death and Life of Great American Cities*; Daniel Patrick Moynihan, "New Roads and Urban Chaos," *Reporter,* April 14, 1960, 13–20; Lewis Mumford, *The Highway and the City* (Westport, Conn.: Greenwood Press, 1963); Caro, *The Power Broker*; Ada Louise Huxtable, "Must Urban Renewal Be Urban Devastation?," *New York Times,* December 12, 1961.

30. Kevin Starr, *Golden Dreams: California in an Age of Abundance* (New York: Oxford University Press, 2009), 245–66; Issel, "'Land Values, Human Values, and the Preservation of the City's Treasured Appearance'"; Katherine M. Johnson, "Captain Blake

versus the Highwaymen; or, How San Francisco Won the Freeway Revolt," *Journal of Planning History* 8, no. 1 (February 2009): 56–83.

31. Milk quoted in Jason Edward Black and Charles E. Morris III, eds., *Harvey Milk: An Archive of Hope* (Berkeley: University of California Press, 2013), 30.

32. Jason Schultz, "Freeway 90210: Opposition and Politics of the Pavement in Los Angeles" (paper, Humanities Honor's Program, University of California, Irvine, June 1, 2004).

33. "Completion of I-95 Only a Matter of Time," *Princeton Packet,* November 7, 1995; "The Chickens Come Home to Roost: Opponents of I-95 Brought Traffic Here," *Town Topics,* March 22, 1995.

34. Alan Lupo, *Rites of Way: The Politics of Transportation in Boston and the U.S. City* (Boston: Little, Brown, 1971), 57–58; Geiser, *Urban Transportation Decision Making,* 270–95; Lenny Durant, office manager of the Black United Front, interview by Cat Lea Holbrook, October 17, 2006, Roxbury Community College Library, https://archive.org/details/InTheSpotlightWithLennyDurantpart1.

35. Lupo, *Rites of Way,* 51–57; Lenny Durant, interview by Holbrook.

36. Quoted in Geiser, *Urban Transportation Decision Making,* 285.

37. Quoted in Gordon Fellman, *Implications for Planning Policy of Neighborhood Resistance to Urban Renewal and Highway Proposals,* national government publication (Waltham, Mass.: Department of Sociology, Brandeis University, 1970), 32.

38. "Inner Belt Mural Goes in C'Port," *Cambridge Chronicle,* September 18, 1980.

39. Robert Nichols, *The Expressway: A Play in Three Scenes,* Judson Archives, box 15, folder 3, New York University Fales Library and Special Collections.

40. Quoted in Jane Lee Keidel, "An Expressway Bridges a Gulf between People," *Baltimore Sun,* August 17, 1969.

41. Robert Gioielli, "We Must Destroy You to Save You: Highway Construction and the City as a Modern Commons," *Radical History Review,* no. 109 (Winter 2011): 62–82.

42. Sugrue, *The Origins of the Urban Crisis.*

43. Lewis, *Divided Highways,* 53–54.

44. U.S. Public Roads Administration, *Toll Roads and Free Roads,* 76th Cong., 1st sess., House Document no. 272 (Washington, D.C.: U.S. Government Printing Office, 1939), 99.

45. Ellis, "Visions of Urban Freeways," 155–57; Mohl, "The Interstate and the Cities: Highways, Housing, and the Freeway Revolt" (research report, Poverty and Race Research Action Council, 2002), 5–6.

46. U.S. National Interregional Highway Committee, *Interregional Highways,* 78th Cong., 2nd sess., House Document no. 379 (Washington, D.C.: U.S. Government Printing Office, 1944), 69–70.

47. Kenneth T. Jackson, "Race, Ethnicity, and Real Estate Appraisal: The Home Own-

ers' Loan Corporation and the Federal Housing Administration," *Journal of Urban History* 6, no. 4 (August 1980): 419–53. For a different perspective on the HOLC and its role in redlining, see Amy E. Hillier, "Redlining and the Home Owners' Loan Corporation," *Journal of Urban History* 29, no. 4 (May 2003): 394–420.

48. Home Owners' Loan Corporation, Los Angeles City Survey Files, Lincoln Heights, Record Group 195, National Archives, Washington, D.C.

49. There is now debate about the impact of the city survey files on the racial geography of the American city, as new evidence suggests that the FHA's *Underwriting Manual* actually played a greater role in enforcing racial segregation in the postwar urban regions. My point, however, is simply to underscore the fact that federal agencies like the HOLC and FHA actively and deliberately considered race in their approach to urban policy at midcentury, providing a racial lens through which other policy makers, like BPR officials, "read" the urban landscape. See Hillier, "Redlining and the Home-owners' Loan Corporation."

50. Mohl, "Race and Space in the Modern City," 109–10.

51. Cobo quoted in Sugrue, *The Origins of the Urban Crisis,* 47–48.

52. Robert O. Self, *American Babylon: Race and the Struggle for Postwar Oakland* (Princeton: Princeton University Press, 2003); Jeff Norman, *Temescal Legacies: Narratives of Changes from a North Oakland Neighborhood* (Oakland, Calif.: Shared Ground Press, 2003); Walter Hood, *Urban Diaries* (Oakland, Calif.: Spacemaker Press, 1997).

53. Ralph Abernathy wrote a letter to JFK protesting the destruction of his home and church. His pleas for assistance were granted though the rest of his community was destroyed. See Rose and Mohl, *Interstate,* 106–7.

54. Mohl, "The Interstate and the Cities," 102–18.

55. Altshuler, *The City Planning Process.*

56. Raymond A. Mohl, "Race and Space in the Modern City"; Milan Dluhy, Keith Revell, and Sidney Wong, "Creating a Positive Future for a Minority Community: Transportation and Urban Renewal Politics in Miami," *Journal of Urban Affairs* 24, no. 1 (2002): 75–95.

57. Mohl, "Race and Space in the Modern City," 113–14.

58. As far back as 1954, the California Division of Highways proposed a five-hundred-foot-wide swath of concrete through Sugar Hill, one of the most prosperous black neighborhoods in the nation. Sugar Hill resident Floyd Covington, former Urban League director, organized the Adams Washington Freeway Committee and pleaded before the California State Highway Commission in Sacramento to reroute the freeway, arguing that blacks had limited options for relocation. African Americans in Santa Monica also protested this particular freeway route, as it would bisect that city's small coastal black community. After hearing such protests, the state Highway Commission stalled in its decision for several months but ultimately proceeded with its original plan. Josh Sides,

L.A. City Limits: African American Los Angeles from the Great Depression to the Present (Berkeley: University of California Press, 2003), 124; Miguel Marcello Chavez, "Las Cuatro Esquinas: The Chicana and Chicano Movement in the West Side of Los Angeles, 1963–1979" (PhD diss., University of California, Los Angeles, 2010).

59. *Miami Times* quoted in Mohl, "Stop the Road," 685.

60. Graciela Valenzuela, interview by author, May 4, 2013.

61. Ibid.

62. Caro, *The Power Broker,* 837–94.

63. Norman, *Temescal Legacies,* 71–93.

64. Lizabeth Cohen, *A Consumer's Republic: The Politics of Mass Consumption in Postwar America* (New York: Alfred A. Knopf, 2003); Greg Hise, *Magnetic Los Angeles: Planning the Twentieth Century Metropolis* (Baltimore: The Johns Hopkins University Press, 1997). On Lakewood, see D. J. Waldie, *Holy Land: A Suburban Memoir* (New York: W. W. Norton, 1996).

65. Nell Irvin Painter, *The History of White People* (New York: W. W. Norton, 2010); Matthew Frye Jacobson, *Roots Too: White Ethnic Revival in Post–Civil Rights America* (Cambridge, Mass.: Harvard University Press, 2006).

66. "The Battle Lines of Baltimore," *Innovation Magazine,* July 1969, Movement against Destruction Collection, Langsdale Library Special Collections, University of Baltimore, series 8, box 1.

2. "NOBODY BUT A BUNCH OF MOTHERS"

1. Vivian Sobchack, "Cities on the Edge of Time: The Urban Science Fiction Film," *East West Journal* 3, no. 1 (December 1988): 4–19; see also Sobchack, *The Limits of Infinity: The American Science Fiction Film, 1950–1975* (South Brunswick, N.J., and New York: A. S. Barnes; London: Thomas Yoselloff, 1980); Vivian Sobchack and Kathleen McHugh, eds., "Beyond the Gaze: Recent Approaches to Film Feminisms," special issue, *Signs: Journal of Women in Culture and Society* 30, no. 1 (Autumn 2004).

2. John D'Emilio and Estelle Freedman, *Intimate Matters: A History of Sexuality in America* (New York: Harper and Row, 1988); Estelle Freedman, *No Turning Back: The History of Feminism and the Future of Women* (New York: Ballantine Books, 2002); Daniel Horowitz, *Betty Friedan and the Making of "The Feminine Mystique": The American Left, the Cold War, and Modern Feminism* (Amherst: University of Massachusetts Press, 1998); Stephanie Coontz, *A Strange Stirring: "The Feminine Mystique" and American Women at the Dawn of the 1960s* (New York: Basic Books, 2011); Ruth Rosen, *The World Split Open: How the Modern Women's Movement Changed America* (New York: Viking, 2000); Jane Gerhard, *Second Wave Feminism and the Rewriting of American Sexual Thought, 1920–1982* (New York: Columbia University Press, 2001).

3. Alison Lurie, *The Nowhere City* (New York: Coward-McCann, 1965).

4. Cherrie Moraga and Gloria Anzaldúa, eds., *This Bridge Called My Back: Writings by Radical Women of Color* (Watertown, Mass.: Persephone Press, 1981); Alma M. Garcia, *Chicana Feminist Thought: The Basic Historical Writings* (New York: Routledge, 1997); Ellen DuBois and Vicki Ruiz, eds., *Unequal Sisters: A Multicultural Reader in U.S. Women's History,* 2nd ed. (New York: Routledge, 1994).

5. Betty Friedan, *The Feminine Mystique* (New York: W. W. Norton, 1963), 5.

6. Elaine Tyler May, *Homeward Bound: American Families in the Cold War Era* (New York: Basic Books, 1988); Clifford Edward Clark, *The American Family Home, 1800–1960* (Chapel Hill: University of North Carolina Press, 1986); Gwendolyn Wright, *Moralism and the Model Home: Domestic Architecture and Cultural Conflict in Chicago, 1873–1913* (Chicago: University of Chicago Press, 1980); Alice T. Friedman, "Just Not My Type: Gender, Convention, and the Uses of Uncertainty," in *Ordering Space: Types in American Architecture and Design,* ed. Karen A. Franck and Lynda H. Schneekloth (New York: Van Nostrand Reinhold, 1994), 331–44; Dolores Hayden, "Model Houses for the Millions: Architects' Dreams, Builders' Boasts, Residents' Dilemmas," in *Blueprints for Modern Living: History and Legacy of the Case Study Houses,* ed. Elizabeth A. T. Smith (Cambridge: MIT Press, 1989). For specific analyses of the role of highway construction in shaping domesticity in postwar America, see Dolores Hayden, *Redesigning the American Dream: Gender, Housing, and Family Life,* rev. and expanded ed. (New York: W. W. Norton, 2002); Martin Wachs, "Men, Women, and Urban Travel: The Persistence of Separate Spheres," in *The Car and the City: The Automobile, the Built Environment, and Daily Urban Life,* ed. Martin Wachs and Margaret Crawford (Ann Arbor: University of Michigan Press, 1992).

7. Michelle Nickerson, *Mothers of Conservatism: Women and the Postwar Right* (Princeton: Princeton University Press, 2012), 4.

8. Ibid.; see also Lisa McGirr, *Suburban Warriors: The Origins of the New American Right* (Princeton: Princeton University Press, 2001).

9. Caro, *The Power Broker,* 879–82.

10. Mumford quoted in Robert Fishman, "Revolt of the Urbs: Robert Moses and His Critics," in *Robert Moses and the Modern City: The Transformation of New York,* ed. Hillary Ballon and Kenneth T. Jackson (New York: W. W. Norton, 2007), 122–29.

11. "New Traffic Plan/Project That Would Put New Roads in Washington Sq. Park Upset by Women," *New York Times,* May 28, 1952.

12. Quoted in Douglas Martin, "Shirley Hayes, 89, Won Victory over a Road," *New York Times,* May 11, 2002; "Washington Sq.: No Autos! City to Ban Buses Too," *Village Voice,* April 15, 1959.

13. Jacobs, *The Death and Life of Great American Cities,* 360.

14. Alice Sparberg Alexiou, *Jane Jacobs: Urban Visionary* (New Brunswick, N.J.: Rutgers University Press, 2006), 55.

15. Fishman, "Revolt of the Urbs," 361.

16. Nickerson, *Mothers of Conservatism,* 45.

17. Eliza Nichols, interview by author, April 20, 2013; Mary Perot Nichols, "Village Wins Major Victory; City Plans Trial-Closing of Washington Square to Traffic," *Village Voice,* October 29, 1958.

18. William Barrett, "Bohemia Gone Bourgeois," *New York Times,* April 4, 1954.

19. "Housing and Building: Whither the Village?" *Interiors,* August 1951, 10.

20. Jacobs, *The Death and Life of Great American Cities,* 83.

21. Fishman, "Revolt of the Urbs"; Lewis Mumford, "Mother Jacobs's Home Remedies," *New Yorker,* December 1, 1962, 173; "Short Reviews," *Scientific American* 206, no. 4 (April 1962): 186; Edward Chase, *Architectural Forum,* April 1962.

22. Jacobs, *The Death and Life of Great American Cities,* 23.

23. Ibid., 371.

24. Robert A. M. Stern, Thomas Mellins, and David Fishman, *New York, 1960: Architecture and Urbanism between the Second World War and the Bicentennial* (New York: Monacelli Press, 1997), 259–60.

25. Alexiou, *Jane Jacobs,* 107–11.

26. Lindsay quoted in Sam Roberts, ed., *America's Mayor: John V. Lindsay and the Reinvention of New York* (New York: Columbia University Press, 2010), 144.

27. Nancy Rising, interview with Kenneth R. Geiser Jr., July 28, 1969, in Geiser, *Urban Transportation Decision Making,* 119–20.

28. Geiser, *Urban Transportation Decision Making,* 125.

29. Fisher quoted in Norman G. Rukert, *The Fells Point Story* (Baltimore: Bodine and Associates, 1976), 92.

30. "Fells Point House Has History," *Baltimore Sun,* October 19, 1995; "Lucretia Fisher, City Preservationist," *Baltimore Sun,* November 8, 2011. See also Geiser, *Urban Transportation Decision Making,* 164.

31. Rose and Mohl, *Interstate,* 132.

32. Kenneth Durr, "The Not-So-Silent Majority: White Working Class Community," in *From Mobtown to Charm City: New Perspectives on Baltimore's Past,* ed. Jessica I. Elfenbein, John R. Breihan, and Thomas L. Hollowak (Baltimore: Maryland Historical Society, 2002), 225–49.

33. Barbara Mikulski, "Anti-Expressway Speech," June 29, 1971, Movement against Destruction (MAD) Archives, Maryland Department, Enoch Pratt Free Library; "The 'Road' That Turned Anger into Unity," *Baltimore Sun Magazine,* November 13, 1977, 42–43.

34. Mikulski quoted in Durr, "The Not-So-Silent Majority," 233.

35. Barbara Mikulski, "Who Speaks for Ethnic Americans?," *New York Times,* September 29, 1970. This piece was initially delivered as a speech before the Urban Task Force of the United States Catholic Conference in June 1970.

36. Ibid.

37. Jacobson, *Roots Too*, 6.

38. Virrick quoted in Raymond A. Mohl, "Elizabeth Virrick and the 'Concrete Monsters': Housing Reform in Postwar Miami," *Tequesta: The Journal of the Historical Association of Southern Florida*, no. 61 (2001): 5–37.

39. Caroline Emerson, *Make Way for the Highway* (New York: Golden Press, 1961).

40. Patricia Preciado Martin, *Days of Plenty, Days of Want* (Tucson: University of Arizona Press, 1988).

41. Stephen Pitti, *The Devil in Silicon Valley: Northern California, Race, and Mexican Americans* (Princeton: Princeton University Press, 2003), 105–6.

42. Lorna Dee Cervantes, "Beneath the Shadow of the Freeway," in *Emplumada* (Pittsburgh: University of Pittsburgh Press, 1982), 11–14; Eric Avila, "The Folklore of the Freeway: Space, Identity, and Culture in Chicano Los Angeles," *Aztlán: A Journal of Chicano Studies* 23, no. 1 (1998): 15–31; Tey Diana Rebolledo, "Tradition and Mythology: Signatures of Landscape in Chicana Literature," in *The Desert Is No Lady: Southwestern Landscapes in Women's Writing and Art,* ed. Vera Norwood and Janice Monk (New Haven: Yale University Press, 1987).

43. Cervantes, "Freeway 280," in *Emplumada,* 20–21.

44. Judith Baca, interview by author, November 3, 2011.

45. In 1984, the International Olympic Committee agreed to sponsor a marathon for women for the first time in Olympic history.

46. "Downtown's New Main Street," *Los Angeles Times,* November 6, 1971.

47. Home Owners' Loan Corporation, Los Angeles City Survey Files, Record Group 195, National Archives, Washington, D.C.

48. Mike Davis, *City of Quartz: Excavating the Future in Los Angeles* (New York: Verso Press, 1990), 230.

49. Ibid., 221.

50. Helena Maria Viramontes, interview by Michael Silverblatt, "Bookworm," August 16, 2007, on KCRW, http://www.kcrw.com/etc/programs/bw/bw070816helena_maria_viramon.

51. Helena Maria Viramontes, *Their Dogs Came with Them: A Novel* (New York: Atria Books, 2007).

52. Miguel León-Portilla, *Broken Spears* (1962), quoted in ibid., [iv].

53. Viramontes, *Their Dogs Came with Them,* 6.

54. Ibid., 225.

55. Ibid.

56. Émile Zola, *L'Assommoir* (1876; repr., New York: Penguin Books, 1970), 367.

57. Juana Gutierrez, quoted in Mary Pardo, *Mexican American Women Activists: Identity and Resistance in Two Los Angeles Communities* (Philadelphia: Temple University Press, 1998), 73.

58. Hayden, *Redesigning the American Dream*; Wachs, "Men, Women, and Urban Travel."

3. COMMUNITIES LOST AND FOUND

1. D. Irene Key, "Trouble in Paradise Valley: A Review of a Musical-Comedy-Whodunit," *Michigan Citizen*, December 20, 2003; Brent Dorian Carpenter, "Detroit's Black Bottom History Revisited," *Michigan Citizen*, April 17, 2004.

2. U.S. Public Roads Administration, *Toll Roads and Free Roads*, 97–99.

3. Mumford quoted in Joseph F. C. DiMento and Cliff Ellis, *Changing Lanes: Visions and Histories of Urban Freeways* (Cambridge: MIT Press, 2013), 38.

4. Ellis, "Visions of Urban Freeways," 204.

5. Holston, *The Modernist City*, 53–55; James Scott, *Seeing Like a State: How Certain Schemes to Improve the Human Condition Have Failed* (New Haven: Yale University Press, 1998), 109.

6. Robert Moses, director, *Arterial Plan for New Orleans* (New York: printed by Steidinger Press, 1946), 8.

7. Bureau of Governmental Research, *Plan and Program for the Preservation of the Vieux Carré: Historic District Demonstration Study* (New Orleans, La.: Bureau of Governmental Research, December 1968), 1–5. Marcou, O'Leary, and Associates served as the prime consultants in the preparation of this report.

8. Moses, *Arterial Plan for New Orleans*, 5.

9. Lewis, *Divided Highways*, 200.

10. Bureau of Governmental Research, *Plan and Program for the Preservation of the Vieux Carré*; J. Mark Souther, *New Orleans on Parade: Tourism and the Transformation of the Crescent City* (Baton Rouge: Louisiana State University Press, 2006); Lewis, *Divided Highways*, 201.

11. Souther, *New Orleans on Parade*, 59; Rose and Mohl, *Interstate*, 106.

12. William M. Blair, "Volpe Vetoes a Freeway to Save French Quarter in New Orleans," *New York Times*, July 10, 1969.

13. Federal Highway Act of 1966, Pub. L. No. 89–574, § 15(a), 80 Stat. 771, as amended 23 U.S.C. § 138 (Supp. V 1975); Department of Transportation Act, Pub. L. No. 89–670, § 4(f), 80 Stat. 934 (1966), as amended 49 U.S.C. § 1653(f) (Supp. V 1975); National Historic Preservation Act of 1966, Pub. L. No. 89–665, § 1, 80 Stat. 915 (codified at 16 U.S.C. § 470 [Supp. V 1975]).

14. Relocation and Management Associates, Inc., *Lower Manhattan Expressway Tenant Occupancy Survey* (New York: n.p., October 1960), 22.

15. Stephanie Gervis, "Artists, Politicians, People Join Fight for Little Italy," *Village Voice*, August 30, 1962; Sharon Zukin, *Loft Living: Culture and Capital in Urban Change* (New Brunswick, N.J.: Rutgers University Press, 1982), 48–49.

16. Roberta Brandes Gratz, *The Battle for Gotham: New York in the Shadow of Robert*

Moses and Jane Jacobs (New York: Nation Books, 2010), 95–119; see also Gratz, *Cities Back from the Edge: New Life for Downtown,* with Norman Mintz (New York: John Wiley and Sons), 305–8.

17. Jane Kramer, "Little Italy's Canyons Are a Festa in Naples," *Village Voice,* September 20, 1962.

18. *Village Voice,* June 17, 1965.

19. "Village Wins: It's a Landmark!," *Village Voice,* March 23, 1967.

20. Ada Louise Huxtable, "Good Buildings Have Good Friends," *New York Times,* May 24, 1970; Huxtable, "Must Urban Renewal Be Urban Devastation?"; Huxtable, "Threatened by Expressway," *New York Times,* July 22, 1965. See also Zukin, *Loft Living,* 48.

21. Dolores Hayden, *The Power of Place: Urban Landscapes as Public History* (Cambridge: MIT Press, 1995), 6–9; Michael DeHaven Newsom, "Blacks and Historic Preservation," *Law and Contemporary Problems* 36, no. 3 (Summer 1971): 423–31.

22. Priscilla Dunhill, "An Expressway Named Destruction," *Architectural Forum* 126 (March 1967): 54–59.

23. "Rondo Days Bring Cultural, Economic Benefits to St. Paul," *St. Paul Pioneer Press,* April 25, 2006.

24. Jimmy Griffin, *Jimmy Griffin: A Son of Rondo,* with Kwame J. C. McDonald (St. Paul: Ramsey County Historical Society, 2001), 18.

25. "Remembering Rondo," *St. Paul Pioneer Press,* July 14, 1999; Floyd George Smaller and Marvin Roger Anderson, "Rondo Days—A Community Festival," interview by Kate Hope Cavett, February 13, 2004, Rondo Oral History Project, Research Center for the Ramsey County Historical Society, St. Paul, Minnesota.

26. David V. Taylor, *Remember Rondo: Celebrating the People, Their Lives and Times* (St. Paul: Rondo Ave., 1983).

27. George H. Herrold, planning engineer, *Report to the Streets and Highways Committee, Submitting a Plan for Highway Approaches to the City for Street Improvement within the City* (St. Paul: n.p., 1942); C. David Loeks, associate city planner, *Information Report to the Planning Board Regarding the Proposed Central Routing of the 'East-West Highway'* (St. Paul: City Planning Board, May 12, 1950).

28. Griffin, *Son of Rondo,* 21.

29. "Pastor Threatens Cops," *St. Paul Dispatch,* September 28, 1956.

30. F. James Davis, *Freeway Exodus: Experiences in Finding Housing as a Result of the St. Anthony-Rondo Freeway Displacement from Western to Lexington Avenues in St. Paul—A Research Report,* with Alice Onque (St. Paul: Hamline University, 1962).

31. "Leave behind Memories," *St. Paul Recorder,* June 28, 1957.

32. "Howard Urges Families Affected by Freeway against Hurried Action," *St. Paul Recorder,* August 3, 1956.

33. Mrs. George Davis, quoted in "Reverend Fights to Keep His Home," *St. Paul Dispatch,* September 28, 1956.

34. *Voices of Rondo: Oral Histories of Saint Paul's Historic Black Community* (Minneapolis: Syren Book Company, 2005).

35. Smaller and Anderson, "Rondo Days—A Community Festival."

36. Yusef Mgeni, interview by Kateleen Hope Cavett, March 21, 2003, Rondo Oral History Project, Ramsey County Historical Society.

37. Constance Raye Jones Price, interview by Kateleen Hope Cavett, February 24, 2003, Rondo Oral History Project, Ramsey County Historical Society.

38. Teresina "Willow" Carter Felix, interview by Kateleen Hope Cavett, April 14, 2004, Rondo Oral History Project, Ramsey County Historical Society.

39. Evelyn Fairbanks, *The Days of Rondo: A Warm Reminiscence of St. Paul's Thriving Black Community in the 1930s and 1940s* (Minneapolis: Minnesota Historical Society Press, 1990).

40. Ibid., 31.

41. Smaller and Anderson, "Rondo Days—A Community Festival."

42. "Celebrate! Heritage, Arts Are Focus of Festivals," *St. Paul Dispatch,* July 22, 1984; "Rondo Avenue Lives Again in Festival," *St. Paul Pioneer Press and Dispatch,* July 5, 1985.

43. Remember Rondo Committee, *Remember Rondo—A Tradition of Excellence* (St. Paul: Pioneer Press, n.d.).

44. "Rondo Days Bring Cultural, Economic Benefits to St. Paul."

45. Mohl, "Stop the Road," 674–706; Dluhy, Revell, and Wong, "Creating a Positive Future for a Minority Community," 75–95.

46. Alwayn Nicholas, *A Brief History of Overtown,* 2004; Special Collections, Miami–Dade Public Library.

47. Joseph Dames II, interview by Electra Ford, August 21, 1997, *Tell the Story,* Oral History Project, Black Archives Foundation, Miami, Florida.

48. Nathaniel Q. Belcher, "Miami's Colored-Over Segregation: Segregation, Interstate 95, and Miami's African American Legends," in *Sites of Memory: Perspectives on Architecture and Race,* ed. Craig Evan Barton (New York: Princeton Architectural Press, 2001), 37–54.

49. Suburbanization, coupled with burgeoning patterns of racial integration during the 1950s, sowed the seeds of Overtown's decline, even before the onslaught of the I-95, as some upwardly mobile black families moved to Miami suburbs that were shedding their residential restrictions, including Opa-Locka and Carol City. This early outmigration chipped away at Overtown's social infrastructure as established institutions—that is, churches, schools, and the like—lost their leaders. See Mohl, "Race and Space in the Modern City," 119–22.

50. Estimates of population decline vary here. The legal scholar Andrea Eaton has found that "more than twenty thousand African American families were displaced in order to build highways in Miami." Another study estimated that at least 40 percent of Overtown's population was lost because of the highways. The effects of the highway can be measured in basic population shifts. While Miami's general population grew by some 36,000 between 1950 and 1970, Overtown witnessed a decrease in its population, from 29,253 to 15,935. Dluhy, Revell, and Wong, "Creating a Positive Future for a Minority Community," 13. See also Andrea Eaton, "Impact of Urban Renewal or Land Development Initiatives on African American Neighborhoods in Dade County Florida," *Howard Scroll: The Social Justice Law Review* 3, no. 49 (1995–96): 49.

51. Rose and Mohl, *Interstate,* 120.

52. Dluhy, Revell, and Wong, "Creating a Positive Future for a Minority Community," 90.

53. M. Athalie Range, interview by Stephanie Wanza, August 28, 1997, *Tell the Story,* Oral History Project, Black Archives Foundation, Miami, Florida.

54. Ingram quoted in Geoffrey Tomb, "Hope Is Rising from the Rubble of Overtown," *Miami Herald,* December 31, 1982.

55. Dorothy Jenkins Fields, "Pride of Place: Overtown," *Miami Times,* n.d., special section sponsored by the Florida Department of State, Special Collections, Black Archives Foundation, Miami, Florida.

56. *Cultural Tourism in the United States: A Position Paper for the White House Conference on Travel and Tourism* (U.S. Department of Commerce and the Presidential Committee on Arts and Humanities, 1995), 3.

57. Fields quoted in Jan Lin, *Ethnic Places* (New York: Routledge, forthcoming).

58. First identified as a project in the Southeast Overtown Park West Community Redevelopment Plan of December 1982, the reconstruction of this part of Overtown has been a goal of the city and of the community that has survived in this area for many years. A master plan with urban design guidelines was sponsored by the BAF in February 1989, and the project continued to be a goal within the Overtown Community Redevelopment Plan of November 1992. Most recently, a 1996 plan for the redevelopment of Overtown produced by the St. John Community Development Corporation likewise supports the redevelopment of this district as the Historic Overtown Folklife Village.

59. Master Plan for Historic Overtown Folklife Village, Miami, Florida, May 1997, sponsored by the Black Archives History and Research Foundation, Duany Plater-Zyberk and Company, Architects and Town Planners, 15–24.

60. Ibid.

61. "Pride of Place: Overtown."

62. Dell Upton, "Preface," in *Sites of Memory,* ed. Barton, x–xi. For a different perspective, see Belcher, "Miami's Colored-Over Segregation," 37–54.

63. Andrew Leong, "The Struggle over Parcel C: How Boston's Chinatown Won a Victory in the Fight against Institutional Expansion and Environmental Racism," *Amerasia Journal* 21, no. 3 (Winter 1995): 965; May Lee Tom, "Remembering Hudson Street," *Chinese Historical Society of New England Newsletter* 2, no. 1 (Spring 1996): 2; "Hudson Street Reunion," *Chinese Historical Society of New England Newsletter* 1, no. 1 (Spring 1995): 5; Adam Smith, "80 Year Chinatown Resident Reflects," *Sampan: The Only Bilingual Chinese–English Newspaper in New England,* March 4, 2005, http://sampan.org/pastissues/2005/0304/neilchin.htm.

4. A MATTER OF PERSPECTIVE

1. Cecile Whiting, *Pop L.A.: Art and the City in the 1960s* (Berkeley: University of California Press, 2006), 107–11.

2. Martin A. Berger, *Sight Unseen: Whiteness and American Visual Culture* (Berkeley: University of California Press, 2005).

3. Quoted in Whiting, *Pop L.A.,* 5.

4. Henry Hopkins, *Artforum,* May 1963, 43.

5. Susan M. Anderson, *Roger Kuntz: The Shadow between Representation and Abstraction,* with an introduction by Peter Plagens (Laguna Beach, Calif.: Laguna Art Museum, 2009), 66–68.

6. Quoted in ibid., 15.

7. Harvey Milk, "Address to the Joint International Longshoreman and Warehousemen's Union of San Francisco and to the Lafayette Club," September 30, 1973, in *Harvey Milk,* ed. Black and Morris, 72.

8. Stephen Nash, *Wayne Thiebaud: A Paintings Retrospective,* with Adam Gopnik (New York: Thames and Hudson, 2000).

9. Wayne Thiebaud, interview by Aaron Zilkowski, March 24, 2009.

10. Ibid.

11. Scott, *Seeing Like a State,* 4–5.

12. City, Planning Board, *Report on a Thoroughfare Plan for Boston,* Robert Whitten, consultant (Boston: Boston City Planning Board, 1930).

13. Thomas N. Tamburri, "Aerial Inventory: Large Scale Aerial Photos Aid Traffic Engineering," *California Highways and Public Works* 42, nos. 7–8 (July–August 1963): 49.

14. Ansel Adams and Nancy Newhall, *Fiat Lux: The University of California,* facsimile ed. (Berkeley and Los Angeles: University of California Press, 2012), 17.

15. Sam Lubell and Douglas Woods, *Julius Shulman: Los Angeles,* forward by Judy McKee (New York: Rizzoli Press, 2011), 21. See also Joseph Rosa, *A Constructed View: The Architectural Photography of Julius Shulman* (New York: Rizzoli Press, 1994); Christopher James Alexander, *Julius Shulman's Los Angeles* (Los Angeles: Getty Research Institute and J. Paul Getty Museum, 2011).

16. Alice Friedman talks about the "glamourization" of architecture in Shulman's work; see Friedman, *American Glamour: And the Evolution of Modern Architecture* (New Haven: Yale University Press, 2010), 87.

17. Holland Cotter, "Art Review. Catherine Opie: A Retrospective of Many Artists, All of Them One Woman," *New York Times,* September 25, 2008.

18. Russell Ferguson, "How I Think, Part I: An Interview with Catherine Opie," in *Catherine Opie: American Photographer* (New York: Solomon R. Guggenheim Museum, 2009), 104.

19. Laura Meyer, "Constructing a New Paradigm: European American Women Artists in California, 1950–2000," in *Art/Women/California, 1950–2000: Parallels and Intersections,* ed. Diana Burgess Fuller and Daniela Salvioni (Berkeley and Los Angeles: University of California Press and San Jose Museum of Art, 2002), 97–119.

20. Cotter, "Art Review."

21. *Catherine Opie: American Photographer,* 83; Maura Reilly, "The Drive to Describe: An Interview with Catherine Opie," *Art Journal* 62, no. 2 (Summer 2001): 82–95; Nan Trotman, "Freeways (1994–1995)," in *Catherine Opie: American Photographer,* 82.

22. Opie quoted in *Catherine Opie: American Photographer,* exhibition catalog (New York: Guggenheim Museum Publications, 2009).

23. Catherine Opie, "Interview with Catherine Opie," July 11, 1997, interview by Collette Dartnell in *Catherine Opie,* exhibition catalog (Los Angeles: Museum of Contemporary Art, 1997).

24. Whiting, *Pop L.A.,* 115–16; Opie, quoted in Reilly, "The Drive to Describe."

25. James Doolin, "Art and Artificiality: Southern California," *Architecture California,* journal of the American Institute of Architects California Council, 14, no. 2 (November 1992): 9–13.

26. Lauren Doolin, interview by author, October 24, 2012.

27. Adrian Maher, "A Helicopter Ride to a New Perspective," *Los Angeles Times,* May 28, 1995.

28. James Doolin, "Murals in the M.T.A. Headquarters Building by James Doolin, 1994–1996" (unpublished manuscript, January 2000).

29. Community newspapers, namely the *Eastside Sun* and the *Belvedere Citizen,* document the placement of freeways to this level of detail during the 1950s and 1960s, as does the California Division of Highways (now California Department of Transportation, or CalTrans), in its journal *California Highways and Public Works.* Of course, one can see them for oneself by simply walking in the neighborhood. See "Set Huge Freeway Building Program," *Belvedere Citizen,* September 19, 1957; "Golden State Freeway Project," *Belvedere Citizen,* March 6, 1958. See also "Freeway Link Near Completion," *Eastside Sun,* August 7, 1958; "Carpet of Concrete Rolls Out," *Eastside Sun,* August 28, 1958. For the official account, see Paul O. Harding, assistant state highway engineer,

"Southern Freeways: Progress Report," *California Highways and Public Works* 43, nos. 5–6 (June–July 1965): 34; Heinz Heckeroth, project engineer, "Design of Interchange Was a Team Effort," *California Highways and Public Works* 37, nos. 11–12 (November–December 1958): 20.

30. Http:/www.census.gov/Press-Release/www/2001/cb01-81.html. See also Lawrence Bobo et al., eds., *Prismatic Metropolis: Inequality in Los Angeles* (New York: Russel Sage Foundation, 1999).

31. Brodsly, *L.A. Freeway*; Avila, *Popular Culture in the Age of White Flight.*

32. Max Benavidez, "Chicano Art: Culture, Myth, and Sensibility," in *Chicano Visions: American Painters on the Verge,* ed. Cheech Marin (Boston: Bullfinch Press, 2002), 10–21. For a more general perspective, see also Eva Sperling Cockcroft, "From Barrio to Mainstream: The Panorama of Latino Art," in *Handbook of Hispanic Cultures in the United States: Literature and Art,* ed. Francisco Lomeli (Houston: Arte Publico Press, 1993), 192–217.

33. Oral History interview with Frank Romero, January 17–March 2, 1997, Archives of American Art, Smithsonian Institution.

34. Ibid.

35. William Stewart Young, *History of Hollenbeck Home* (Los Angeles: Jeffrey Banknote, 1934), 2.

36. Postcard-size photos of Hollenbeck Park, Special Collections, Young Research Library, University of California, Los Angeles.

37. Joseph Eli Kovner, "Boyle Hollenbeck Shall Not Be Divided," editorial, *Eastside Sun,* December 4, 1958.

38. Lyman R. Gillis, "Freeway Loop," *California Highways and Public Works* 38, nos. 11–12 (September–October 1959): 11–17.

39. Heckeroth, "Design of Interchange Was a Team Effort," 20.

40. W. James Gauderman et al., "Effect of Exposure to Traffic on Lung Development from 10 to 18 Years of Age: A Cohort Study," January 26, 2007, www.thelancet.com; Heather E. Volk et al., "Residential Proximity to Freeways and Autism in the CHARGE Study," *Environmental Health Perspectives* 119 no. 6 (June 2011): 873–77.

41. Raul Homero Villa, *Barrio-Logos: Space and Place in Urban Chicano Literature and Culture* (Austin: University of Texas Press, 2000).

42. Oral History interview with Carlos Almaraz, February 6, 1986–January 29, 1987, Archives of American Art, Smithsonian Institution.

43. Ibid.

44. The California Department of Transportation (CalTrans) opened in its District 7 headquarters in downtown Los Angeles in September 2004. Designed by architect Thom Mayne of the Los Angeles–based firm Morphosis, the walls of the building's entrance lobby are decorated with streaming tubes of red and blue florescent lights. Designed by artist Keith Sonnier, the lights evoke the glow of cars passing on freeways at night.

45. Romero interview, January 29, 1997.

46. Almaraz interview, July 31, 1986.

47. Romero interview, January 17, 1997.

48. Tomás Ybarra-Frausto, "Rasquachismo: A Chicano Sensibility," in *Chicano Aesthetics: Rasquachismo,* exhibition catalog (Phoenix, Ariz.: MARS [Movimiento Artistico del Rio Salado], 1989), 6.

49. Amalia Mesa-Bains, "Domesticana: The Sensibility of Chicana Rasquache," *Aztlán: A Journal of Chicano Studies* 24, no. 2 (Fall 1999): 157–67.

50. Holly Adams, "Ruben Ochoa: In a Construction Zone," *Los Angeles Times,* March 7, 2010.

51. Michelle Urton, "Ruben Ochoa," in *Phantom Sightings: Art after the Chicano Movement,* ed. Rita Gonzalez, Howard N. Fox, and Chon A. Noriega (Los Angeles: Los Angeles County Museum of Art and University of California Press, 2008), 180–83.

5. TAKING BACK THE FREEWAY

1. Dan Collins, "Faithful See Image of Virgin Mary," CBS News, April 20, 2005, http://www.cbsnews.com/news/faithful-see-image-of-virgin-mary/; Jennifer Lebovich, "Faithful See Mary on Underpass Wall," *Chicago Tribune,* April 19, 2005; Art Golab, "Our Lady of the Underpass Hasn't Faded Away, Bishop Says," *Chicago Sun-Times,* December 19, 2011.

2. "Imaginative Club Gets Park under Traffic Maze," *Oakland Tribune,* July 23, 1972; "Apgar Thanks," *Oakland Tribune,* April 29, 1972.

3. Walter Hood, *Urban Diaries* (Oakland, Calif.: Spacemaker Press, 1997); Robert Self, *American Babylon: Race and the Struggle for Postwar Oakland* (Princeton, N.J.: Princeton University Press, 2003).

4. Hood, *Urban Diaries,* 14.

5. Jacobs, *The Death and Life of Great American Cities,* 257–70.

6. David Botello, interview by author, August 27, 2009.

7. Hood, *Urban Diaries.*

8. Kellie Jones, *Now Dig This! Art in Black Los Angeles, 1960–1980* (New York: Delmonico Books, 2011), 22–23.

9. Nick Stillman, "Senga Nengudi's 'Ceremony for Freeway Fets' and Other Los Angeles Collaborations," *East of Borneo,* December 7, 2011.

10. Nengudi, in *Shopping Bag Spirits and Freeway Fetishes: Reflections on Ritual Space,* color video with sound, 59 min., dir. Barbara McCullough, 1979.

11. Beverly H. Wright, "New Orleans Neighborhoods under Siege," in *Just Transportation: Dismantling Race and Class Barriers to Mobility,* ed. Robert D. Bullard and Glenn S. Johnson (Gabriola Island, B.C., and Stony Creek, Conn.: New Society Publishers, 1997), 121–44; Lewis, *Divided Highways,* 188–89.

12. Matt Sakakeeny, "'Under the Bridge': An Orientation to Soundscapes in New

Orleans," *Ethnomusicology* 54, no. 1 (Winter 2010): 1–27, quotations on 1; Helen Regis, "Second Lines, Minstrelsy, and the Contested Landscape of New Orleans Afro-Creole Festivals," *Cultural Anthropology* 14, no. 4 (1999): 472–504; Regis, "Blackness and the Politics of Memory in the New Orleans Second Line," *American Ethnologist* 28, no. 4 (2001): 752–77.

13. Sakakeeny, "'Under the Bridge,'" 13–15.

14. Jennifer Kiser, "The Story of the Murals," *UW-NOLA 2010*, University of Wisconsin Bayou-Bienvenue Wetland Restoration and Community Redevelopment Project, June 17, 2010, http://uwnola2010.wordpress.com/2010/06/17/the-story-of-the-murals/.

15. LeRoy E. Harris, "The Other Side of the Freeway: A Study of Settlement Patterns of Negroes and Mexicans in San Diego, California" (PhD diss., Carnegie Mellon University, 1974).

16. Jacob Dekema, "District IX Freeway Report: San Diego," *California Highways and Public Works* 36, nos. 1–2 (January–February 1957): 27–28; "San Diego Awaits Completion of Crosstown Freeway," *San Diego Union*, April 2, 1958.

17. State of California, Department of Public Works, *1968–1969 Annual Report,* Division of Highways, Legal Division, Division of Administrative Services, Division of Bay Toll Crossings (July 1969).

18. State of California, Department of Public Works, Division of Highways, "Report: San Diego: Coronado Highway Toll Crossing," August 1962, 11; State of California, Department of Public Works, Division of Highways, "Report on a Proposed Toll Highway Crossing of San Diego Bay between the Cities of San Diego and Coronado," April 1957, 7.

19. "Crosstown Link Scheduled to Open Today," *San Diego Union*, November 18, 1969; "San Diego Celebrates New Bridge," *San Diego Union*, April 8, 1969.

20. Frank Norris, "Logan Heights: Growth and Change in the Old 'East End,'" *Journal of San Diego History* 26 (Winter 1983): 32.

21. "State Awards Land Lease near Bridge," *San Diego Union*, July 24, 1969.

22. "Chicanos Occupy Bridge Park," *San Diego Union*, April 23, 1970; "Chicano Park Occupation," *San Diego Union*, April 25, 1970; "City Hopes to Own Chicano Park Site," *San Diego Union*, April 29, 1970.

23. "Chicano Park Occupation," *San Diego Union*, April 24, 1970; "Heavens Open Up to Aid Park Plan," *San Diego Union*, April 25, 1970; "Chicanos Vacate Bridge Site," San Diego *Union*, May 1, 1970.

24. "Williams Vows City Gift of Park," *San Diego Union*, May 5, 1970; "City Authorizes $21,814.96 for Coronado Bridge Park," *San Diego Union*, July 1, 1970; *Chicano Park,* videocassette, 58 min., dir. Marilyn Mitford and Mario Barrera, prod. Marilyn Mitford (Red Bird Films, 1988).

25. Pamela Jane Ferree, "The Murals of Chicano Park" (MA thesis, San Diego State

University, 1994), 36; Eva Cockcroft, "The Story of Chicano Park," *Aztlán: A Journal of Chicano Studies* 15, no. 1 (Spring 1984): 82; Mitford and Barrera, *Chicano Park*.

26. Daniel D. Arreola, "Mexican American Exterior Murals," *Geographical Review* 74, no. 4 (October 1984): 409–24.

27. Shifra M. Goldman, *Dimensions of the Americas: Art and Social Change in Latin America and the United States* (Chicago: University of Chicago Press, 1994), 8.

28. Arreola, "Mexican American Exterior Murals," 413.

29. Torres, in Mitford and Barrera, *Chicano Park*.

30. Ferree, "The Murals of Chicano Park," 26.

31. National Park Service, National Register of Historic Place, Registration Form, United States Department of the Interior, December 3, 2012.

32. Benjamin Marquez, *Power and Politics in a Chicano Barrio: A Study of Mobilization Efforts and Community Power in El Paso* (Lanham, Md.: University Press of America, 1985), 56–73; Bradford Luckingham, *The Urban Southwest: A Profile History of Albuquerque–El Paso–Phoenix–Tucson* (El Paso: Texas Western Press, 1982).

33. Miguel Juarez, *Colors on Desert Walls: The Murals of El Paso* (El Paso: Texas Western Press, 1997); Junior League of El Paso, *An Art of Conscience: A Guide to Selected El Paso Murals,* Los Murales Project (El Paso: Junior League of El Paso, 1996), 7.

34. City of El Paso Texas Parks and Recreation, "Lincoln Recreation Center," c. 2007, http://www2.elpasotexas.gov/parks/lincoln.asp; Miguel Juarez, "History on the Murals at Lincoln Park," Lincoln Park Conservation Committee (2009), http://www.lincolnparkcc.info/.

35. "Murals Unveiled at Lincoln Park," Youth Initiative Program Newsletter 10 (El Paso, Texas), October 2007, http://www.elpasotexas.gov/Police/_documents/Oct%20YIP%20Newsletter.pdf.

36. Leon C. Metz, *City at the Pass: An Illustrated History of El Paso* (Woodland, Calif.: Windsor Publications, 1980).

37. Linda B. Hall, *Mary, Mother and Warrior: The Virgin in Spain and the Americas* (Austin: University of Texas Press, 2004), 283–84.

38. Amalia Mesa Bains, "'Domesticana': The Sensibility of Chicana Rasquache," *Aztlán: A Journal of Chicano Studies* 24, no. 2 (Fall 1999): 157–58; Ybarra-Frausto, "Rasquachismo: A Chicano Sensibility," 5–8.

CONCLUSION

1. Eckbo, Dean, Austin, and Williams, *H-3 Socio-Economic Study: The Effects of Change on a Windward Oahu Rural Community,* with Morris G. Fox, consultant (Honolulu [?]: December 14, 1973).

2. Haunani-Kay Trask, *From a Native Daughter: Colonialism and Sovereignty in Hawai'i,* rev. ed. (Honolulu: University of Hawai'i Press, 1999); see also "The Birth of

the Modern Hawaiian Movement, Kalama Valley, Oahu," *Hawaiian Journal of History* 21 (1987): 126–53; Momiala Kamahele, "Iioʻulaokalani: Defending Native Hawaiian Culture," *Amerasia Journal* 26, no. 2 (Fall 2000): 39–65; Davianna McGregor-Alegado, "Hawaiians: Organizing in the 1970s," *Amerasia Journal* 7, no. 2 (1980): 29–55.

3. Eventually, the contract's value mushroomed from an initial outlay of $700,000 to almost $15 million, largely funded by taxpayers through the Hawaii Department of Transportation. See Bob Krauss, "H-3 Sites Yield Clues of Early Islanders," *Honolulu Advertiser*, n.d.

4. Davianna Pomaikaʻi McGregor, "Constructed Images of Native Hawaiian Women," in *Asian/Pacific Island American Women: A Historical Anthology*, ed. Shirley Hune and Gail M. Nomura (New York: New York University Press, 2003), 26.

5. Stu Glauberman, "H-3 Protesters Planning Religious Rites at Site 75," *Honolulu Advertiser*, April 8, 1992; June Watanabe, "Halawa Heiau Vigil Preserved," *Honolulu Star-Bulletin*, April 14, 1993.

6. Pat Omandam, "Late Man's Pleas for Family Bones Went Unheeded," *Honolulu Star-Bulletin*, December 4, 1997.

7. Debra Barayuga, "Work at H-3 Site Halts for Fatal Mishap Probe," *Honolulu Star-Bulletin*, January 27, 1995; Kameʻeleihiwa quoted in Greg Barrett, "Troubles on H-3 Strengthen Beliefs in Power of Supernatural Wrath," *Honolulu Advertiser*, August 4, 1996.

8. Greg Barrett, interview by Lilikana Kameʻeleihiwa, *Honolulu Advertiser*, August 11, 1996.

9. That is, until the construction of the Big Dig in Boston; see McNichol, *The Big Dig*.

10. Rose and Mohl, *Interstate*, 181; McNichol, *The Big Dig*.

11. Norquist, quoted in Mohl and Rose, *Interstate*, 182.

12. Mark Wild, *Street Meeting: Multi-Ethnic Neighborhoods in Early Twentieth-Century Los Angeles* (Berkeley: University of California Press, 2005); Alison Varzally, *Making a Non-White America: Californians Coloring outside Ethnic Lines, 1925–1955* (Berkeley: University of California Press, 2008); George Sanchez, "'What's Good for Boyle Heights Is Good for the Jews': Creating Multiracialism on the Eastside during the 1950s," *American Quarterly* 56, no. 3 (September 2004): 633–61.

13. Thomas B. Gray, *The Aesthetic Condition of the Urban Freeway*, chapter 3, "Strategies," http://www.mindspring.com/~tbgray/prindex.htm.

14. "Rondo Days Bring Cultural, Economic Benefits to St. Paul," *St. Paul Pioneer Press*, April 25, 2006.

15. Joshua Bloom and Waldo E. Martin Jr., *Black against Empire: The History and Politics of the Black Panther Party* (Berkeley: University of California Press, 2013), 13–14.

16. Seely, "The Scientific Mystique in Engineering."

17. Peter Novick, *That Noble Dream: The "Objectivity Question" and the American Historical Profession* (Cambridge: Cambridge University Press, 1988), 483.

18. Jeffery Hou, ed., *Insurgent Public Space: Guerrilla Urbanism and the Remaking of Contemporary Cities* (London: Routledge, 2010); see also John Chase, Margaret Crawford, and John Kaliski, eds., *Everyday Urbanism* (New York: Monacelli Press, 1999).

Index

Adame, Felipe, 173–74

Adams, Ansel, 126, 128

African Americans, 8, 13, 42–43, 46–47, 51, 94, 100–115, 152–53, 155–60, 189, 191, 205n58. *See also* Miami, FL; Oakland, CA; St. Paul, MN

Almaraz, Carlos, 13, 137; artistic technique, 142–43; and Chicano Movement, 142, 146; critical reception of, 145; education of, 141–42; and freeway paintings, 142, 144

American Association for Highway Improvement, 26

American Association of Highway State Officers (AAHSO), 23, 202n9

American Road Builders Association, 26

Anderson, Marvin Roger, 104

assemblage art, 155

Atlanta, GA, 43

Attack of the 50-Foot Woman, The, 53, 54

automobile(s): and highway research, 21; images of, 24; masculine culture of, 80, 86; and modernist city planning, 6, 9, 51; proliferation of, 10, 18, 192

automobile lobby, 26

Automotive Safety Foundation, 41

Autopia Ride. *See* Disneyland

Baca, Judith, 77–81, 84, 85, 120, 177, 197

Baltimore, MD, 38–39, 42, 68–69; Movement Against Destruction (MAD), 38–39; Relocation Action Movement (RAM), 38–39

Banham, Reyner, 132

barrios: aesthetics of, 10, 146, 168, 177; epistemology of, 141, 188; and highway construction, 3, 8, 11, 14, 19, 39, 176; political activism in, 85, 87; representations of, 13, 74–77, 81–83, 138, 140, 144, 147, 169. *See also* El Paso, TX; San Diego, CA; Tucson, AZ

Baudelaire, Charles, 10

Beat the Belt (mural), 36

Bel Geddes, Norman, 24–25, 65

Beneath the Shadow of the Freeway, 74–75, 76

Beverly Hills, CA, 2, 32, 34, 52, 120, 193

Beverly Hills Freeway. *See* Beverly Hills, CA

Birmingham, AL, 43

Black Archives, History, and Research Foundation of South Florida, 112

Boston, MA, 7, 26, 29, 33–36, 71, 127, 193; Central Artery, 15, 116, 126, 149, 186, 201n23; Chinatown, 116; Inner Belt

Expressway, 34–36, 61; Roxbury, 34, 204n34

Botello, David, 13; acclaim for, 145; and Chicano art, 143; and East Los Angeles, 138, 140, 141, 146, 153–54

Boyle Heights (Los Angeles), 41, 47, 120, 127–29, 135–41, 153–54, 177–88

brutalism, 27

Bureau of Public Roads, 20, 21, 23, 27, 39–40, 41

California Department of Transportation (Cal Trans), 19, 120, 216n44

California Division of Highways. *See* California Department of Transportation

Caro, Robert, 31, 48–49, 59

Ceremony for Freeway Fets. See Nengudi, Senga

Cervantes, Lorna Dee, 74, 87

Chamizal region (Texas), 174–76

Charlotte, NC, 43

Chicano art: use of color in, 144–45

Chicano Movement, 13, 87, 121, 137, 138, 166, 168–69, 171, 172, 179, 189

Chicano Park (San Diego, CA), 14, 150, 160–71, 176–77, 178–79, 189

Chinatown: Boston, 116, Houston, 188

Chinese Americans, 8. *See also* Chinatown

Civil Rights Movement, 7, 11, 47, 116, 157, 189, 192

class conflict, 2, 11, 12, 42, 43, 49, 51, 71, 79, 99, 154, 190; cross-class alliances, 34, 38, 46, 101–2, 110; discourse of, 8

Clay, Lucius, 26

Clean Air Act (1970), 30

Clean Water Act (1972), 30

Columbus, SC, 43

Congress of Racial Equality (CORE), 47

Cross Bronx Expressway. *See* New York City

dance, 4, 89, 154–56, 158, 159, 174

Death and Life of Great American Cities, The (Jacobs), 31, 48, 55, 62–65, 96, 153; colorblindness of, 64; critiques of, 64

decentralization, 17, 25, 27. *See also* suburbanization

destruction/demolition, 9, 18, 19–20, 116; in Miami, 112; in Oakland, 43; St. Paul, 104–5

Detroit, MI, 42, 89–90

Disneyland, 24, 114–15

Doolin, James, 132–35

Du Camp, Maxime, 132

East Los Streetscapers, 138, 141. *See also* Botello, David

Eisenhower, Dwight, 26

El Paso, TX, 171–76

engineering profession, 15, 20, 21, 24, 191–92

expertise, culture of, 6, 20–21, 28, 36, 192

Expressway, The (Nichols), 36–38

Fairbanks, Evelyn, 105–6

Federal Aid Highway Act: (1944), 27; (1956), 1, 12, 18, 19, 21, 23–24, 26, 27, 58; (1966), 21, 96, 187; (1973), 187

Federal Highway Administration, 21, 187

Federal Housing Administration (FHA), 40, 49

Feminine Mystique, The (Friedan), 12, 56, 57

feminism, 90, 192; and Chicanas, 87; second-wave, 7, 12, 52, 55, 56

Fields, Dorothy Jenkins, 112, 113, 114

Fisher, Lucretia, 68–69, 73, 87, 96

folklore, ix–x, 4, 150, 178, 184, 189, 190, 191–92, 193–94
freeway revolt, 1–2, 5, 19, 29–39, 50–52, 65–73, 190, 193; and environmentalism, 30, 192
freeway shootings, 143
Freeway 280 (Cervantes), 75, 77
Freidan, Betty. *See Feminine Mystique, The*
Futurama, 24, 25, 91

Galbraith, John Kenneth, 35
Gans, Herbert, 31
Gaye, Marvin, 14
Gayle, Margot, 98
gender, 12, 52, 55, 86, 87, 120, 155; and the modernist city, 63, 64, 84; and urban space, 57, 75, 77, 80
gentrification, 51, 62
ghettos, 3, 8, 10, 176, 178
Goez Art Studio and Gallery, 138, 141. *See also* Botello, David
Great Wall of Los Angeles, 77, 78
Greenwich Village. *See* New York City

Haussmann, Georges-Eugène, 9–10
Hayes, Shirley, 65, 73
Highway Research Board, 21, 41
Historic Overtown Folklife Village, 113–15, 117, 213n58
historic preservation, 30, 93, 96, 117, 192
Hitting the Wall (mural), 78–81
Hockney, David, 120, 121, 132
Hollenbeck Park (Los Angeles), 138–40, 154
Holston, James, 6
Home Owners' Loan Corporation (HOLC), 39, 40, 41, 49, 205n49
Hood, Walter, 152–53, 177, 178

Houston, TX, 188
Huxtable, Ada Louise, 31, 98

impressionism, 10
infrapolitics, 4
Interregional Highways (Bureau of Public Roads), 40
Interstate 5: Los Angeles, CA, 24, 127, 131, 133, 136, 137, 139, 154; San Diego, CA, 160–63
Interstate 10: El Paso, TX, 172, 176; Los Angeles, 136, 137; New Orleans, 94, 157–59, 160, 161; Phoenix, AZ, 188; Tucson, AZ, 74
Interstate 40 (Nashville, TN), 43
Interstate 75 (Detroit, MI), 89–90
Interstate 93. *See* Boston, MA: Central Artery
Interstate 94 (St. Paul, MN), 3, 45, 101, 103–7
Interstate 95: Miami, FL, 3, 46, 72, 109, 111, 114, 189; Princeton, NJ, 32–33
Interstate 110 (Harbor Freeway, Los Angeles), 78–79, 80, 133, 154, 155
Interstate 280 (Bay Area, CA), 30, 74, 75, 77, 124, 125
Interstate 395 (Miami, FL), 111
Interstate 405 (Los Angeles), 56
Interstate 580 (Oakland, CA), 44, 152
Interstate 605 (Seattle, WA), 67
Interstate 980 (Oakland, CA), 44, 152
Interstate Highway Act. *See* Federal Aid Highway Act: 1956
interstate highway construction: architecture of, 27, 79–80, 150, 151, 177, 188, 189; and the Cold War, 26–27, 181; corporate sponsorship of, 25; and downtown redevelopment, 25–26; health effects of, 140;

as infrastructure, 4–5; and labor, 11, 26; opposition to (*see* freeway revolt); racial consequences of, 2–4, 7–8, 205n49; and scientific mystique, 21–23, 28; visual perspective of, 25, 125–26; and white flight, 49–50
Interstate H-3 (Honolulu, HI), 14, 181–86, 220n3

Jacobs, Jane, 13, 31, 55, 59–67, 73, 96, 99, 125, 153, 193
Journey, The (Martin), 73–74

Kansas City, MO, 43
Kennedy, G. Donald, 23
Kuntz, Roger, 122

labor unions, 11, 26
LaCasse, Bernard, 36
L'Assomoir. See Zola, Emile
Le Corbusier, 92, 202n15
Lincoln Park. *See* El Paso, TX
Los Angeles, x, 7, 13, 56, 77–79, 119; East Los Angeles, 3, 47, 49, 81–85, 120, 121, 129, 135–46, 150, 151, 153–54, 171, 188, 189; Metropolitan Transit Authority, 134–35; redlining of, 41
Lower Manhattan Expressway (LOMEX). *See* New York City
Lurie, Alison, 55
Lynch, Kevin, 35

MacDonald, Thomas H., 21, 23, 40, 41
Magic Motorways (Bel Geddes), 24–25
Make Way for the Highway (1961), 72–73
Martin, Patricia Preciado, 73–74
Massachusetts Institute of Technology (MIT), 35–36
memory, culture of, 104–6, 108–9, 115, 116

Mexican Americans, 8, 47, 73–85, 87, 120, 135–46, 160–78, 191. *See also* Chicano Movement; Chicano Park; San Jose, CA
Miami, FL, 3, 7, 13, 26, 72, 91, 100, 116, 186, 189; and highway planning, 46–47; Overtown, 3, 109–15, 213n50; racial segregation in, 111. *See also* Historic Overtown Folklore Village; Virrick, Elizabeth
Mikulski, Barbara, 69, 71, 73, 97
Milk, Harvey, 32
Milwaukee, WI, 186
modernism, aesthetic, 11
modernist city, 6, 16, 17–18; as anti-historical, 92, 118; birth of, 8; decline of, 51, 193; fantasies of, 24–25; gendered critique of, 63, 86–87, 191; and highway construction, 92–93; racial consequences of, 15, 179, 190
modernization, 7, 10; cultural interpretations of, 11; racial critique of, 83, 84, 85; racial disparities of, 5, 8, 178
Montgomery, AL, 43
Moses, Robert, 9–10, 59, 61, 64, 92
motherhood, politics of, 57–58, 85
Mothers of East Los Angeles (MELA), 85
Moynihan, Daniel Patrick, 31, 35
Mumford, Lewis, 31, 36, 59, 64, 91
muralism, 138, 160, 167–70. *See also* Chicano art
music, 4, 10, 89, 155, 156, 157, 158, 159. *See also* second-line parades

Nashville, TN. *See* Interstate 40
National Advisory Council on Historic Preservation, 96
National Association for the Advancement of Colored People (NAACP), 47
National Automobile Association, 26

National Environmental Policy Act
    (1970), 30
National Highway Trust Fund, 23, 29
National Historic Preservation Act
    (1966), 13, 30, 90, 96, 187
National Register of Historic Places, 96,
    112, 189
Native Americans, 8, 182–86
Nengudi, Senga, 154–55
New Orleans, 1, 7, 26, 29, 43, 51, 62, 90,
    99, 116; Treme, 94–95, 157–60; 161;
    Vieux Carre, 13, 30, 92–93, 95–96, 98,
    100, 193; Vieux Carre Commission
    (VCC), 93, 94
new urbanism, 113, 187
New York City, 90, 96–99; Cross Bronx
    Expressway, 59, 153; Greenwich Vil-
    lage, 31, 36, 59–63, 65, 97–98; Harlem,
    31; Little Italy, 97; Lower Manhattan
    Expressway (LOMEX), 36, 65, 96–98;
    SoHo, 65, 97–98, 193
New York City Landmarks Preservation
    Commission, 97–98
Nichols, Mary Perot, 62, 208n17
Nichols, Robert, 36–37
NIMBYism, 71
Norquist, John, 186
Nowhere City, The (Lurie), 55–56

Oakland, CA, 7, 31, 42–44, 49, 152–54,
    178
Ochoa, Ruben, 146
Opie, Catherine, 129–32
origin–destination survey, 23

Parent–Teachers' Association (PTA), 60,
    67
Paris, 8–10
Parsons, Talcott, 36
Pate, Alexs, 107

Phoenix, AZ, 188
photography, 4, 13, 14, 120, 128, 129,
    130; verisimilitude of, 140. See also
    Adams, Ansel; Opie, Catherine;
    Shulman, Julius
Polyforum Siqueiros (Mexico City), 167.
    See also Siquieros, David Alfaro
pop art, 122, 123
Princeton, NJ, 2, 32–33, 193
progress: as cultural ideology, 7, 15, 19,
    28, 51; gendered critique of, 87
public housing, 11, 17, 27, 201n21
Purifoy, Noah, 155

race, 7–8, 11–12, 147; and the built
    environment, 100; construction of,
    190, 191; critical race theory, 120;
    and highway construction, 2–3, 15,
    19, 20, 39–48; and historic preserva-
    tion, 13, 99–100; and public infra-
    structure, 4–5
Range, M. Athalie, 112, 213n53
redlining. See Home Owners' Loan Cor-
    poration (HOLC)
Report on the Thoroughfare Plan for
    Boston (1930), 126, 127
Rising, Nancy, 67, 71, 73
Romero, Frank, 13–14, 177; acclaim for,
    145; and Chicano politics, 142, 145,
    146; and East Los Angeles vantage
    point, 137–38, 141; and freeway shoot-
    ings, 143; and use of color, 144
Rondo Days Festival, 101, 106–9, 115, 117,
    190
Rondo Oral History Project, 104
Royal Chicano Air Force, 167

sal si puedes, 74–75; as cultural imperative
    of barrios, 76
San Diego, CA, 160–71

San Diego–Coronado Bay Bridge, 160, 162–64

San Francisco, CA, 7, 25, 37, 71, 74; Embarcadero Freeway, 32, 33, 186; and environmental movement, 30; and freeway revolt, 29, 31–32, 51, 62, 193; representations of, 123–25

San Jose, CA, 74

Sargent, Francis, 34

Seattle, WA, 67–68

second-line parades, 157–59

Sesame Street, 31

Shulman, Julius, 127–29, 138

Siqueiros, David Alfaro, 167–68

sixties, the, 7, 28–29

slum clearance, 17, 38, 41, 63, 179; and highway construction, 11, 50

Smaller, Floyd George, 106, 107

St. Paul, MN, 3, 12, 13, 45, 91, 100; Rondo–St. Anthony neighborhood, 101–9. *See also* Rondo Days Festival

suburbanization, 1, 11, 17, 27, 28, 42, 49; and African Americans, 56, 152, 212n49; and women, 12, 57

technical expertise, 21, 27

Their Dogs Came With Them (Viramontes), 81–85

Thiebaud, Wayne, 123–25

Toll Roads and Free Roads (Bureau of Public Roads), 39–40, 91, 138

Torres, Salvador, 166, 167, 169, 180

traffic survey, 21

Tucson, AZ, 73–74

United Auto Workers, 26

United States Department of Transportation Act (1966), 187

United States Urban Mass Transportation Act (1970), 187

Urban Land Institute, 26, 41

Urban League, 47, 205n58

urban parkways, 27

urban renewal, 3, 17, 34, 38, 48, 49, 59, 78, 179; and highway construction, 11, 28, 41, 62, 97

Valenzuela, Graciela, 47–48, 87

Village Voice, 62, 96, 97

Viramontes, Helena Maria, 81–85, 120

Virrick, Elizabeth, 72, 73

Volpe, John, 95

Von Eckardt, Wolf, 31

Warhol, Andy, 122. *See also* pop art

Washington Square Park. *See* New York City

Watts riots, 11, 28, 154, 155

white flight, 48–50, 129, 178

whiteness, 48–50, 71; visual culture of 120–21, 146–47

Whyte, William, 31

Zola, Emile, 10, 84

ERIC AVILA is associate professor of history, Chicano studies, and urban planning at UCLA. He is the author of *Popular Culture in the Age of White Flight: Fear and Fantasy in Suburban Los Angeles.*